THE VIENNA
WOODS KILLER

THE VIENNA
WOODS KILLER

A WRITER'S DOUBLE LIFE

JOHN LEAKE

Granta Books
London

Granta Publications, 12–14 Addison Avenue, London W11 4QR

First published in Great Britain by Granta Books 2007

First published in the United States in 2007 by Sarah Crichton Books,
an imprint of Farrar, Straus and Giroux, as *Entering Hades: The Double Life
of a Serial Killer*

A CIP catalogue record for this book
is available from the British Library.

1 3 5 7 9 10 8 6 4 2

Printed and bound in Great Britain
by William Clowes Limited, Beccles, Suffolk

To Johnny Marciano, for his faith.

To my parents, Sam and Kathy Leake, for their patience.

If a lion could speak, we couldn't understand him.

—WITTGENSTEIN

AUTHOR'S NOTE

The names and identifying characteristics of some individuals depicted in this book have been changed. In particular, I have used the names Carolina, Jennifer, Susanna, Daphne, Manu, Elisabeth, Joanna, Katharina, Lela, Maria, Anna, and Mrs. Müller in place of the real names of certain women involved in these true events.

CONTENTS

PART III

PART I

A MYSTERY

ON JULY 11, 1991, a solar eclipse occurred in the sky over Los Angeles. At 10:12 a.m., the moon began to move in front of the sun, and by 11:28 it covered 69 percent of it. That morning, a couple of men and their children drove up to Corral Canyon Road in Malibu, northwest of the city, to watch the event.

The Malibu hills are a landscape of rugged beauty, hostile to residential development. During the dry season the resinous brush, desiccated by the Santa Ana wind, sometimes sparks into swift-moving conflagrations that incinerate everything in their path. About two miles inland, an old fire road branches off to the right of Corral Canyon Road and ascends a steep hill. With its panoramic view and isolation, the grassy mesa at the top draws the occasional couple seeking the thrill of sex under an open sky. A few empty wine bottles and discarded underwear bear witness to their encounters.

The men and children were seeking the mesa's high vantage point to watch the eclipse, but as they reached the top, they were too horrified by what they saw lying on the ground to pay attention to the sky. When they called the L.A. County Sheriff's Department at 11:15 a.m., the first man to talk said he'd discovered a dead body, but as he started to give directions to its location, he became upset and started cursing. A calmer man then got on the phone and described where the body lay, and a couple of hours later, Deputy Sheriff Ronnie Lancaster was directed to the scene.

A cheerful native of Amarillo, Texas, Lancaster had seen much of the evil that men do, but he seldom allowed it to put him in a bad humor. Bodies shot and stabbed were part of the territory, and like all good detectives, he'd trained his mind to view them as evidence, not as the personalities they once were. The one thing he'd never gotten used to was decomposition. When the call came in about a murdered woman off Corral Canyon Road, Lancaster didn't ask for a description of the crime scene, as he always preferred to approach it without preconceived notions. But he did have one question: "Is it a decomp?"

"Yes, it is."

"Oh, *man*," he said to his partner. "It's a decomp. There's gonna be maggots, and that means I'm gonna have nightmares." They arrived at the base of the fire road at 2:45 p.m.—the hottest time of the hottest day he could remember. Reaching the top of the mesa soaked in sweat, he found the area cordoned off with a group of sheriff's deputies and park rangers standing around. Deputy Knudson, the first to have arrived at the scene, filled them in.

"I got the call at 11:51 and headed here. An Aero unit flew over before I arrived and directed me to the site. The guys who found her called the Malibu Station, but they didn't say who they were or wait for me to get here. The decomp is advanced, but you can see from her breasts she's a female."

The heavy-set corpse was lying on its back, twenty yards west of the dirt road, underneath a laurel sumac shrub. Her face was obscured by maggots streaming out of her nose, mouth, eyes, and ears. Her T-shirt was hiked up to her shoulders, exposing her bloated belly and breasts. Around her neck was a tightly knotted bra. Otherwise she was clothed. The pockets of her blue jeans were turned out; no I.D. was present.

"Boys, we're gonna solve this one!" Lancaster exclaimed. "This is the work of a boyfriend or husband; all we gotta do is find him and case closed."

"What if it's a hooker?" his partner asked.

"What would a hooker be doing up here? They take care of business a block or two from where they get picked up, and we've gotta be twenty-five miles from where the nearest streetwalker would be." The inspectors continued working the crime scene, and at 5:20 p.m., the coroner recovery team arrived to collect the body.

Lancaster was glad the day's work was ending. He knew he wasn't done yet—that he'd have to go over the whole thing again with a forensic pathologist. But at least he could take a break from it. He walked over to the edge of the hill, to where the fire road began its descent to Corral Canyon Road. The view of Santa Monica Bay was spectacular, and for the first time that day he thought about the beauty of the landscape. He'd always associated a pretty countryside with the feeling of peace. To have committed such a horrible crime in such a lovely place seemed especially perverse.

That night he had nightmares, and the next day, still feeling haggard, he bumped into Lieutenant Christianson at the Homicide Bureau.

"Just heard from the coroner. They fingerprinted that girl from Corral Canyon Road, and guess what? She *is* a prostitute. Nice call, Lancaster."

"You've gotta be kidding!"

"She's got numerous arrests on her record."

"Well, what the hell was she doing up there on that hill?"

"That's for you to find out. You can start with the coroner. The autopsy's tomorrow morning at eleven o'clock."

Autopsies didn't bother him too much, though it sometimes troubled him when a victim stared at him. A dead man's eyes don't close, and they may catch you in their gaze. Sherri Long didn't have eyes to stare at him because they'd been eaten by maggots. In their place were empty black orbits. Lancaster felt his knees go weak as Dr. Ribe opened her skull to reveal "a large seething central mass composed of several thousand active maggots, mostly large." They had devoured all of her brain except "50 cc of pale gray soup," which was collected for toxicology, as well as a few live specimens of the larvae. From their species and length, a forensic entomologist could deduce how long the victim had been lying in the place where she was found, and if she had first lain somewhere else.

In Dr. Ribe's estimation, the victim had been dead four to seven days. "From the anatomic findings and pertinent history," he ascribed the death to "ASPHYXIA due to or as a consequence of LIGATURE STRANGULATION."

To Deputy John Yarborough, the girl strangled with her bra in Malibu sounded familiar, as he'd recently read LAPD teletypes about prostitutes who'd been murdered in the same way downtown. He showed the print-outs to Lancaster, who contacted Detective Fred Miller at LAPD Homi-cide. When Miller heard the story of the girl murdered in Malibu, he figured the killer he'd been hunting had struck again.

The killer had struck first on the night of June 19, 1991. Twenty-year-old Shannon Exley was popular with the truckers who delivered groceries to the produce district off Seventh Avenue in downtown L.A. They liked her blond hair and youthful looks. Performing for them was rough and dirty work, but she needed the money to support her crack habit. On the evening of June 19, 1991, she called her father before she went to work and told him that she was trying to get her life in order.

Her last customer picked her up on Seventh sometime after mid-night and drove east, across the L.A. River to the Girl Scout Center on Seventh and Fickett. In the vacant lot behind it, surrounded by eucalyp-tus trees, no one saw his car or heard her screams, so he could have taken all the time he wanted with her.

The location indicated he had planned the killing, because it wasn't a place where Seventh Avenue hookers turned tricks. Normally they drove only a block or two with their customers and parked in the neighboring warehouse district. Shannon would not have proposed driving to an iso-lated place, miles from her corner. The killer must have scoped it out in ad-vance, because he wouldn't have spotted it at night. From where he picked her up, he knew where he was taking her, and when to slow down for the right turn into the narrow lane that dead-ended next to the wooded lot.

The killer had strangled her with her own bra. Detective Miller knew of prostitutes getting manually strangled, beat up, shot, and stabbed, but he'd never heard of a hooker strangled with her own bra, the bra left tightly bound around her neck. Not only was it kinky, it ap-peared to have been practiced. Miller sensed that whoever had mur-dered Shannon Exley had probably murdered women before, and would probably do so again.

———

Miller had known from a young age that he wanted to be a detective. Raised in San Antonio, Texas, he moved with his family to L.A. when he was in high school. After a stint in the U.S. Army, with a tour of duty in Vietnam, he joined the LAPD. Those were the days of the television series *Dragnet* and *Adam-12*, when its officers had a reputation for being the best in the world. Only the toughest and smartest cops could police a city like Los Angeles, with its giant size, ethnic complexity, large amount of crime, and chronic shortage of police manpower.

At the downtown Robbery and Homicide Division, Miller had investigated cases with legendary detectives such as John "Jigsaw John" St. John, Badge Number One. By the summer of 1991, he'd probably worked on or been privy to as many serial murder investigations as any cop in the country. Over the years he'd supplemented his experience by reading the literature on serial murder that came out of the FBI, and he attended its seminars in L.A. He believed the most important lesson to be drawn from the analysts at Quantico was this: a good homicide investigator doesn't wait for the pattern to emerge that proves separate murders are the work of the same killer, but looks for signs that any murder is the work of a man who will do it again. By recognizing the signs and staying in contact with police divisions throughout the city, a detective could get onto a killer's trail quickly.

Miller figured the world's oldest profession was also its oldest target for men who kill for pleasure. As purveyors of sex for money, prostitutes are ready-made victims for sexual sadists. In the modern, car-driven world, they are also the only women in society who routinely get into the cars of strangers. One of the biggest cases of Miller's career was a prostitute strangler who ran amok in the mid-1980s. For two years, every time a woman was murdered and dumped outdoors, Miller examined the crime scene to determine if it was the work of the same hand. It was painstaking work, with days of talking to possible witnesses and nights of surveillance. But Miller loved the challenge, above all the intellectual challenge. It was like a game of chess—the city its board—comparing, calculating, connecting. He never forgot the adrenaline rush when he finally arrested the man he'd hunted for so long. In April 1989, Louis Craine was convicted of murdering four women.

In June 1991, Miller was head of the Homicide Special Section—"special" because it worked on complex cases requiring attention over potentially long periods of time. Every morning he came into his office on the third floor of the LAPD Parker Center and read teletype reports of homicides from all over the county. On Monday morning, June 24, 1991, he saw a report on the Exley murder. Detectives in the Hollenbeck Division, east of downtown, were investigating it after she'd been found the previous Thursday. Miller contacted them to learn more about the case.

Girls picking up litter in the lot behind the Girl Scout Center on the morning of June 20 found the body. She was lying on her belly, nude except for her T-shirt hiked up over her breasts and a pair of blue socks. The rest of her clothing was missing. No I.D. was present, but taking her fingerprints at the coroner's revealed her identity and her record of arrests for prostitution. A follow-up investigation indicated she'd recently been working on the corner of Seventh and Towne.

Miller told the Hollenbeck detectives about his concern that Shannon Exley's murderer might be the sort of man who would kill again, which meant that they probably wouldn't find him among her social circle. Maybe the killer had been her customer before, but it was unlikely she knew him. That's what made investigating the murder of a hooker so tough. In 1991, L.A. County had 4.5 million male inhabitants, plus thousands of tourists, plus the truckers from all over the country who made deliveries to the city. Shannon Exley could have gotten into the vehicles of fifteen different strange men on the night she died.

A week later, Miller saw a teletype about a dead girl found in a freight company parking lot on Myers Street in Hollenbeck, and contacted the same detectives working the Exley case. A homeless man foraging for firewood in the industrial zone along the L.A. River had found her lying on her back underneath a big rig trailer with a bra tightly knotted around her neck. Most of her clothing was missing; a sock, T-shirt, and hypodermic syringe lying near her body were the only articles at the scene. Her fingerprints and a follow-up investigation revealed her story.

Thirty-three-year-old Irene Rodriguez had arrived in L.A. in April 1991 on a Greyhound from El Paso, Texas, where she'd been living with her common-law husband and their four children. Child-bearing hadn't altered her girlish figure—maybe her heroin habit had kept her slender—and her face had fine features, with large, widely spaced brown eyes. She had visited her parents in L.A. just before Mother's Day, but instead of returning to her husband and children in El Paso, she stayed, turning tricks to support her drug habit. Her roommate saw her for the last time at 8:00 p.m. on Friday, June 28, as she was leaving the apartment to go to work on Seventh.

"He's done it twice," Miller told the Hollenbeck detectives. "I wouldn't be surprised if he does it again this coming Fourth of July weekend. Keep a watch on your area, and we'll put Seventh under surveillance."

On the evening of July 3, Sherri Long went to work on Sunset Boulevard in Hollywood, which lies about seven miles from Seventh Avenue in downtown. Like a lot of girls from the Midwest, she had moved to L.A. hoping for a more exciting life. The warm weather, the glamour and stimulation of life in the great city of movies and music were to be a happy change from Michigan. But after her arrival she learned that an elementary education and a few hundred dollars didn't go very far in the City of Angels. She drifted into the wrong crowd, got into drugs, and began the downward slide.

Tourists from all over the world make pilgrimages to Hollywood to see the mythical site. They arrive at the "Walk of Fame" at Sunset and Vine, and process down Sunset. Good observers might notice signs posted on medians at certain intersections that read NO TURNS 11:00 P.M. TO 7:00 A.M. NIGHTLY. Don't mind those girls standing on that corner on the opposite side of the street; just keep going straight. Nowadays it's hard to tell the pros from the teenyboppers, but in the summer of 1991, there was no mistaking it: Sunset Boulevard between La Brea and Fairfax was the biggest outdoor girl-flesh market in America. The drag got a publicity windfall in June 1995, when Hugh Grant couldn't resist the temptation standing on the corner of Sunset and Courtney.

From Hollywood, Sunset Boulevard runs about seventeen miles west, through Beverly Hills and Brentwood, all the way to the Pacific

Ocean. Running west from the end of Sunset, the Pacific Coast Highway hugs the Malibu coast, with the shoreline on the left and the
foothills of the Santa Monica Mountains rising from the right. Twelve
miles up the coast, the highway intersects the base of Corral Canyon
Road, which ascends to the mesa where lovers like to go.

After dusk, when the stars come out, the landscape seems even
more primeval, its dark serrated ridges silhouetted by the night sky. The
moon reflects off the dry grass, illuminating the countryside like film
exposed day for night. Behind the peaks to the southeast, a skyward-
radiating glow is the only reminder that just fifteen miles away lies one
of the largest cities on earth. The mesa is so serene that the sounds of
nature, usually drowned out by people and machines, become audible.
Had anyone been in its vicinity at around midnight, July 3, 1991, he
might have heard—rising above the distant surf and the trickle of nearby
Solstice Creek—Sherri Long's scream.

After her body was found eight days later, Lancaster and Miller met
with detectives from Hollenbeck and Long Beach at the Hollenbeck
Station on July 15. The Long Beach detectives were investigating the
murder of a black prostitute named Alice Duval, whose body had been
found on June 10, lying in a field, strangled to death. It was possible her
murder was part of the same series, though her killer had asphyxiated
her with his hands instead of with her bra. All the detectives had seen
women manually throttled, but none strangled with her bra, the bra left
tied around her neck. The knotting also looked similar, though only the
crime lab could make that judgment. It was a job for "the Boa."

Dr. Lynne Herold at the L.A. County Sheriff's Department crime
lab got her training in one of the busiest laboratories of forensic pathology in the world, the Los Angeles County Department of Coroner,
"responsible for the investigation and determination of the cause and
manner of all sudden, violent, or unusual deaths in the County." Every
time one of L.A. County's residents expires without a physician attending within twenty days prior, he or she must be examined by the coroner,
who receives about eighteen thousand cases annually.

When Dr. Herold was at the department (1982–89) it received

about three thousand possible homicide victims per year. Her job was to figure out which of the deceased had indeed been murdered. By the time she transferred to the sheriff's crime lab in 1989, she had examined about twelve thousand people who'd been shot, stabbed, strangled, and bludgeoned.

At the crime lab, which reviews about seventy thousand cases per year, she analyzed physical evidence in all kinds of crime. She had a flair for it, and detectives from both the LAPD and the Sheriff's Department relied on her for help with investigative leads. Though she didn't know it, among themselves they sometimes called her "the Boa." The origin of the name was a mystery. Maybe it had something to do with her pet python Penelope, who some mistook for a boa constrictor.

The python and the boa immobilize their prey by wrapping their coils around it. Homicidal men sometimes immobilize and kill their victims by wrapping material around their hands, limbs, and throats. Dr. Herold had seen countless variations of binding, gagging, and strangling. Often the material could lead to the killer, as in the case of the murdered woman found in a parking lot in Orange County. Her body was encased in a sheet of plastic wrapped with orange tape. None of the big retailers or hardware stores carried the tape, but the airline baggage department where her husband worked used it. He was what Dr. Herold called "felony dumb."

Sometimes a killer may use an unusual material and fashion it in an unusual way. There was the case of the murdered girl found in an alley, rolled up in a tarp lashed with an assemblage of wire coat hangers. The killer had unwound, interlocked, and rewound the hangers so that they fit together like links in a chain. The hooks all faced in the same direction except the two at the top of the circle, which faced opposite directions. It was a strange instrument for bundling a tarp—time-consuming to make and less suitable than a roll of tape or twine. A VICAP search turned up a victim in Louisiana, bundled in a tarp lashed with the same kind of coat-hanger chain, and it just so happened that the boyfriend of the girl's mother, who was already under suspicion, had been in the same part of Louisiana, visiting his uncle, at the time that victim disappeared.

The coat-hanger chain must have had symbolic significance to the killer, because he had no practical reason to use it. In most cases involving a ligature, it is a functional means of immobilizing the victim or bundling the body. For the killer who created the coat-hanger chain, the bundle was not just a means to an end but an end in itself. The chain meant something to him. It was the peculiar expression of a peculiar idea, which set it apart from thousands of other victims bundled with cords.

Dr. Herold had seen victims bound with all kinds of tape, rope, extension cords, speaker cable, telephone cords, and electrical wire; in most cases the killer simply lashed the cord around the victim and tied it with a few overhand knots. The overhand—"the knot that ties itself," as some American Indian tribes called it, because it naturally forms tangles in nets and other lines—is effective for simple purposes and easy to tie. It also happens to be the only knot the majority of people know, so in crimes in which a complex knot is used, it may be useful in pointing to a suspect.

On July 16, 1991, a deputy from the sheriff's department picked up the three bras from the coroner and delivered them to Dr. Herold at the crime lab. She opened the three brown paper bags (plastic, which traps moisture and breeds bacteria, is used only in movies) and laid out the bras on her table. Strange. None of them had wire-enforced cups, which meant that the entire articles could have served as the ligatures. A bra is a cord that runs around a woman's torso with suspenders over her shoulders. The killer could have grasped the ends with his hands, turned it once around the woman's neck, and pulled. The slender bands of elastic material that run through a bra make a ready-to-use tourniquet that will constrict the carotid arteries with little force. But this killer apparently didn't care about simplicity. Out of each victim's bra he'd made an instrument whose complexity exceeded the application of simple strangulation.

First of all, he'd used a tool. With a sharp instrument (probably a knife) he'd cut one of the shoulder straps from the top of the cup and made an incision along a side panel, which created an eye through which he ran the shoulder strap. The cut in the side panel also separated the top and bottom elastic bands. Running the shoulder strap between them enabled him to exert force over three cords, with less friction in between them. Had he not dismantled the bra, he would have had only one (though again, just one would have sufficed). The slip component enabled him to play with the constriction. The final knot that held the ligature in place had an intricate, braided quality, though it was tied too tightly to tell the precise combination of loops without untying it.

All three were tied off at enormous tension. The neck of the slightly built Rodriguez was compressed to a circumference of six inches, the medium-built Exley's to seven, and that of the heavy-set Sherri Long down to eight. That the killer had used far more pressure than was necessary (only five pounds per square inch applied to the carotid arteries) to asphyxiate his victims wasn't unusual. What stood out was how he'd taken such care to tie the nooses at maximum tension, rather than releasing them, even just a little, after the women became lifeless.

So the ligatures shared the same distinct points:

1. Each was made from an intimate article of the woman's own clothing.

2. Each was dismantled with a tool, even though it was already lethal without preparation.

3. Each had incisions in the same places.

4. Each was left around the victim's neck and tied off at maximum tension.

5. Each had a knot holding the ligature in place that was more complex than the usual series of overhands.

It was significant that the killer had used the women's bras instead of bringing a ready-to-use ligature with him. He'd brought a cutting tool; he could have just as easily brought along a piece of cord. Given the bra's effectiveness as a ligature, one might expect it to be a common tool in strangulation murders. Yet among hundreds of cases of women murdered by men, these were the first three Dr. Herold had ever seen in which the women had been strangled with their own bras.

She didn't speculate about why the killer had strangled the women the way he had. She would only state her opinion that, in comparison to the hundreds of cases of ligature strangulation she had examined, the three bra ligatures were unique. Nevertheless, it was reasonable to infer from them that the killer was experienced. An inexperienced strangler may have trouble telling when his victim is dead, and he may be surprised when she starts to regain consciousness after he takes the pressure off her carotid arteries. Cases have been documented of stranglers returning to the crime scene to make sure their victims are dead. The killer who strangled the prostitutes with their bras had developed a method for ensuring they wouldn't revive. That suggested he'd had trouble in the past with a victim living to tell the tale of her ordeal to the police.

"What do you think?" Detective Miller and his partner James Harper asked Lynne Herold a few days later.

"For all three, I think you should be looking for the same guy," she said, confirming what Detective Miller already suspected. With the Hollenbeck detectives, he and Harper visited the crime scenes and went over every detail. The killer picked up the first girl, Shannon Exley, on Seventh and drove straight for two miles, across the L.A. River and into Boyle Heights. At Fickett Street he turned right. Thirty yards down the narrow street, Fickett dead-ends at a steep embankment of the Pomona Freeway. Just to the left of the dead end was a chain-link gate that could be opened onto a little parking lot behind the Girl Scout Center. He apparently strangled her in the car or on the ground of the parking lot, adjacent to the lot surrounded by trees. A trail in the grass indicated where he'd dragged her body about twenty feet and dumped it at the base of a eucalyptus—a waste of time and effort, given that it had done nothing to conceal the body.

With the second girl, Rodriguez, he did almost exactly the same thing. He picked her up on Seventh and kept driving straight and over the bridge. But instead of continuing into Boyle Heights, he turned left on Myers Street, just east of the river. Through the concrete cityscape of warehouses he drove until he reached the intersection of Mission and Myers, where he turned left into the parking lot by the river. The same routine: strangle the girl, either in the car or on the ground next to the car, and drag her body underneath something, in that case a big rig trailer. It was the same gesture that didn't really conceal her body.

Everything matched up, though one thing puzzled Miller. For the second girl, why had the killer chosen that particular parking area? For his first victim, the empty lot surrounded by trees was a one-of-a-kind near downtown, but the parking lot behind the loading dock offered no apparent advantage over a number of ill-lit spots among the warehouses, many of which had the advantage of being closer to the turnoff from Seventh. So it was odd that he drove so far north, almost all the way to the First Street Bridge.

One night Miller and Harper drove the killer's route, examining the spots he could have chosen, trying to glean why they compared unfavorably with the place he'd chosen for his ritual. Maybe it just felt right to him. Or was there something special about the parking lot by the river?

Miller and Harper also spent hours around Seventh and Gladys in a surveillance van, noting license plates and talking to the girls. The women understood they weren't there to arrest them but to solve the murders. Some women *wanted* to talk to them about their traumatic experiences. Some began to cry at the mention of their murdered friends.

"Shannon was such a nice girl," one said, with tears streaming down her face. "Why would someone do that to her?" Miller wondered the same. In listening to prostitutes, he got depressed by the viciousness they described—of men beating them up and forcing them to perform humiliating acts. It was a testament to the terrible power of drugs that many of the girls stuck with the job. In LAPD jargon, women who sold their bodies for drug money were called "strawberries." Miller sometimes wondered where the name came from. Maybe it was from the red hypodermic "track marks" that resembled the skin of a strawberry. Both the murdered women were strawberries—Exley cocaine, Rodriguez heroin.

He sensed the killer was more refined than the typical pig who assaulted girls. Not that he was above brute violence. He'd hit both women in the face and Rodriguez in the abdomen hard enough to cause internal damage. Still, his work was methodical and controlled. He probably got the girls where he wanted them without a struggle, and savored his power over them with the devilish noose he made out of their bras.

Was he a trucker? Most of the johns around Seventh and Gladys were. They drove in from all over the country, dropped their trailers at the docks, and then cruised for girls in their cabs while the freight was unloaded. Truckers also work with cords and knots for tying down freight. One long-haul trucker, who was observed picking up girls on Seventh, happened to be a registered sex offender, and so Miller and Harper visited his company to look at his driving logs. Extrapolating from his times at weigh stations, they determined that he wasn't in Los Angeles on the mornings the girls were murdered.

From the start, Deputy Lancaster at the Sheriff's Department had questioned the trucker hypothesis because it was based on little more than the location of the first two murders. If someone saw a trucker in the area at the critical times, he could account for it by saying he was there for his job. But what about the third murder? After committing the first two near his place of work, why would a trucker then take the third victim all the way up to Malibu? And something else: a few days after Sherri Long's autopsy, Lancaster made contact with her brother in Michigan, who'd occasionally spoken with her before her disappearance. She'd called him collect a few times, and his phone bill indicated numbers in Hollywood. If the killer were a trucker who favored the area he knew from his job, why would he drive to Hollywood to pick up the third one?

A month later, Lancaster tracked down Sherri's ex-boyfriend. He refused to come to the station, but he agreed to meet at a restaurant, provided his mother and sister could come along. The thirty-year-old man said he couldn't have murdered Sherri Long because he'd only just gotten out of jail for beating her up. Good alibi; at any rate, it checked out.

"We were living together at the Peppertree Motel in Hollywood earlier this year. I got tired of her drug use and prostitution; that's why I beat her up. I haven't seen her since I went to jail." His sister was more helpful. She'd gotten to be friends with Sherri and had, not long before she disappeared, taken some clothes to her at the Hollywood Vine Motel.

In the summer of 1991, the Vine was a popular workspace for Hollywood hookers. With its hourly rates, a sex worker might check in and out several times per night, perhaps looking up at the famous HOLLY-

WOOD sign on the hillside above as she returned to her post on Sunset. Lancaster dropped in and showed the manager a picture of Sherri Long. He recognized her, said she was a regular customer, but that he hadn't seen her for a month. The register showed she'd checked out for the last time at 11:00 on the night of July 3.

Lancaster tried to imagine the sequence of events. After picking up Sherri Long near or on the main drag, the killer probably once again just kept going straight, this time down Sunset, all the way to the Pacific Coast Highway, where he turned right and headed up the Malibu Coast. What did he tell her when she suggested they go back to the Vine? Maybe he said he was headed to a party in Malibu and needed a date. Whatever he told her, it must have put her at ease, because it's a long drive from Hollywood to Corral Canyon Road, with a lot of stoplights at which she could have jumped out of the car. How strange that he'd driven her so far.

Even stranger was how he'd stopped killing. It's a rule of thumb that serial killers don't just stop. Getting away with their murders tends to embolden them to murder with greater frequency. At first Miller and Lancaster thought he'd moved on to a different town, yet their statewide queries and an FBI VICAP search yielded no matches. In the weeks following July 3, no other law-enforcement agencies in the United States reported similar cases of prostitute murder—another fact that undermined the trucker hypothesis. The killer struck three times in L.A. within a fourteen-day period, with nine days of cooling off between the first and second, and five days between the second and third. The detectives braced for a fourth murder, but it never happened.

And so, seemingly out of nowhere, a killer had materialized in Los Angeles in June 1991, murdered three of the city's streetwalkers with a refined modus operandi, with increasing frequency, and then stopped. As summer turned into fall, the case went cold, but Detective Miller didn't forget it. He often thought about the three women strangled with their bras and wondered who had murdered them.

CHAPTER 2

NO APPARENT MOTIVE

A SERIAL KILLER is the most mysterious and devious of criminals, because he has no apparent motive for committing his crimes. He kills strangers, which distinguishes him from most murderers, who have some relationship with their victims (their motive is born out of their relationship). Because he murders strangers, investigators cannot find leads by examining his victims' acquaintances.

He gains nothing from his murders (other than fleeting sexual gratification), nor does he avenge a wrong or eliminate a rival. His motive is an inner urge to assault, sexually abuse, and kill, nurtured by endless fantasizing. A few serial rapists and killers have video-recorded their crimes; the videos (seized by the police) show them to be exquisitely aroused by their victims' cries of pain, and callous to their pleas for mercy. To a normal human being, the tormentors appear to be monsters in human guise.

Centuries before the FBI agent Robert Ressler coined the expression "serial killer" and described them as a distinct category of murderers, their depredations were recorded. In 1440, the French nobleman Gilles de Rais was convicted for raping and murdering hundreds of boys. A few decades later, pamphlets printed on the recently invented movable-type press reported the bestial murders of the Wallachian (now Romania) Prince Vlad Tepes ("the Impaler"), or Vlad Dracula. In 1610, the Hungarian countess Erzsebet Bathory was imprisoned for torturing and murdering hundreds of girls in her castle. Historians tend to regard these tyrants as different from modern serial killers, but Rais's and Bathory's modus operandi of luring victims into their castles was used in 1890s Chicago by Herman Webster Mudgett, aka Dr. H. H. Holmes, whose three-story hotel was known in the neighborhood as "the castle."

The incidence of serial murder (and the means to detect it) has greatly increased in modern times. The first graphic depictions of the ritual—abduction, sexual abuse, torture, and murder—were penned by the Marquis de Sade while he sat in the Bastille prison in Paris in 1784–89. Following Sade's death, the cities of Europe and America grew rapidly, with ever increasing numbers of people encountering each other on the streets. During the 1870s, many sexual murders were reported in France, Italy, Britain, and the United States, and some of the murderers confessed to experiencing orgasm when they killed their victims.

In 1886, Richard Freiherr von Krafft-Ebing, a professor of psychiatry at the University of Vienna, published the first clinical description of a mental condition he called "sadism," after the Marquis de Sade. A sadist, he explained, is one who gets or tries to get sexual gratification by inflicting pain and humiliation on another.

Two years later, in 1888, Jack the Ripper murdered a series of prostitutes in the Whitechapel area of London. That he was never caught partly accounts for why he is still the most legendary serial killer in history. Assisting the investigation was the surgeon Dr. Robert Bond, who wrote a sophisticated profile of the unknown offender.

The Ripper terrorized the prostitutes of London's East End, but Peter "the Vampire" Kürten terrorized the entire city of Düsseldorf, Germany, in 1929, murdering children, women, and one man. After Kürten was arrested, he spoke at length about his crimes with the psychologist Karl Berg, who wrote a book about him titled *The Sadist*.

In the 1970s, analysts at the FBI and other American law-enforcement agencies began a broad, systematic study of serial rapists and murderers. After World War II, America became an increasingly individualistic and mobile society, increasingly plagued by predatory offenders. With its large population living under one federal jurisdiction, its single language, its uncensored news media, and its advanced police agencies, America in the 1970s and '80s was an ideal laboratory for studying criminals who comprise a tiny percentage of humanity.

Serial killers are rare. In the 1980s, the FBI estimated that, at any given time, there were about thirty-five in the United States (then a nation of about 240 million people) who had committed murders but had not yet been detained. In 1988, the FBI agent Robert Ressler published *Sexual Homicide: Patterns and Motives*, based upon interviews of thirty-six convicted offenders, twenty-nine of whom were serial killers. Twenty-nine is a small number of people, but it's a huge number of serial killers to analyze. Countries with relatively small populations may not experience a single one for decades.

In America, he may be only one in 6.8 million, but just one active serial killer—especially if he's intelligent and organized—can take an enormous toll on society and present the greatest challenge to investigators. When one struck three times in Los Angeles in the summer of 1991, Detective Miller was already familiar with the challenge.

Six thousand miles to the east, in Vienna, Austria, a series of prostitute murders in the spring of 1991 had taken the city's police investigators by surprise. Never had any of them seen anything like it. Ernst Geiger, head of Vienna Homicide, figured it was going to be tough to find the killer. He had no idea of the true challenge that lay ahead.

CHAPTER 3

THE FEAR IN THE RED-LIGHT DISTRICT

PROSTITUTE IN VIENNA MURDERED: THREE STILL MISSING read the front-page headline of the May 22, 1991, edition of the newspaper *Kurier*.

> *Four prostitutes have gone missing without a trace from the Penzing neighborhood of Vienna. On Monday, one of them—Sabine Moitzi, 25—was found strangled in the Scots Woods by a hiker.*

Now there is grave concern for the lives of the three still missing.
In the red-light district the fear of death prevails.

Kurier crime reporter Peter Grolig got the scoop. From his contacts in the Vienna police, he learned that the four women had disappeared from the same part of the red-light district in April and the beginning of May. After the last woman vanished on May 7, Grolig heard there was speculation at police headquarters that all of them might have been murdered by an "eerie prostitute killer," because the disappearance of four hookers from the same neighborhood within such a brief period was unprecedented. And then the first body was found in the Vienna Woods on May 20.

Heavy rains in April and the beginning of May had kept the hikers away, but with June approaching, the warm weather beckoned. It also promoted putrefaction. A sixty-two-year-old retiree, walking a path through the Scots Woods (a section of the Vienna Woods) near the Sign of the Cross Meadow, noticed the smell first. Scanning the forest floor among the stumps and dead leaves, he saw a corpse.

A patrol officer dispatched to the scene could see it was no suicide, and an investigative team soon arrived. Ernst Geiger, head of Homicide, examined the body. The young woman was naked except for a leotard hiked up around her shoulders. Lying face down with her legs spread wide apart and her arms extended forward, she appeared to be melting into the compost of the forest floor—literally returning to the soil. A layer of bluish gray fungus spread over her body, giving her a ghostly appearance. Foxes had chewed the flesh off her right leg. Her killer had arranged her corpse to cause outrage. He had planted her face in the dirt, spread her legs, and situated her backside so that her anus and genitals would face upward, gaping toward the viewer. It was the ultimate obscene gesture, an expression of mocking hatred.

A stocking was bound around her neck, and an autopsy later confirmed that she had died from strangulation with her own panty hose. Fashioning the nylon material into an elaborate noose, the killer had applied tremendous force and then tied it off. The slip component indicated he might have alternately tightened and relaxed the pressure to prolong her agony. However long it had taken, it had been a terrifying death.

Though the killer had left her jewelry on her body, he had scattered some of her clothing and the contents of her purse in a large radius around her. Geiger imagined him tracing a circle, tossing her personal effects from side to side. He had also sprinkled soil and leaves over her, slightly camouflaging her, but not enough to prevent her from being discovered. It was more of a gesture than a proper burial, as though the killer had wanted her to be found eventually. He had not felt rushed, but had been confident of being alone. Given the risk of a hiker showing up during the day, even in bad weather, he must have carried out the ritual late at night. Among the scattered articles, the investigators could find no apartment key and no documents identifying the victim.

Geiger had never seen anything quite like what lay before him. He sensed he wasn't looking at a dump site but at a murder scene. The killer had taken the girl into the woods at night—itself a frightening experience—and strangled her among the trees, in the darkness, where no one could hear her screams. The Vienna Woods, which arc around the western half of the city, are in places dense and primeval. In no other major city in Europe does the urban zone so abruptly give way to forest— a clear boundary between civilization and wilderness across which no prostitute would drive with a client at night. What tricks had the killer used on her?

It didn't take long to identify the victim; her husband had filed a missing-person report the previous month. Twenty-five-year-old Sabine Moitzi was a bakery salesgirl by day, but unknown even to her husband, she occasionally worked as a "secret prostitute" (meaning she wasn't registered with the Office of Health, as prostitutes are required to be by law in Vienna). The delicately built brunette had fallen into the trap of heroin addiction, and her wages at the bakery didn't cover the cost. At around 11:00 on the night of April 16, her friend Ilse dropped her off at an intersection near the railyard of the West Train Station. The neighborhood has long been low-rent, the home of down-and-outers such as the art school reject Adolf Hitler, who had once lived in a building near Sabine's corner. When Ilse passed by ten minutes later, Sabine was gone. Her body was found five weeks later, and its state of decay indicated she had been dead about that long. The streets that run east-west through the district lead directly to the Vienna Woods. Her killer had probably picked her up and driven straight to the place of her death.

The second body was found three days later, on May 23. A woman looking for her guinea pig's favorite food found the naked corpse of Karin Eroglu instead. Karin had disappeared on the night of May 7 from her corner, just a few blocks from where Sabine had last been seen. She'd been driven ten miles outside the city, even deeper into the woods. Her body lay in a grove of spruce trees, thirty yards from the nearest road. She was a heavy woman; the strongest of men would have struggled to carry her that distance. Most likely her killer had forced her to walk to the spot where her corpse would later be found. The blunt-force trauma to her face indicated he had savagely beaten her. From her leotard he had fashioned the same kind of ligature that was found around Sabine Moitzi's neck. He had taken the rest of her clothing with him. Once again he had placed the body face down, leaving her jewelry. Once again the primitive burial gesture—a tree branch laid across her head. But this time he had left a trace of himself. Under her body was the torn-off fingertip of a rubber surgical glove, a clue he had planned the killing.

Two women murdered in the same way—Geiger knew it was only a matter of time before the corpses of the other two missing women, Silvia Zagler and Regina Prem, turned up. His investigators questioned everyone they could find who had known the murdered and missing, and constructed the following chronology:

APRIL 8, 1991: Silvia Zagler was last seen on her corner. Her body had not yet been found, but Geiger believed it would be, somewhere in the Vienna Woods.

APRIL 16, 1991: Sabine Moitzi was last seen on her corner. Her body was found on May 20 in the Vienna Woods.

APRIL 28, 1991: Regina Prem was last seen walking back to her corner from a hotel. Her body had not yet been found, but Geiger believed it would be, somewhere in the Vienna Woods.

MAY 7, 1991: Karin Eroglu was last seen on her corner. Her body was found on May 23 in the Vienna Woods.

All the women were from the lowest class of street prostitution. Not very attractive, none of them had strong pimps to stake out corners for them near the neon-lit nightclubs. They were pushed off to the fringes of the district, to lonely, ill-lit corners. No one was looking after them, which was doubtless why the killer had selected them.

He had struck on average once every ten days, on a Sunday, Monday, or Tuesday night, when the traffic in the neighborhood was light and when most of the residents of the surrounding apartment buildings were already at home asleep. After murdering Karin Eroglu, he stopped, and it was notable that the first body was found at about the time he could be expected to strike again. That suggested he had seen the newspaper report on May 22 and decided to cool it. How long would he cool it? How long *could* he?

Geiger's experience with murderers in general was small compared to that of an American big-city cop like Detective Miller in Los Angeles. At the time the prostitutes disappeared, he was a thirty-six-year-old police lawyer who had just been appointed head of Homicide. Through hard work and study, he had come a long way from the poor rural village of his birth.

His role model, Uncle Ernst, had been the prize pupil of the philosopher Ludwig Wittgenstein, who had taught for two years at the local grammar school. The eccentric genius had taught the children with missionary zeal. He sent "Geigerl" (little Geiger), as he called Uncle Ernst, to an elite Gymnasium in Vienna. Geiger followed in his uncle's footsteps and went to the capital for his education, though it wasn't the son of a steel magnate who paid for it but the socialist government of Chancellor Bruno Kreisky.

At the University of Vienna he'd earned his law doctorate in record time, forgoing the idle, enchanted life of most students in the city. He'd worked hard, and it had paid off, at least in terms of advancement. From his first post in the quiet suburb of Hietzing he'd shot up the ranks as no one in the history of the Vienna police had.

Yet sometimes it seemed as if he'd gotten all dressed up with no place to go, because most crime in Vienna was simple. A melancholy streak in the Viennese caused them to kill themselves more often than others, and when they did kill others, they were usually sloppy about it. Most of the murder investigations Geiger had overseen were cases of domestic abuse turned lethal.

The Vienna Homicide section was small because homicide in the city was rare. In 1990 the number of murders hit a thirty-year high of 50 in a city of 1.5 million. In the same year, 983 murders (many gang-related) were committed in Los Angeles, then a city of 3.5 million; about another 1,000 were committed in the other cities of Los Angeles County, which had an aggregate population of 6 million.

While postwar America was increasingly plagued by violent crime, in Austria the trend went the other way. After the turmoil of the first half of the twentieth century: the dissolution of the monarchy in 1918, the civil war in 1934, the crime and destruction of the Nazi period (1938–45), and the oppression of the Four Powers occupation (1945–55), the Austrians were determined to create political and social harmony. On a visit in 1983, Pope John Paul II called the country of 7.5 million an "Isle of the Blessed" for its apparent elimination of the social ills that afflicted most other countries.

In 1991, Vienna was (and still is) a mellow city of coffeehouses and classical music. Administered by a large civil service with a zeal for urban planning and regulation, the city is one of the cleanest and safest in the world. The Viennese have a deeply ingrained law-and-order mentality, and visitors are often surprised to see them waiting patiently for the green signal at a crosswalk, even if there are no cars in sight of the intersection.

That's not to say that the Viennese don't have a dark side, and many chafe at the strict regulation of life (without ever actually breaking the rules). It's probably no coincidence that Freud, the theoretician of neuroses, was a Viennese. Many Austrian authors have written about their resentment and loathing of their society's staidness and narrow-mindedness.

Law and order also prevail in Vienna's red-light district. Though prostitution is legal in Vienna, it is highly regulated. The police tolerate a certain amount of nefarious activity in "the milieu," as the Viennese call the world of prostitutes and pimps, so long as it doesn't result in violence and public disorder. The neighborhoods where hookers work are just as safe as the rest of the city. While prostitution is a high-risk occupation in most cities, in Vienna the homicide rate among hookers was no higher than that of the general population.

That all changed in the spring of 1991, when the "Vienna Woods Killer" (as the press called him) started striking. How exactly had he gotten women so far out of the city, alone in the forest, while he made a noose out of their underwear? They wouldn't have gotten to that point without a fight, and though weaker than most men, they could still punch, kick, scratch, and bite. Some were handy with a can of mace.

It seemed likely the killer had avoided a struggle in the city, because it would have been difficult to drive with a kicking and screaming woman trying to jump out at every red signal light. He had to have quickly immobilized them, or to have tricked them into *agreeing* to drive into the woods with him. However he'd done it, it was with skill, because he appeared to have a perfect score. Geiger's investigators didn't turn up a single prostitute who told of a client *attempting* to drive her into the woods but failing to pull it off when she resisted or fled.

In the days and weeks following the discovery of the first body, investigators spent hours talking to prostitutes and pimps, noting descriptions of violent or perverse customers and trying to track them down for an interview. They examined numerous sex offenders and tapped all their informants in the red-light district for anything they might have heard. They received about 130 credible-sounding tips, and they did their best to evaluate all of them.

Because of the prominence of the case in the media, there was a barrage of tips from women trying to settle scores with abusive and unfaithful ex-husbands and boyfriends. A number of men could hypothetically be regarded as a suspect in one of the murders. Per standard procedure, the investigators looked at the men known to have had regular contact with each of the girls. But given the probability that all the women had fallen prey to the same killer, Geiger understood that the only true suspect was one who could be placed at the abduction scene of not just one woman but of all four.

Ironically, the women disappeared just as *The Silence of the Lambs* was making a sensation in Vienna's cinemas. No one had ever seen a bad guy like Hannibal Lecter, so eloquent, charismatic, and cunning. Dr. Lecter became a celebrity, and at the very moment he was stimulating interest in serial killers, the Viennese got their own.

The newspapers produced a steady stream of reports on his crimes. Even Austria's most serious periodical, *profil* magazine, joined the media frenzy. "Streetwalkers Die: A Series of Murders Shakes the Austrian Prostitution Scene" was the title of a long feature in their June 3, 1991, edition. For most readers, the unknown killer was fascinating, like a character out of *The Silence of the Lambs*. The inspectors thought of him as Vienna's version of Jack the Ripper, and a report published by the Association of Police Inspectors referred to him by the English moniker "Jack the Struggler," a misspelling of "Jack the Strangler."

Things were different in the red-light district. While the good burgers of Vienna could read about the Strangler in the safety of their coffeehouses, the girls on the street had to live with him. Particularly shocking was the news that Karin Eroglu had been murdered. Sabine Moitzi was a novice, but Karin was an old pro. The only time her friends had worried about her was when she'd married a Turk for $5,000. "What if someday he returns to Turkey and insists on taking you with him?" her best friend had asked her. Maybe the Ottoman sieges of Vienna, when hundreds of girls had been hauled off to Turkey, still lingered in the collective memory. In the end, Karin disappeared not into the hinterland of Anatolia but into the nearby Vienna Woods. If the killer got her, he could get anybody. Like the East End of London in the summer of 1888, Vienna's red-light district at the end of May 1991 became a place of fear.

CHAPTER 4

A DRAMATIC APPEAL

CONSPICUOUSLY ABSENT from the media coverage of the murders were mourning relatives. Like many prostitutes, the murdered and missing women had little contact with their families, or they had grown up in orphanages. No one came forth to talk about them as they'd been in life, and so the public never learned anything about them other than their names and ages and where they had last been seen. The exception was Rudolf Prem, the husband of the still missing Regina Prem.

She had grown up in an orphanage and held various menial jobs, and according to Rudolf, two years after she met him she realized she could make a lot more money turning tricks. They had a child and got married, and Rudolf quit his job as a plumber to stay home and look after the boy, who was under the impression his mother worked as a waitress. With her earnings she had furnished their apartment and built a playroom for their child, and just before she disappeared, she bought him a new navy suit for his first communion.

"She was an insanely good mother," Rudolf explained to *profil* magazine. "She'd let herself be torn into pieces for the boy."

Nights on the street had aged the thirty-three-year-old woman. For a while she'd been addicted to Rohypnol sleeping pills and landed in the Steinhof nerve clinic. When she got out, she put on her work clothes and returned to her corner.

The intersection of the Linzerstrasse and the Flachgasse lies in the "free zone" of the red-light district, near the rail yard of the West Train Station, away from the nightclubs, with their neon lights and traffic. At 9:45 p.m. on Sunday, April 28, 1991, Rudolf dropped her off for her appointment with a regular client, a wine salesman. Usually she finished around 2:00 a.m. and called Rudolf to pick her up. When she didn't call that morning, he drove to her corner and saw she wasn't there. Her colleague Erika, who stood on the opposite corner, hadn't seen her all night. They drove to various dead-end streets where Regina serviced her customers, but couldn't find her. They then went to the Hotel Rudolfshohe, where Regina sometimes went with high-paying clients. The porter had seen her that evening; she'd paid her bill and left at 11:30. The sausage vendor across the street said the same thing: Regina walked out of the Rudolfshohe around 11:30 by herself. She must have then returned to her corner and encountered her last customer.

On May 24, 1991, *Kurier* journalist Peter Grolig reported Rudolf's claim that he had seen the "Phantom of Graz"—an unknown killer who had recently murdered prostitutes in the city of Graz, 120 miles south of Vienna—in a Vienna red-light establishment. *Viennese* magazine had just published a report on "the Phantom" in its May edition, illustrated with a composite sketch of a man whom a witness claimed to have seen leaving the apartment of one of the victims. On May 28 a homicide inspector traveled to Graz to determine if there were parallels between the Graz and Vienna murders, and he concluded there weren't.

On May 28, Peter Grolig reported Rudolf's "dramatic appeal" to the killer: "I don't want to believe she's dead. Maybe she's been abducted and locked up somewhere. But if the lunatic has killed Regina, he should at least say where her body lies. My wife deserves a decent burial." He described Regina's clothing: a red suede leather jacket, a white skirt, and white high heels. If she was still alive, he would pay 10,000 Schillings ($1,000) for information leading to her.

CHAPTER 5

A SPECIAL QUALIFICATION

ON MONDAY, JUNE 3, ten days after the second body was found, a reporter for the ORF (Austrian Broadcasting Corporation) arrived at police headquarters for an interview with Chief Max Edelbacher about the murders. The reporter introduced himself as Jack Unterweger and said he was producing a story for *Journal Panorama* (the highest quality current-events radio program in the country).

Unterweger explained that he was a freelance reporter who'd gotten the assignment because of a special qualification. His aunt had been a prostitute who was murdered by her last customer in 1967. From her he'd learned about the lives of prostitutes; from losing her, he understood what the girls in the red-light district who'd lost their friends were going through. The previous Friday, he had interviewed a few of them while they stood on their corners.

To Edelbacher, the reporter asked cogent questions about the search for the unknown killer. Though the police chief preferred not to go into detail about the running investigation, in this case, he had no cards to hide.

Despite a number of leads, so far we have obtained no positive result. What we are really missing is material evidence, because the prostitutes we have found so far had already been lying there for a relatively long time, and any material traces that may have been left were destroyed by the bad weather. It rained very hard for a long time.

To the entire country he had admitted it—*he had nothing*. This killer, the likes of whom he'd never seen, was a phantom. Four women had vanished and no one had seen a thing. "It must be very frustrating for an officer to, so to speak, run into such a dead end," the reporter said. *Frustrating indeed*.

At the same time the reporter Jack Unterweger produced the radio story, he also researched and co-wrote an article on the murders for the weekly newspaper *Falter*. For the *Falter* piece he took a more editorial tone, asserting that, while the fear of the unknown killer was understandable, the press was responsible for whipping it into hysteria. Most journalists, he claimed, were incapable of understanding what the prostitutes were going through. Their reporting was aimed solely at satisfying the "greedy voyeurism" of their middle-class readership—its "appetite for sex, blood, and tears." The prostitutes also read the reports, which caused them to live and work in a state of panic. Their fear caused them to suspect *everyone*, and to give the police a superabundance of tips. Trying to check them all caused the investigators "to lose valuable time in the search for the real murderer."

In other words, the fear itself had become as much a problem as the real risk of falling prey to the unknown killer. It was a good point—the same made by the Viennese director Fritz Lang in his 1931 film *M*—the first ever about a serial killer, inspired by the Peter Kürten case two years earlier.

According to Unterweger, the cops were also struggling to overcome the distrust of prostitutes and pimps. While the girls were wary of the police, he assured them that he—the nephew of a murdered prostitute—really understood their world and was someone they could trust.

While the massive increase of police presence in the district might deter the killer, it was also bad for business, because many customers were family men who didn't want to risk being observed by the police, pulled over and questioned with a girl in the car. While interviewing hookers for *Falter*, Unterweger was questioned three times by passing cops.

"What can they do now?" one girl asked him. "It's already too late to catch him. They should have taken the missing-persons reports more seriously. If [Austrian chancellor] Vranitzky's daughter disappeared, they wouldn't wait till she was found by a mushroom hunter."

"We are also human beings," another woman said, lamenting that mainstream society wasn't concerned about them. "Many overlook the fact that we provide a valuable social service."

Unterweger agreed. "We should be glad that there is a red-light district. Instead of banning and damning it, we should support it." To him, "the dead in the Vienna Woods are another argument for why society should do more to provide security for prostitutes, from medical insurance to assistance in getting out of the profession. The more securely integrated a prostitute is in society, the more she can work in safety, with less chance of falling victim to a crime," he explained.

On June 5, a couple of days after Unterweger interviewed Chief Edelbacher, his story "The Fear in the Red-Light Milieu" was broadcast on *Journal Panorama*. In the introduction, the announcer stated that Vienna wasn't the only city in Austria in which prostitutes had been killed. In recent years, streetwalkers had also been murdered or gone missing in the cities of Graz and Bregenz (385 miles west of Vienna, near the Swiss border). Yet the fear was most current in Vienna, as two murdered women had just been found in the woods and two more were missing. The program announcer also stated Unterweger's special qualification: his aunt was a prostitute "murdered in 1967 by her last customer." All over the country, people driving home for work or sitting in their homes tuned in and heard the prostitutes talking about their fears.

UNTERWEGER: Friday night, shortly after 11:00 in the Vienna Felberstrasse. Light rain, little traffic, few customers driving by the prostitutes standing in the street. Despite the unsolved murders and the still missing girls, business goes on, even if it's not as good as before. The first woman I speak with is named Susanne. She is twenty-six years old, has been in the profession for five years, and cuts a very attractive figure in her work clothes—a tightly fitting leotard, leather jacket, and high heels, all in black . . . She is feeling the pressure of the unsolved murders.

SUSANNE: Of course I'm afraid! Every car that stops, you think to yourself, That's the murderer! Sure it scares me. I don't get into cars anymore.

UNTERWEGER: How would you protect yourself?

SUSANNE: You can't protect yourself, because anything can happen on the streets. Maybe the murderer will get you, maybe someone else will. Anything can happen.

SABINE: When you read about it, it gives you a very bad feeling, and sometimes you get goose bumps all over your body just thinking about it. But you've still got to get out on the street to work, because the bills still have to be paid. You can't just stay at home and wait till he's caught. That could take months, and they may never catch him at all.

UNTERWEGER: You knew two of the victims personally. One of them was from Vorarlberg. The other one—the one from here in Vienna—was actually standing on your corner when she [*His voice wavers.*] . . . when she fell into the hands of the murderer—right here where you're standing!

SABINE: Yeah, when I get into a car, my friend writes down the license number, so if he kills me, the license number will be the murderer's. Then the police will easily track him down.

Among the people who listened to the broadcast was Chief Edelbacher. Of all the media reports about the killer, he was most interested in the *Journal Panorama* story. The state-sponsored ORF, with its monopoly on radio and television broadcasts, was the most important news organization in the country. *Journal Panorama* wasn't the radio equivalent of a tabloid crime section but a program with an audience of educated listeners—the sort of people who count in Austrian society and government.

There was also the issue of the man who had produced the program. At dinner a couple of days earlier, Edelbacher had been surprised by his wife's reaction when he mentioned that he'd been interviewed about the murders by an ORF reporter with the unusual (in Austria) name "Jack." Jack Unterweger was his full name.

"Jack Unterweger!" his wife exclaimed. "Don't you know who that is?"

"No."

"*Mensch*, Unterweger is that guy who got a life sentence for murdering a woman and who wrote a crazy book in prison. He was released last year!"

CHAPTER 6

ONE YEAR EARLIER

FREE AFTER FIFTEEN YEARS: JACK UNTERWEGER, 40 was the headline in the May 23, 1990, edition of the Vienna newspaper *Kurier*.

> *He is a bestselling author, has written seven books, and wants to film his novel* Purgatory *a second time. The talk is of Jack Unterweger, 40 years old, ex-prisoner in Stein, with a life sentence for the murder of an 18-year-old girl. In his single-occupancy cell he became a literary figure. Today, Wednesday, after more than 15 years of incarceration, the prison doors have opened for him.*

The report was illustrated with a photograph of Unterweger sitting in front of Café Landtmann (located on Vienna's grand boulevard, the Ringstrasse), wearing a silk, double-breasted glen-plaid suit on top of a snow-white shirt. Striking a pensive pose, he held his hand to his chin, displaying his gold rings and bracelet. His eyes were concealed by a pair of trendy dark glasses.

Most of the newspapers in the country ran similar stories in their culture sections, because Jack Unterweger's release from prison was a significant cultural event. Not only was he a renowned author, he was also the country's most high-profile rehabilitated offender.

In his youth he'd been a thief and pimp whose criminal career had culminated in the murder of an eighteen-year-old girl in December 1974. A year and a half later, at the age of twenty-five, he was convicted of the crime and sentenced to life in prison. He'd already begun keeping a diary in 1974, and after his arrest, he passed the time in his cell by writing reflections on various subjects. Three years after his conviction, he completed correspondence courses on literature and narrative writing, and began submitting children's stories to the ORF, which ultimately broadcast about fifty of them on its radio program for children.

His children's stories were perceived as a celebration of the love he had never known as a child. One woman, a music teacher and single mother, was so moved by them that she visited him in prison, and later testified at his parole hearing that a man who wrote such tales was "full of love." He followed up his children's stories with a play and a volume of poetry.

In 1982, the seminal year of his career, the prestigious literary magazine *Manuskripte* published his autobiographical novel, *Purgatory*, in serial form. The German publisher Maro printed the book a year later, the newspaper *Die Zeit* gave it a full-page review and the murderer Jack Unterweger became a celebrated author.

In 1988 *Purgatory* was again presented to the public in a film adaptation, first in the cinemas and then on ORF television. To be sure, many Austrians never read the book or saw the film. The people who were most interested in Jack were intellectuals. They comprised a small but influential portion of the citizenry, and in the 1980s they became fascinated by the story of his childhood and youth.

CHAPTER 7

PURGATORY

My hands, sweaty with fear, were twisted onto my back and the steel
shackles snapped around my wrists . . . I awake . . . Trembling . . .
Fearfully I gaze into the unknown darkness of the next minutes.

So *Purgatory* opens, with the narrator in prison, having a nightmare
about being put into handcuffs. Emerging from the dream into the
"strangling stillness" of his cell, he contemplates his past and wonders if
his future has been lost irrevocably. The thought of spending the rest of
his life in prison brings him to the brink of despair.

Sometimes during these moments before dawn I think I should
take my leave . . . A new package of razor blades lies ready. Also a
long leather strap. I have prepared for the minute of the last deci-
sion. I see my body go to sleep, with a final convulsion fleeing from
this lonely vegetative life. Is that the answer?

At the moment Jack was handcuffed, his life—at least his life in
freedom—ended. From thenceforth he was confined by the prison
walls. The vine-covered hills above and the Danube River below were
views of the world into which he wasn't allowed to venture. It was as if
he had died and gone, not to hell, but to purgatory.

In Catholic theology, purgatory (German: *Fegefeuer*, "cleansing fire")
is the place of sinners not condemned to hell but not yet fit to enter
heaven. In purgatory they suffer punishments in order to be redeemed.
Dante portrayed it in the second book of the *Divine Comedy*. Unlike
those who enter hell and are told to "abandon all hope," those who enter

purgatory have reason for hope. Their punishment directs them to think about their sins and to atone for them.

The title *Purgatory* prompted associations with canonical literature and with weighty moral and theological concepts. It also conveyed the idea that Jack wasn't a lost soul—that his imprisonment would eventually end and he would emerge from it redeemed. It was as if he was telling the reader: *I will one day leave this prison because I deserve to leave it.*

After the narrator of *Purgatory* decides that suicide is not the answer, his mind wanders back to his earliest memories—to the place where his journey to prison began. He was born on August 16, 1950, into a land still struggling to recover from the most destructive war in human history. His birth coincided with the midpoint of the Allied occupation of Austria (1945–55), when the nation and its capital were divided into four zones controlled by the United States, Britain, France, and the Soviet Union. The period was vividly portrayed in *The Third Man*, shot on location in bombed-out Vienna in 1948. As this was one of Jack's favorite films, it's tempting to think that he identified with the charismatic villain Harry Lime (played by Orson Welles), who led a double life in Vienna. Maybe the American occupation soldiers in the film's background made him think of his own father.

> *Of my paternity I knew only a name . . . The G.I. came from Trieste, his home was in New Jersey . . . Perhaps he gave coveted dollars or silk stockings for it. Perhaps it was a great but doomed love between the soldier and a girl who was too young and without the means to be my mother.*

Jack's mother, a country girl named Theresia Unterweger, left home in her late teens and worked as a waitress and barmaid, occasionally committing acts of theft and fraud. Like many Austrian girls, she discovered that the American soldiers occupying her country were better provisioned than Austrian boys, and could show her a better time. As Stephen Ambrose wrote in his World War II history *Band of Brothers*: "In Austria, where the women were cleaner, fairer, better built, and more willing than in any other part of Europe, the G.I.s had their field day."

When Theresia was pregnant with Jack, she was jailed for fraud, but released a few weeks before he was born. When he was old enough to drive, he loved to make long road trips, and his favorite novel was Jack Kerouac's *On the Road*, so it seems prophetic that his mother was on the road to the Austrian city of Graz when she went into labor. She named the infant after its absent father, who she claimed was an American soldier named Jack Becker whom she'd met in Trieste the previous autumn. Three years after Jack's birth, she married an American soldier in Salzburg named Donald van Blarcom. Jack never met his stepfather, but he saw photographs of the young officer, to whom he bore a striking resemblance, which caused him to conclude that Donald van Blarcom, and not Jack Becker, was his father.

When he was two years old, his mother was again arrested, and he was placed in the custody of his grandfather in Carinthia, the southernmost state of Austria. And so Jack spent his early life in the alpine countryside, though it didn't feature the panoramic vistas of *The Sound of Music*. His childhood cottage is situated in a valley that confines its inhabitants to a narrow strip of ground at its base. The sheer, densely wooded slopes rise above, creating a claustrophobic atmosphere. In *Purgatory*, Jack depicted his cottage as equally cramped and oppressive:

> *My eyes burned from the smoky air in the low little room. The women prattled, the men played cards . . . I was the house and court fool, a slave, educated by Grandfather to be a fraud's accomplice. I sat on his lap . . . playing dumb. Later I moved to my uncle's lap and betrayed his cards to Grandpa . . . I was the ace in his sleeve. His fists were my teacher, and I was a good student.*

Thus begins Jack's account of his childhood, abandoned with his violent, schnapps-swilling grandfather in the middle of nowhere, without proper food and clothing, and, above all, with no motherly love. The further the reader gets into the story, the more he is impressed with the thought: It's no wonder this poor child became a criminal.

A recurring theme in the novel is Jack's quest for his mother. He yearns for her to come and take him away from his unhappy world, but she never does. His grandfather tells him that she is a "tramp with no time for you." Later in the story, he travels to Salzburg to search for his mother, and although he doesn't find her, he does track down her sister Anna, a Salzburg prostitute. Aunt Anna is kind to him, and later in the story he is overwhelmed with grief when he learns that she has been "murdered by her last customer."

CHAPTER 8

REHABILITATION

THOUGH THE LITERARY merits of *Purgatory* are debatable, the book wasn't judged by its literary merits alone, because no one read it without the knowledge that its author was a prison inmate. He lived not in the café society of his fellow authors but in a cage with criminals, which made his voice all the more surprising and powerful.

To show the world that he was a special inmate, he gave televised readings in the prison auditorium that were attended by intellectuals and government officials. Later he was allowed to attend the premiere of his play *End Station Prison* at the Vienna People's Theater. Wearing a tuxedo, he was greeted at the entrance by a group of fans and press photographers. Afterward he remarked how strange it was that the first time he set foot in a theater was to watch his own play performed.

A short (5'6"), slender man with delicate, youthful features, he had a particularly strong effect on women, many of whom have described him as looking like a "little boy." When he read from his works, he seemed sensitive and thoughtful. As Alfred Kolleritsch, the editor of *Manuskripte*, later recalled: "At his reading in Stein, he was so tender, and at that moment we decided we had to get him pardoned."

So began the campaign to spring Jack from prison. In 1985, Austria's intellectual elite wrote letters to the then-president, Rudolf Kirchschläger, asking him to pardon the incarcerated author. Jack reminded his advocates of the French criminal and author Jean Genet—a celebrated figure among Austrian writers who came of age in the 1960s—and they saw themselves as fulfilling the same function that Jean Cocteau and Jean-Paul Sartre had fulfilled decades earlier when they successfully petitioned the President of France to release Genet from his life sentence (which he'd received for his tenth burglary conviction). President Kirchschläger refused to pardon Jack, pointing out that under Austrian law, an offender sentenced to life in prison must serve at least fifteen years, and that Jack had served only ten.

After serving fifteen years, a murderer sentenced to life in prison may be considered for parole, depending on the nature and motive of his crime. If, upon reviewing his case, a Judges' Senate grants him a hearing, he must undergo a psychiatric examination. Unless a court-appointed psychiatrist testifies that the murderer no longer poses a threat to society, he may not be released. In Austria, murderers sentenced to life in prison typically serve eighteen to twenty years. Jack's advocates resolved to get him paroled as soon as possible—fifteen years after he was arrested on January 17, 1975.

On the grounds of *Purgatory*, they claimed he should be set free, as they believed the act of writing his life story, and the self-reflection that it required, had transformed him. In his letters to prominent persons and in his press interviews, Jack emphasized how literature had enabled him to overcome the chaos of his earlier life.

When the Austrian director Willi Hengstler made *Purgatory* into a movie, Jack was allowed to attend the film festival at which it was first screened, and afterward he told the audience: "In working on this book, I wrote three different drafts. By the time I got to the third draft, I no longer recognized the person I was writing about as being myself. Through the process of self-analysis through writing, I was freed from the pressure of my childhood, mother, etc."

With statements such as these, Jack gave the impression of self-awareness. "Insofar as personal development is evident in literature, Jack Unterweger has fully realized it," wrote Arno Pilgram, University Lecturer of Criminal Sociology to President Kirchschläger. "I don't know

him personally, but I have read his autobiographical novel *Purgatory* . . ."
wrote Ernest Bornemann, Austria's most eminent sexual researcher, to
the then–justice minister, Egmont Foregger. "The clarity and great literary quality with which Jack Unterweger described his childhood made a
great impression on me," wrote Elfriede Jelinek, winner of the 2004 No-
bel Prize in Literature, to the Krems court, where Jack's parole hearing
was to be held.

Some of his advocates asserted that the entire project of criminal rehabilitation hinged on Jack. "As we know," wrote senior ORF journalist
Peter Huemer to the director of the Stein prison, "the rehabilitation success of our prisons is not overwhelming. I don't say that to be critical; I
mean only that the example of Jack Unterweger as a successfully rehabilitated offender would be a significant and opportune result. Otherwise
one must doubt the earnestness of the state's dedication to rehabilitation."

"Apart from general humanitarian considerations, the credibility of
the Justice Ministry with respect to rehabilitation stands or falls with the
person of Jack Unterweger," wrote Gerhard Ruiss, general secretary of
the Austrian Authors' Council.

Jack also had advocates within the Justice Ministry among officials
who were members of the Socialist Party. In 1970 the Socialists won an
absolute majority and appointed the ideologue Dr. Christian Broda Minister of Justice. Using his party's advantage in Parliament, Broda oversaw
the passage of a sweeping reform of Austria's criminal-justice system
based on the concept of *Resozialisierung* (resocialization). Broda believed the justice system shouldn't punish offenders but treat their anti-
social behavior as a doctor treats an illness. He spoke of one day creating
a "prisonless society."

During the 1970s and 1980s, many ranking officials within the Justice Ministry Section for Penal Executions (Section V) shared Dr. Broda's
dream, and starting in 1977, the then-director of Section V, Dr. Wolfgang
Doleisch, took a personal interest in Jack and occasionally visited him at
Stein prison. After his retirement from the ministry, Dr. Doleisch continued to help Jack in various matters and was the strongest witness at his
parole hearing. As word spread of Jack's significance for the cause, he

became known as "the *Paradefall* [parade case or poster boy] of the successfully rehabilitated offender."

At a closed parole hearing on April 27, 1990, court-appointed psychiatrist Dr. Gerhard Kaiser stated his favorable prognosis for Jack's future in free society on the grounds that his literary vocation had given him constructive work into which he could channel his energy. His writings had won him recognition, which meant a great deal to him.

Representing Jack at the hearing was the Viennese arts and entertainment lawyer Georg Zanger, who submitted a statement of support for his release signed by a "who's who" of writers and artists. The statement concluded with the assertion that "Austrian justice will be measured by the Unterweger case."

On May 23, 1990, after fifteen years and four months of incarceration, Jack became a free man.

CHAPTER 9

FREEDOM

HE'D BEEN ARRESTED at the age of twenty-four and was reentering the world at the age of thirty-nine (three months before his fortieth birthday). Immediately he got to work doing what he did best—seducing women.

"He was polite, charming, very well-groomed and dressed, and therefore a darling of the girls," a juvenile parole officer recalled of her experience with Jack when he was fifteen. A few days after his parole hearing, he visited a nurse at her flat near the General Hospital. The next day he met the wife of an ORF crew member in the Café Museum and then returned to her apartment. "We were alone, undisturbed . . . Greed devoured beauty," as he described the encounter in his diary.

Another pleasure of being free was dressing as he pleased. Since puberty he'd been keenly interested in clothes, and he often wore suits and dinner jackets. Pimp and disco disc jockey were suitable occupations for wearing flashy outfits, and becoming an author gave him a greater outlet for his desire to dress up. At his first reading in freedom, he wore a seventies disco–era snow-white silk suit with a red rose in the lapel.

For his first few months of freedom, Jack was a darling of Vienna's radically chic. What made him interesting was not his "rehabilitated offender" status but his "wild, ex-con artist" status. The romantic notion that artists and writers are exceptional, creative people who don't abide by the rules of ordinary society has long been an article of faith among Vienna's large population of state-subsidized artists and writers. Because the Nazis had waged such a thuggish campaign against what they deemed "degenerate art," the pendulum swung to the opposite extreme in postwar Vienna, and no one dared call an artist or writer a degenerate.

Various magazines did illustrated stories on Jack, some portraying him as a dandy, some as an ex-con wearing only blue jeans, his body covered with prison tattoos. The contrast between the two personae was striking. One night he met a woman at an upscale champagne bar in Vienna's historical center. Wearing a glen-plaid suit and bow tie, he was the picture of a gentleman, but when he got the woman back to his apartment and took his clothes off, she was so startled by his fully tattooed body that she ran out.

Shortly after his release, a portrait photographer took some shots of him in the attic of an old apartment building, a place of shadows and cobwebs. The spooky setting seemed fitting for a portrait of a murderer, and Jack got into the spirit. Among the things stored in the attic was a coiled rope, and he suggested using it as a prop. With the photographer and his assistant watching, he threw the rope over a rafter and tied the ends into a noose. Wearing his favorite double-breasted suit and red bow tie, he posed as a hangman and as a suicide.

His love of clothes was matched by his love of cars. A week after his parole hearing he acquired the same model of Mercedes he'd had just before he'd been arrested sixteen years before. It was the first of six cars he would own during his first year of freedom, registering them with the vanity license plate W JACK 1 (the "W" indicating "Wien"—Vienna).

CHAPTER 10

BEST FRIEND

TWENTY-SEVEN-YEAR-OLD Margit Haas worked for *Viennese* magazine, managing its restaurant and bar guide. It was a perfect job for her, because she loved going out on the town, checking out new places, and meeting new people. To her, the most interesting places in Vienna were its redlight establishments.

Vienna has long been known for its prostitution industry. Shakespeare's *Measure for Measure* is partly set in a Viennese "bawd house" owned by Mistress Overdone. Through the centuries, the red-light district has developed its own distinct customs, codes, and dialect.

In Viennese dialect, a pimp is called a *Strizzi*—a word that derives from the Czech word for "uncle." To be a major *Strizzi*, one has to be not only tough and ruthless but also smart and charismatic. Margit liked hanging out in nightclubs with *Strizzis*—exotic characters who told countless funny stories. They were more entertaining than the people from her own social background—people who were so staid, so *bourgeois*. Margit had grown up with wealth and culture in a palace formerly owned by the Rothschild family, and though she was grateful for her good fortune, since her adolescence she'd been interested in the underbelly of society.

As a teenager she began reading "outsider" literature—Henry Miller, Jean Genet, Charles Bukowski, Jack Kerouac. While Jack Unterweger was still in prison, she read one of his newspaper interviews and was fascinated. A few weeks after he was paroled, she saw photos of him in *free life* magazine, wearing only blue jeans, his thirty-nine-year-old body still slender and muscular, the skin of his upper body etched with tattoos. The photos were striking, their green hue exaggerated, giving them a painted appearance. Like a portrait by Schiele, they were erotic and ugly at the same time.

A few months later, her job at *Viennese* gave her an excuse to call him. She was doing a survey on where the city's prominent people liked to dine and was annoyed that no one would give her a direct answer. Everyone needed time "to think about it." In other words, they needed time to calculate which place fit whatever image they were trying to project. Then she called Jack.

"Unterweger," the voice answered.

"Mr. Unterweger. Hello, this is Margit Haas from *Viennese* magazine. We're doing a survey on the restaurants where prominent Viennese like to dine."

"Aha, so now I count among the prominent?"

"Ummm, yes, I—"

"That's very flattering."

"Yes, well, if you'd like to think about it, I can call you back tomorrow."

"Why would I need to think about it? I can tell you right now."

Margit laughed.

"Why are you laughing?"

"I'm not laughing at you. It's just that, for everyone else I've called it's not so easy to name their favorite restaurant."

"I suppose being prominent isn't easy," he said. "Anyway, where I like to go, especially if I have a woman with me, is the Café Cobenzl." Surely he's joking, Margit thought. The Café Cobenzl was a kitschy tourist trap in the Vienna Woods, overlooking the city from the Cobenzl hill. It was on the same grounds as the Castle Cobenzl, where Johann Strauss and his orchestra used to play in the summer. Like many tourist places, it had a stale air of nostalgia.

"Do you know the Cobenzl?"

"Of course. My parents used to go there to grope each other in the parking lot back in the fifties."

"My apartment suffices for that, but I like the Cobenzl."

"What about it?"

"Naturally the view. The food isn't bad either." Now that she thought about it, Margit realized that the Cobenzl wasn't so bad.

"I guess it is a romantic place," she said.

"I like the drive through the woods—the intimacy of being close to-gether in the car, where I can smell the woman's perfume. And there's that feeling of anticipation of soon reaching our goal."

He's flirting with me, she thought, and decided to flirt back.

"Yes, I know the feeling. It's especially nice if you're hungry and you know that soon you'll be sitting down to a glass of wine and something to eat."

"Exactly. So you, too, like the Cobenzl."

"I like to drive out to the country for dinner."

"Your readers will probably think I'm old-fashioned. Why shouldn't I be? I am about to turn forty, you know."

"You think forty is old?"

"Yes."

"I take it your advanced age isn't slowing you down."

"No, I live with much more gusto than I did in my youth. Maybe some evening you'll join me for a drive up to the Cobenzl."

"Maybe I will."

Margit noticed that her colleague Christine was listening. "Who was that?" she asked.

"Oh, just the woman killer Jack Unterweger," Margit replied, trying to be as provocative as possible. Christine was shocked, but also curious. She wanted to know everything.

A couple of days later, the same scene played itself out when Margit walked into the office to find Hermi, a young secretary, very excited.

"Margit, an attractive man was just here looking for you. He didn't introduce himself, but he left this." It was an envelope containing a pho-tograph of Jack for the survey. "He had a big German shepherd with him. Who is he?"

"That was the woman killer Jack Unterweger." Just like Christina, Hermi was shocked and intensely curious. The only thing that Margit knew about Jack's crime was the bare fact that he had murdered an eighteen-year-old girl in 1974. She didn't know the identity of the vic-tim, why he had murdered her, and how he had murdered her, but the epithet "woman killer" held a mysterious fascination for her, and for the other women as well. She wondered why. Maybe they were turned on by the idea of being near evil without the risk of being harmed by it.

A few days later she walked into the office to find Hermi in a state. "Check it out!" she said, holding up a pair of tickets. "Mr. Unterweger has invited us to the premiere of his play!"

Margit's most vivid memory of *Dungeon* was Jack's introduction to it. As he walked onto the stage wearing a white suit, she was struck by how small he looked. So small, like a little boy. Afterward a reception was held at the Reiss Bar, near the Crypt of the Capuchins, in which seven hundred years of Hapsburg monarchs are entombed. She approached him at his table and ended up chatting and sipping champagne with him until closing time. They then drove to her favorite club in Vienna.

Jack's car, a white 1972 Mustang Mach I with the license plate W JACK 1, suggested that he was stuck in the seventies. Driving to the Motto, she thought about how strange it must be to sit in prison for fifteen years and then be transported back into the world. Jack had not incorporated the world of 1990 into his being. Fifteen years earlier the Mustang had been a favorite car of Viennese pimps.

The Motto strove to break free of Vienna's staidness by going to extremes. The entrance was like that of a vault, and only the radically chic and flamboyantly erotic were buzzed in. Everything about the place was designed to inflame lust, from the sumptuous flower arrangements to the pornographic films projected on the walls of the bathrooms.

Margit wanted to see how Jack would react to a place of such infernal sensuality, and was surprised that it irritated him. But as was his talent, he tuned out the surroundings and focused on her. She could tell he wanted her, and she let him stroke her thigh under the table.

"What do you think of my favorite club?" she asked.

"You are playing with *Feuer* [fire], you know," he said. She leaned closer to him. "With *Fegefeuer* [purgatory]," she answered. He saw his opportunity with her lips so close, and she felt his tongue, small and pointed, thrust into her mouth.

"Your meal is served." They looked up to see a young waiter standing

over them. The smirk on his face suggested he was happy to interrupt
the scene. Margit figured he was jealous, for even at forty, Jack still had
boyish good looks.

At six o'clock they left the midnight blue interior of Motto and
stepped out into the gray morning of the street. In the narrow alley he
pushed her up against the wall of an apartment house and thrust his leg
between her thighs. She felt the surprising strength of his delicate frame
pushing against her, but her arousal was gone and she pushed back.

"It's time to go home," she said.

He backed off. "Shall I give you a lift?" he asked.

"That would be nice."

As they drove along the Wienzeile, past the Secession building,
where Gustav Klimt and Egon Schiele exhibited their paintings, she
rummaged through her purse, looking for her house key.

"Why did you kill that girl back then?" she asked. He was silent for
a moment, and then spoke.

"Well, you know from *Purgatory* that my mother abandoned me with
her alcoholic father when I was a baby. For so long I was full of rage
against her, and I think it affected all my thinking and feeling. At the
time I met that girl, I was living at rock bottom, using drugs and alcohol,
with no money and no home. But I did have a serious girlfriend. This
other girl—the one I killed—she really came on to me, and something
about her irritated me. Something about the way she looked and talked
reminded me of my mother. I hit her once, and then couldn't hold myself back. I don't know why. I think at that moment I thought of her as
my mother. It was as if my mother, and not her, stood there before me."
He sighed. "I wish I could undo it."

"How do you feel about your mother now?"

"I'm on pretty good terms with her. She lives in Munich, and I visit
her from time to time." They were driving through the Schwarzenberg-
platz, past the overbearing Stalinist monument to the Unknown Soviet
Soldier, or Unknown Soviet Rapist, as wags call it.

"And your father?" she asked.

"I never met him, but I'm pretty sure he's living in New Jersey. I'm
thinking about making a trip to find him. I can't wait to see the surprise

on his face when he meets his Austrian son." They drove up Prinz Eugen Strasse, the grounds of the Belvedere Palace on their left.

"Turn right here," she said. They arrived at her parents' house, where she had her own wing. If Jack was surprised by the place, he didn't show it.

"Wonderful. I can't find my key."

"It's not so early. What about just ringing the bell?"

"I don't want to wake up my parents. They don't ask questions, and I don't want them to start." He thought for moment and said, "You're welcome to sleep at my apartment. You can lock yourself in the guest room." Without a hint of self-consciousness or self-pity, he revealed what it was like to live for the rest of your life with the stigma of a murder conviction. No matter what the circumstances were or how many years passed, people would always be afraid of you. She felt tenderness for him, and began to fumble in her purse again to conceal her emotion. *She wasn't afraid of him.* At least she didn't think she was.

The evening inspired her to read *Purgatory*, and a couple of days later, lying in her bedroom at around 2:00 a.m., she reached the midpoint of the book, in which Jack leaves home and starts hanging around prostitutes. Near the Klagenfurt train station he chats one up, and she is so charmed by him that she agrees to give him a favor the next day, free of charge. Right as Margit reached the sex-charged scene, her phone rang.

"Am I disturbing you?" said Jack's voice.

Margit burst out laughing.

"Why are you laughing—I was afraid you'd yell at me for waking you up."

"I was just reading the scene in *Purgatory* where you screw a girl in the train station bathroom."

"Oh, I see," he said, also laughing. So began the first of many telephone conversations. As their friendship developed in the autumn of 1990, they chatted at least three times a week, sometimes for up to three hours at a time. Like Margit, Jack was a night owl and often called past midnight. She loved to smoke, drink a glass of wine, and listen to his voice. He was a gifted conversationalist, especially on the subject of people, of whom he was an acute observer. He often met people in publishing circles—people whom Margit had known for years—and he had a talent for grasping their personalities after speaking with them only a few minutes. Margit was often amazed at how quickly he figured someone out.

Margit liked a lot of things about Jack. His energy, intensity, and spontaneity—his gift for seizing the day—were qualities she admired. Most of the time he was an entertaining companion, but sometimes he could be bitter and cynical, and his occasional monologues about the stupidity and injustice of society were tedious. She sensed that the root of his problem was his unrealistically high expectations of life in a free society.

It stung him that his play *Dungeon* wasn't a smash hit, and while touring it (as director and lead actor) to various cities, he often called her to complain. The tour was well planned and marketed, and the play got good reviews, so why didn't more people come to watch it? One night in December he called from a city near the Swiss border in a foul mood, complaining that he wasn't making enough money with the play. She listened to him vent his frustration and tried to console him. Later that night he called her again, and she was surprised by how different he sounded. During their second conversation he was relaxed and good-humored, as though he'd dropped all the weight he'd been carrying a couple of hours earlier.

A few months later, in February 1991, Jack prepared for a tour of another one of his plays—a short piece about AIDS titled *Scream of Fear*. He explained to her that he'd become concerned about the disease when he was in prison, as some of his fellow inmates were apparently infected. She was glad to see him preparing for the tour with enthusiasm. One day he gave her copies of the playbill and placards that he was putting up all over town advertising the Vienna premiere.

CHAPTER 11

PATRONESS

THE AUTHOR AND JOURNALIST Sonja Eisenstein was walking through the passage from the Karlplatz subway station to the Vienna Opera in early March when she saw a notice taped to the wall that froze her in her tracks. Her eye was initially caught by the name of the playwright. She'd heard about his parole the year before, so she wasn't surprised he was producing a play. What made her blood run cold was the title: SCREAM OF FEAR. She knew its origin because she'd studied the crime he'd committed in December 1974. Though his play was purportedly about the fear of AIDS, she knew the title didn't refer to the scream of one who has just learned he is HIV-positive. The natural reaction to that would be shocked silence, tears, or nausea. No, Jack was thinking about a scream of fear in a context far removed from a medical clinic.

Scream of Fear premiered in Vienna on February 17, 1991, and then toured seven other cities. The protagonist, a young man named Jürgen, has been hospitalized with flulike symptoms. In the opening scene, he is sitting in his hospital room ("a cross hanging crooked on the wall behind him") arguing with a nurse on the phone:

JÜRGEN: . . . No, I'm not aggressive . . . I can become healthy here. No, I'm not malicious . . . (*He hangs up and probes his thyroid.*) A suspicion! Only a suspicion . . . Swollen thyroid? Suspicion, damn it! Should I talk? Tell the story? To whom? (*Laughs shrilly, hysterically.*) With whom should I talk about this?

A few scenes later, Jürgen is questioned by his lover Hans Peter.

HANS PETER: What is the truth? You are evading my question.

JÜRGEN: Many lies are often the truth, just as the truth is also often regarded as lies. Who knows the difference? . . . Winners never get
hauled before a court. Only losers, because the winner makes every
lie into the truth.

When a member of an AIDS help group asks him his address, he
says, "Felserstrasse 28, second floor." Though there is no "Felserstrasse"
in Vienna, Felberstrasse 28 is located is the middle of what was, in 1990,
the main drag for street prostitution, along the rail yard of the West Train
Station. Club 28 is a nightclub where prostitutes congregate in the Felberstrasse.

After Jürgen receives the third positive HIV test result, he doesn't
scream with fear but laments that he will be removed from society:

JÜRGEN: The time of lies has passed. Tested positive three times! . . . Precautions. (*Laughs.*) A death sentence would be more suitable . . .
Orders and duties and no more rights . . . A delinquent with no right
for a final wish.

Sonja met Jack in 1975, while he was in the Salzburg jail awaiting
trial for the murder he committed in December 1974. From a friend she
had heard about the delicate-looking boy accused of murder, and she
was curious to learn more about him. She wrote him a letter, a correspondence ensued, and she was impressed by his penitential spirit. He
admitted that he'd murdered the girl, and he wrote of his deep sorrow—
sorrow he thought about escaping through suicide. In a poem he sent to
her, he imagined death as a lover who would take him in her embrace
and free him from his pain.

LOVE POEM TO DEATH

You come to me again,
you don't forget me.
And till the end is the agony,
And the chain breaks.

Still you appear strange and distant,
and are alive, Death.
You stand like a cool star
over my distress.

But then you will be near and full of flame.
Come, lover, I am here.
Take me, I am yours.

Sonja was moved by the lyricism of the verses. She praised his native talent and encouraged him to cultivate it.

Sonja didn't attend his trial in Salzburg, though she knew he would be convicted, given his admission (to her) that he'd committed the crime. After his transfer to Stein prison, she suggested he finish high school, and she offered to pay for it. He took correspondence courses and scored his highest mark in religion. After he received his diploma in February 1978, she paid for a correspondence course on narrative writing. He completed it with characteristic energy and was soon ready to get started. His goal: "to write his way to freedom."

Soon it became apparent that he was probably going to succeed, but the more Sonja got to know him, the more she was troubled by his success. On a couple of occasions he betrayed her trust, revealing a ruthless side of his character that was eerily incongruous with her initial impression of a sensitive boy. He had an almost supernatural ability to win helpers and advocates, whom he used to obtain privileges and influence that seemed inconceivable for a prison inmate.

As her misgivings grew, she researched the murder he committed in 1974, and what she discovered terrified her. Years later (after Jack had reached his goal of "writing his way to freedom"), when she saw the notice for his play *Scream of Fear*, she went home and wrote a letter to the editor of Austria's largest-circulation newspaper: "Jack Unterweger is a shark in the Austrian cultural scene. His madness is like the AIDS virus, an agent of destruction that threatens all of society. No one is safe from him."

The editor didn't publish her letter.

———

The tour of *Scream of Fear* ended on March 22, 1991, and a few days later, Jack took a long drive across northern Italy. On Friday, March 29, he called Margit and told her that he'd totaled his beloved Mustang Mach I in a race in the mountains and had left the wreck in Italy. Unscathed himself, he had returned to Vienna by train and was wondering if she would like to meet him for a coffee. They met that Sunday afternoon, which was Easter, and drove up to at the Café Cobenzl in the Vienna Woods. He'd never mentioned to her before that he owned a second car—a VW Passatt. It wasn't flashy like his wrecked Mustang, but at least it got better gas mileage.

At sunset, as they strolled along a nearby vineyard with Jack's splendid male German shepherd Joy (similar to the shepherd he'd owned in 1974), Margit felt hungry and suggested they go for some sushi. They got into his car, but instead of driving back to town, he took the Höhenstrasse that runs through the Vienna Woods, meandering around the western city limit. Margit didn't have a strong sense of direction, so at first she thought he was just taking a different route back to town. But then she began noticing the signs to Vienna that he kept passing. Just as they passed a sign for the Scots Court restaurant (located in a part of the Vienna Woods called the Scots Woods), he slowed down to a walking pace and peered around into the surrounding forest.

"What are you doing?"

"I want to look at something."

"And you intend to drive back to town this way?"

"What do you mean? This is the normal way."

At first Margit wasn't sure, and then, about a mile past the Scots Court restaurant, on the left side of the road, she saw a familiar landmark—the Villa Fuchs, designed by the famous architect Otto Wagner.

"Jack, that's the Villa Fuchs—this is totally wrong!" It was strange enough that Jack encircled half the city rather than driving into it. Odder still was his insistence that it was the correct route.

CHAPTER 12

A COINCIDENCE

WHEN CHIEF EDELBACHER learned that the reporter Jack Unterweger was an ex-convict—paroled exactly one year before the prostitute murders—he requested a background check, which confirmed that Unterweger was well known in literary and intellectual circles. During his year of freedom he had published two novels and produced two plays, for which he had received generous subsidies from the Ministry of Education and Culture. Strangely enough, he also happened to be on the list of possible suspects for the murders.

On Friday, May 31, 1991—the day Unterweger interviewed prostitutes for his radio story—a retired police inspector called headquarters and advised the Homicide section to examine him as a possible suspect for the prostitute murders. The tip wasn't brought to Edelbacher's attention, and before the chief learned about it, Unterweger showed up at headquarters to interview him.

Edelbacher thought about the reporter. Small, neatly dressed and groomed, he had a friendly and respectful manner, and when he asked questions, he seemed frank and sincere. He was engaging, frequently making and holding eye contact, and listening attentively. And as one would expect of a writer, he was very articulate. Everything about him seemed to support the prevailing opinion that he—Jack Unterweger, a forty-year-old author and journalist—was *not* the same man as the twenty-four-year-old punk who'd murdered a girl sixteen years earlier.

Then there was the source of the tip—an old, eccentric cop from the little city of Salzburg. According to his younger colleagues, he was zealous and perhaps prone to tunnel vision. Inspector August Schenner looked as if he'd just stepped off the set of a detective film. Everything about him, from the khaki mackintosh he wore when it was cool and rainy (in Salzburg, most of the time) to his precise speech laced with forensic terminology, said "homicide inspector." A handsome man with a splendid head of silver hair, in his youth he'd resembled the American actor George Nader, famous in German-speaking countries for his portrayal of the pulp-fiction New York FBI agent Jerry Cotton in a series of film adaptations. Like agent Cotton, Schenner drove a sixties Jaguar E-Type, even though it was beyond his means.

When Schenner had called police headquarters, he'd spoken with an officer who considered the tip so implausible that it belonged far down the list. A background check on Unterweger revealed factual errors in Schenner's statement (at least as it was reported by the officer with whom he spoke). The retired inspector claimed that Unterweger had, "a long time ago," murdered two prostitutes in Salzburg. Yet, according to court records, Unterweger had murdered a girl in Germany who wasn't a prostitute. Schenner had apparently investigated him for a different murder in Salzburg, but Unterweger hadn't even been prosecuted for it.

All of the above raised doubts about Schenner's credibility. He appeared to be fixated on an old case he'd failed to solve. At any rate, Edelbacher knew that if they were going to detain Unterweger, they would need more than the tip of a retired cop ruminating about sixteen-year-old cases.

And so Chief Edelbacher put Unterweger under surveillance, and the observation seemed to confirm the notion that he'd been rehabilitated. He led the sort of life one would expect of a writer and freelance journalist, often at home, presumably in his study, or hanging out in his neighborhood café. He frequently met people for lunch and for an evening cocktail at an upscale place in the inner city.

Unlike many paroled offenders, who never found their way in free society, Jack Unterweger appeared to be a successful man with a lot to lose. After his parole he moved into a big apartment in a posh part of town, drove a nice car, was invited to give newspaper and television interviews, and was surrounded by women—all of which seemed difficult to reconcile with Schenner's tip.

Why would Jack Unterweger risk losing his life of excitement and success for the pleasure of strangling hookers? To do that, he'd have to be insane, and he clearly wasn't. The reporter who interviewed Edelbacher was calm, thoughtful, and rational. He concluded by wishing the police the best of luck, and afterward he sat on the couch in the chief's office, drinking a coffee, chatting about various topics.

From experience, Edelbacher knew that true crimes aren't like the intriguing plots of novels and films. The notion that a writer and journalist would cruise around killing hookers and then interview the chief of police about the investigation—maybe in Hollywood, but never in real life.

CHAPTER 13

COWBOY

ON JUNE 10, Jack Unterweger again appeared at Edelbacher's office and said that he was about to leave for Los Angeles, where he intended to do a story on crime and law enforcement. He said he wanted to meet some police officers, perhaps drive around on patrol, and was wondering if Edelbacher had any contacts at the LAPD. The chief replied that he didn't, but that he looked forward to meeting Jack upon his return to hear about his research. It was notable that Edelbacher did not, at that moment, tell Jack about the tip from Salzburg. If he had considered the tip plausible, he might have asked Jack to remain in the country.

For his arrival at LAX on June 11, 1991, Jack put on a striking outfit. White pants, white snakeskin cowboy boots, a white cowboy hat, and a white coat emblazoned with a bright hibiscus print topped off a Navajo vest. He'd packed up in Old Europe and gone West, and he'd be damned if he didn't dress the part. In *Purgatory* the child Jack occasionally tells people, "My papa is an American who owns a ranch." Jack the adult wanted to be a cowboy, albeit of the urban variety. He cut a figure walking through the terminal, and he knew it. Twice he stopped and asked a passerby to take his picture. At Marathon he rented a car with his fake driver's license (on which was written in German: "By .06 percent blood alcohol drive only wheelbarrows") and drove downtown to the Hotel Cecil on Main Street between Sixth and Seventh.

The Cecil is located in the "historic district" of downtown Los Angeles, built in the early decades of the twentieth century. Designed to withstand earthquakes and fires, the district's buildings are of solid masonry, richly ornamented, and no more than fifteen stories high. With its humane architecture and scale suitable for foot travel, the neighborhood is one of the few in L.A. with real urban character, but that didn't stop everyone who could afford to live somewhere else from abandoning it in the fifties and sixties. A few blocks to the southeast are the "missions," which provide food and shelter to the largest stable population of homeless people in the United States. The downscale quality of the neighborhood may be gleaned from a sign on the wall of a shoe store around the corner from the Cecil:

NO LOITERING

DEFICATING [sic]

URINATING

LAPD.COD 347.5

Seventh Avenue, which intersects Main near the entrance to the Hotel Cecil, runs southeast through the "garment district," rows of shops piled with cheap textiles, and then passes through the "wholesale produce district," warehouses of groceries trucked in every day to feed the city. In 1991, Seventh was a popular drag for prostitutes. On Sixth and Wall, two blocks from the Cecil, lies the LAPD Central Facilities, the downtown headquarters of patrol officers. So, in the vicinity of his hotel, Jack could find plenty of hookers and cops, the two kinds of professionals in which he was most interested.

A security guard stood at the entrance of the Cecil, and in the lobby a number of scruffy characters, some drunk, a couple apparently schizo-phrenic, milled about. The hotel embodied a motif that ran through all Jack's magazine articles about L.A.—the existence of extreme destitu-tion in the heart of a city known for its wealth. In the low-rent districts of Vienna, such as the Penzing neighborhood near the West Train Sta-tion, it was impossible to find such seediness. Yet even in the most mis-erable places he could find what he was looking for. From the middle of the lobby he saw her. She was a pretty girl, with lustrous dark hair and big cinnamon eyes.

Carolina saw the slender, fair-skinned man looking around the lobby.

"What's this guy doing?" she said to Jennifer, the other receptionist. Probably because of the heat, Jack had taken off his caballero outfit. With his clean white trousers, turquoise oxford shirt, and elegant pos-ture, he seemed out of place in the Cecil. He looked at them and began to walk toward the reception desk.

"Who is he gonna talk to, me or you?" said Carolina playfully.

"Me," said Jennifer. At nineteen she was nine years younger and also pretty. The man reached the counter, for a second looked at Jennifer, who smiled coquettishly, and then turned to Carolina, speaking to her through the hole in the bulletproof glass surrounding the reception area.

"How much for a room?" he asked in a foreign accent.

"Our rooms are available on a weekly basis. It comes to about twenty-five dollars per night."

"Sounds good. I'll stay for five weeks."

"Are you sure you want to stay here? It's not a nice place, and this is a rough part of town. You shouldn't be wearing that gold necklace here."

He smiled as though he was amused by her warning. "I need to be here for my work." He pulled a folded document out of his wallet and showed it to her. She saw his picture and the word *Presse* printed on it.

"I'm a journalist from Austria, and I'm writing articles about the dark side of L.A.—homeless people, drug addicts, and prostitutes. I believe I've come to the right place."

"I see. You're welcome to stay here, just be careful and don't wear that necklace or that ring."

"This one?" he said, holding up his hand to show the ring, an emerald set in gold.

"Yes. You have to pay a week in advance, and if you want a phone in
your room, you have to pay a security deposit."

"It's a deal!" he said with a grin.

Of course Carolina warned the handsome man about the place. She was
thinking about quitting, so she didn't care if her boss heard about her
scaring off a guest. What was she doing there anyway?

Ten months earlier she'd been working as a nanny for a well-to-
do family when she contracted a case of adult-onset chicken pox that
bound her to bed for a month. The parents replaced her, and though she
could have pleaded for their sympathy, she thought it was time to move
on to something bigger than babysitting. She trained to be a medical assistant and found part-time work at a clinic. It was an okay job, but it
didn't pay much, so when she heard through a friend's sister about the
receptionist job at the Cecil, she took it without giving it much thought.
She needed the money.

Jack returned to the reception an hour later and resumed his conversation with Carolina.

"What are the people in Austria like?" she asked him.

"Would you like to see an Austrian woman?" he asked as he pulled
out his wallet.

"Sure," she said.

He handed her a photograph of a tall slender girl with large breasts,
long brown hair twisted into braids, and green eyes.

"My God, she's beautiful!" said Carolina. "You should marry her."

"She's just a friend."

"What's her name?"

"Susanna."

"Do a lot of Austrian girls look like that?"

"A few. You are also beautiful."

"Oh, thank you," she said, knowing that she wasn't as beautiful as
the girl in the photograph.

"It was nice talking with you," he said. "I think I'll go for a walk."

"I wouldn't do that, now that it's dark. This isn't a safe neighborhood."

"Don't worry about me." He held up his hand and pointed at his throat. "See. No jewelry; nothing to steal."

She watched him as he walked across the lobby and out into the summer night.

A couple of days later Jack met a group of Austrians and Germans who worked in the film industry, including the *Stern* magazine Hollywood correspondent, Frances Schoenberger, at Café Hugo on Santa Monica Boulevard. Over breakfast he spoke about his plans in L.A.—a radio story about the city's "dark side" and a magazine story about the "Strong Women of L.A.," with a focus on Cher. Frances told him it would be impossible for him to get an interview with Cher, which irritated him. He defiantly said that he would find a way. He said he also wanted to interview the writer Charles Bukowski (a friend of Frances's ex-husband) and to pitch his stories to movie producers. Finally, he hoped to track down his father—an American G.I. who'd returned to the States a few years after Jack was born.

"I once went through my mother's letters and found some he'd written from an army base back in the fifties, but naturally he's no longer there, and I don't know how to find his current address." Frances was touched by his desire to find his father, as she had never known hers, and so she volunteered to help him. She spent the next couple of afternoons calling agencies in Washington, D.C., trying to find the address of Jack's father. She didn't succeed. A few days later, on Monday, June 17, she met Jack again at the Hugo and broke the bad news, which he took hard.

"On a brighter note, my ex-husband said he'd be happy to talk to you about Bukowksi," she said, and handed him the number.

Jack spent the next few days sightseeing, and every afternoon he got back to the Cecil before 5:00 p.m. so he could chat with Carolina before she got off work. He longed to see her alone, but each evening at the end of her shift she lingered for only a few minutes before heading home to her place in Echo Park. He hated saying good night and watching her get on the city bus, leaving him to spend the night alone.

On the morning of June 20 (a few hours after Shannon Exley was picked up by her last customer at the intersection of Seventh and Towne, a few blocks from the Hotel Cecil), Jack had a meeting with Frances's ex-husband Michael Montfort. On his way to the appointment he stopped at Marathon to return his car, because the windshield on the passenger side was broken. He told the clerk that a stone had struck it on the freeway. After exchanging the damaged Toyota for a new Pontiac Sunbird, he headed up to the Hollywood Hills.

Michael Montfort and his ex-wife, Frances, had remained on amicable terms, living across the street from one another to share the parenting of their daughter. Montfort was a photographer, and in 1977 he got an assignment to shoot a portrait of Charles Bukowski for the cover of the German magazine *Rogners*. The author was known for his irascibility, so Montfort brought a case of wine along to oil the shoot, and the two men became friends. Over the years they collaborated on projects, including *Shakespeare Never Did This*, a documentary about Bukowski's travels through his native Germany. *Horsemeat* depicted two days in the life of the author at his favorite place, the Santa Anita racetrack.

Montfort showed Jack his collection of Bukowski's works and interview recordings, which Jack copied onto cassettes. Montfort explained that, though Bukowski's autobiographical characters were hard-drinking and womanizing bachelors, he had long been married to the same woman and lived a quiet and private life. Over seventy years old, he wasn't in the best of health. In short, he no longer gave interviews.

Jack was determined to meet Bukowski and planned to track him down at the Hollywood Park racetrack. He felt a kinship with the American author, whose works were first published in German by Maro, the publisher of *Purgatory*. Bukowski's depiction of downtown L.A. in *Erections, Ejaculations, Exhibitions, and General Tales of Ordinary Madness* was probably the initial inspiration for Jack's L.A. trip.

Jack also modeled his image after the German actor Klaus Kinski (with his fascinating portrayals of Jack the Ripper, the Marquis de Sade, and Dracula), whose autobiography, *I Am So Wild about Your Strawberry Mouth*, was an inspiration. Kinski and Bukowski borrowed ideas from the French writer Louis-Ferdinand Céline, and in Bukowski's last novel, *Pulp*, the protagonist is stalked by Céline at the Hollywood Park track.

Jack spent the next couple of days at the Gay and Lesbian Pride parade. With its zany outfits and overt sexuality, it was his kind of event, and in the photos he posed for, he appeared to be enjoying himself. He got a few shots of himself with Bobby Etienne (a nightclub performer with a flair for Tina Turner routines) as she rolled slowly by in her white Rolls. The Sisters of Perpetual Indulgence, a group of women and men dressed up like nuns, probably reminded him of a real nun back in Austria whom he sometimes visited at her convent. In West Hollywood Park he posed, wearing his cowboy hat, with two muscular men dressed up like female cheerleaders.

He disapproved of the use of children, wearing makeup, holding up signs that read I'M PROUD OF MY GAY DADDY or WE LOVE OUR LESBIAN MOTHER. He also didn't like the men and women pretending to masturbate with live snakes, or the masochists piercing themselves with large needles. In an article he wrote about the event for *Tirolerin* magazine, he concluded: "We should keep our fingers crossed that the worldwide gay movement doesn't suffer a setback as a result of these negative manifestations. Especially when they are captured on television, brutal images of the greedy sexual impulse may generate revulsion and prejudice instead of understanding."

On Monday morning, June 24 (the same morning that Detective Fred Miller read the teletype about the Shannon Exley murder), Jack visited the LAPD Parker Center to obtain permission to ride with patrol officers. He also wanted to arrange an interview with Chief Daryl Gates to discuss racial tensions in L.A. following the Rodney King beating. Unfortunately, the chief wasn't available.

A few blocks south of the Parker Center is the LAPD Central Facilities. On the morning of Tuesday, June 25, Sergeant Steve Staples entered the ugly brown building at Sixth and Wall, and as he passed the watch commander's office, he saw Lieutenant Taylor talking with a short man in a baggy, cream-colored linen suit.

"Hey, Staples," Taylor said, "this gentleman is a journalist from Austria. His name is Jack— What was your last name?"

"Unterweger," said the man.

"Yeah, Unterweger," said Lieutenant Taylor, making a mess of the pronunciation. "He's got permission for a ride-along, so go ahead and take him."

Staples didn't like ride-alongs. If it was a busy day, he preferred to drive alone so he could concentrate. If, on the other hand, the streets of the Central Division were quiet, he felt obliged to make conversation with the ride-along, and not every journalist was a good conversationalist. But this guy was different. First of all, he was a European. Staples had never been to Austria, and the only thing he really knew about the country was that it was where Arnold Schwarzenegger came from. *Terminator 2* was due in the cinemas on July 3, and billboards for the movie were all over town.

"So you're from Austria, like Arnold Schwarzenegger?" said Staples after they'd gotten under way.

"Yeah, I was born in the same state."

"Is this your first time in L.A.?"

"Yeah."

"Where are you staying?"

"On the west side, I've got some friends over there." The "west side" of L.A. comprises the neighborhoods near the ocean, like Venice and Santa Monica. In fact, Jack was staying downtown, just two blocks from Central Facilities.

"What do you think of the city?" Staples asked.

"I like it. There's a lot more going on than in Vienna."

"Yeah, there's a lot going on; too much from a law-enforcement perspective."

"That's what I'm here to learn about. I'm writing an article for an Austrian police journal about crime in Los Angeles." Another lie. Though Jack read the police journal, he didn't write for it. He probably sensed that Staples wasn't interested in talking to journalists, so he needed to set himself apart from other reporters. The "police journal" ruse gave the L.A. cop the impression that Jack was writing for Austrian cops. It would encourage Staples to answer his questions with care and candor.

"So it's your officers who will be reading it?" he asked, taking the bait.

"Yeah. We don't have much crime in Austria, so our police aren't as experienced. My article is about your methods."

"Well, I'd be happy to tell you about what I do."

"What sort of crime do you handle?"

"Mostly control street sales of narcotics. If we can suppress the drugs, we can suppress a lot of other crime as well."

"What other crime?"

"So much crime is associated with drugs. The gangs shoot each other to protect their market or to muscle into others. People rob and steal to pay for their drug habit. Girls turn tricks to pay for theirs. Pretty much every hooker in this city has a drug habit."

"I see," said the journalist.

He rode along for the entire four-hour shift. He was curious about everything, took lots of photos, and wanted to see every part of Central Division. He was particularly interested in narcotics, asked countless questions about them. He also wanted to know exactly how the L.A. authorities process someone arrested for a serious crime.

Toward the end of the ride-along, as they were driving up Seventh, Staples remembered a story.

"I'd just started on patrol and was driving along here when I saw the most beautiful black girl standing on the corner. She had the longest legs I've ever seen, and long black hair. I knew she was a hooker, and I decided to let her know I'd seen her. I did a U-turn and pulled up to the curb. As I got close, I saw she wasn't a beautiful woman, after all, but a man in drag! I guess that was my first taste of how weird this town can be."

The journalist grinned. "That's a funny story."

The patrol sergeant would later recall how the journalist, for all his curiosity about crime, didn't ask a single question about prostitution.

At 2:00 p.m., they stopped at a seafood restaurant on Central and Sixth. Staples liked the informal atmosphere of the place, which served the best grilled swordfish in town. The journalist seemed to like it, too, though he made an observation that stuck in the policeman's head. Before he cut into his fish, he picked up the little white roll that came with each entree and eyed it as though he were trying to identify it.

"You don't have very good bread in this country, do you?"

A couple of days after his ride-along with the Austrian journalist, Sergeant Staples walked into the squad room and saw Jack flirting with a group of female patrol officers—pretty black women, their athletic bodies emphasized by their form-fitting uniforms. The journalist must have said something funny, because they were laughing. He took a few snapshots of them and got their cards. Something about the scene prompted Staples to stop and watch. He noticed how the journalist didn't talk to any of the men or ask them to pose for photos—only the women. Was he doing research or trying to get a date?

Jack spent Wednesday, June 26, trying to find Charles Bukowski at Hollywood Park, but he didn't succeed. That evening he walked around the neighborhood near the Hotel Cecil with a tape recorder and microphone, interviewing hookers. At around midnight, a Latina named Jenny climbed up the fire escape and knocked on his window. He let her in, and for thirty dollars she gave him a blow job.

The next morning, equipped with his "Homes of the Stars" map, he found Zsa Zsa Gabor's house in Bel Air and rang the bell. Her "Saxon Prince" husband answered the door and told him that his wife gave interviews to Austrian journalists only for money. He then drove out to Cher's house on the Pacific Coast Highway in Malibu (a half mile before the turnoff to Corral Canyon Road) and didn't get beyond the gate. He gave Frances Schoenberger a call.

"Are you sure you can't help me get an interview with Cher?"

"I told you, Jack, it's impossible. Try to understand that she only gives interviews when she thinks it's in her interest to give one."

"Well, I have my own way of doing things," he replied. "You would be surprised at how I can find people and talk to them. For example, right now I know where you are. Exactly where you are." It was chilling the way he said that. She had never invited him over or given him her address.

"Look, Jack, I'd like to help you find your father, but I can't help you get an interview with Cher."

"Very good, I'll talk to you later."

On the morning of July 1 (two days after Elisabeth Rodriguez was picked up by her last customer on Seventh Avenue, a few blocks from the Cecil), Jack told the receptionist (Carolina was off duty) that someone had broken into his room and stolen his stuff. Because of the poor security, he would be checking out. The next morning he drove to Hollywood and checked into the Sunset Orange Motel at the intersection of Sunset Boulevard and Orange Street (now an In-N-Out Burger).

In Hollywood he continued researching "The Dark Side of Los Angeles," interviewing drug-addicted hookers. As he wrote in a story about L.A. for *Tirolerin* magazine, they were women who "came with dreams and now sell themselves on Sunset and Hollywood Boulevards . . . They move to the city by the thousands, hoping for a better life, while thousands of others (some dead) leave."

On July 3, the day after he moved to Hollywood, he drove to Santa Monica for a morning on the beach, and after lunch he headed up to Malibu to visit the filmmaker Robert Dornhelm to pitch making his autobiography into a movie. With copies of *Purgatory, Dungeon,* and his screenplay *Love Till Insanity,* he drove up the Pacific Coast Highway to Malibu and got lost trying to find the director's house. Driving the canyon roads, he turned onto a dead-end street with a panoramic view and asked a woman to take his picture. It shows him standing next to the rear deck of a house with the ocean spreading out behind him. The most notable thing about the image is his clothing—the same ensemble he'd worn for his arrival in L.A. Following the photo op, he found the address he was looking for.

Robert Dornhelm was put out by the Austrian in the outlandish outfit who appeared at his house that afternoon. The way his fellow countrymen just dropped in when they were in town irritated him. The filmmaker had moved to L.A. in the seventies, and he'd slowly but surely gotten work in American cinema. People back home imagined him to be, like Arnold Schwarzenegger, a bright example of an Austrian who'd realized the American dream in Hollywood. But unlike the provincial Schwarzenegger, Dornhelm was a Viennese with friends among the city's intellectual elite. The man who showed up at his house introduced himself as Jack Unterweger and said he'd gotten his address from the ORF journalist Peter Huemer. *Annoying.*

For his part, Jack was probably disappointed by the director's house—a shack compared to Madonna and Sean Penn's villa across the street. Dornhelm and his wife were about to break ground for a house worthy of the property, which commanded a view of the bay below, but until it was completed, they had to make do with a bungalow.

Dornhelm's irritation was inflamed by Jack's assertiveness. He thrust his books into the director's hands and said, "You are just the man to make a film of my life story. You know where I'm coming from, and my books are your kind of material." Dornhelm looked at the covers of Jack's books, *Purgatory: The Journey to Prison* and *Dungeon.*

"Why are you so interested in prison?" he asked.

"Because I just got out a few months ago."

"Really, what did you do?"

The question made Jack visibly uncomfortable. "Well, back in my youth a very unfortunate thing happened, and a girl got killed."

"I see," said Dornhelm, realizing that he was talking to a convicted murderer. Irritation gave way to curiosity. "Can you tell me what happened?"

"When I was a child I was abandoned by my mother. She left me with her father, a violent alcoholic. As I grew up, I longed for her to come back and take me away from that painful world, and though she turned up occasionally to get something, it was never me. She'd get my hopes up, but then always go away again. I guess I started to hate her, and when I encountered this girl, years later, at a time when I was living at rock bottom, something about her—the way she looked and talked—reminded me of my mother. We got into an argument and I hit her once, and then everything seemed to go blank. Later I realized I'd killed her."

Dornhelm knew Jack was giving him a "psychological" version of the crime—a plea of temporary insanity. The great Viennese director Otto Preminger had dissected the idea in *Anatomy of a Murder*—a drama about the hazards of judging a character not on his actions but on the mental state that preceded them.

"And now you're working in journalism?" Dornhelm asked.

"Yes, that's one of the reasons I'm here in L.A. I'm writing a story about the city's crime. I've gone for rides with the police, learning how they deal with it. I suppose my youth has qualified me to write about cops and criminals."

"Yes, why not? If it's a world you once knew."

"Unfortunately, it's a qualification that also haunts me. You know, anytime a woman is murdered, at any place in the world I've visited, the cops are always going to try to pin it on me. Once a murderer, always a murderer."

"Yes, I can imagine," said the filmmaker.

They continued talking until sunset.

"I'll take a look at your books, and perhaps we can talk about them later," the director said. Jack clearly sensed that Dornhelm wasn't interested. Looking dispirited, he got in his car and drove down the hill.

From Malibu he drove back into the city, to Carolina's duplex in Echo Park. Though she hadn't given him her address, he knew where she lived because he'd once followed her home from work. He parked and walked down the driveway to her apartment on the back side of the duplex. She wasn't home, but some Arab immigrants who lived on the front side were, and they invited him to wait for her in their apartment. Through the window he saw a car pull into the driveway. Carolina got out with a Mexican man who worked at the Cecil, and together they entered her place.

First the disappointment at Dornhelm's, and then the appearance of a rival at Carolina's—July 3, 1991, wasn't a happy day. From Echo Park he drove back to Hollywood.

The next day he met Carolina at a shopping center in Echo Park, where they strolled around and then went for a coffee. As they were parking in front of the café, Jack suddenly exclaimed, "Don't move! Just hold still." He pushed her legs to the side, reached down to the floor-board, and picked up a small plastic bag of powder.

"What is it?" she exclaimed.

"Poison."

"Let me see it!"

"No. It's bad stuff. It could kill you." He tore open the bag and dumped the powder into the gutter.

"But what's it doing in your car?"

"A homeless man I interviewed near the missions must have dropped it. He told me he'd talk to me if I'd give him a lift. God, I hate drugs. Never use drugs!" For five minutes he searched the car, and when he was satisfied the homeless man hadn't dropped anything else, they went into the café.

That evening (Jack recorded in his diary) they made love for the first time. Saturday they strolled around Silver Lake; Sunday they went to a Latino festival at Echo Park, where he invited her to stay with him in Vienna. After sleeping on it Sunday night, she decided she would, and on Monday she quit her job at the Hotel Cecil. That night she stayed with him at the Sunset Orange Motel. At 2:00 a.m. the phone rang and Jack talked for a long time in German.

"Who was that?" she asked when he hung up.

"Just a friend in Vienna." Actually it was Mrs. Müller, the neglected wife of a Viennese manufacturer who had set Jack up in his apartment. As he noted in the diary he diligently kept over the years, though he spoke in an intimate way with Mrs. Müller, Carolina had no way of knowing it because she couldn't understand German.

The next morning, July 9, he said he wanted to move because the motel manager complained about him bringing a woman into the room and wanted to charge him a double-occupancy rate. At least that's what he told Carolina. She helped him move his things into the Hollywood 8 on Cahuenga.

They spent his last week in Los Angeles together—days on the beach at Santa Monica, lunches at Le Petit Four on Sunset, and sunset dinners at Gladstone's in Malibu. The only night she wasn't with him was Friday, July 12, when he went to a party in Hollywood hosted by the

Austrian socialite and caterer Klaus von Ott. The entire Austro-German film crowd showed up, including Frances Schoenberger. She was surprised to see that Jack had penetrated so deep into the Hollywood scene. Maybe he did have a special way of meeting people. On the other hand, his clothes were wrong. With his short-sleeve shirt exposing his tattoos and his gold chain, he looked more like a pimp than a screenwriter.

"What have you been doing?" she asked.

"Mostly research for magazine stories. I've been driving around with cops and talking with street people downtown. I'm especially excited about my story on L.A. prostitution. It's shocking that the girls in this city sell themselves—will do anything—for only thirty dollars."

"It's a sad world," she said.

"The best thing I've done here is rescue the Latina receptionist at my hotel from her boss. She's going to fly over and stay with me in Vienna in a few weeks."

"That's wonderful."

The party gave Jack an opportunity to say farewell to most of the people he'd met in Hollywood. As his departure drew near, he realized he probably wasn't going to fulfill his dream of getting a story made into an American movie. On Sunday he and Carolina drove to Elke Sommer's house in Bel Air, where the Austrian actor Günther Ziegler was staying. Carolina waited in the car while Jack handed him a stack of manuscripts.

"I don't think it will happen," he said as they were driving away. She saw the disappointment in his face and felt sorry for him.

"You must have hope," she said.

CHAPTER 14

ZIGZAG

"JACK UNTERWEGER, murderer and writer. His lifelong story, today on *Zick Zack!*" said Elisabeth Scharang, the ORF radio show's host.

> *You know the stuff that crime stories are made of, but Jack Unterweger's story begins after the denouement, when the perpetrator is caught and put in a cell, where one doesn't gladly look. The perspective is too hopeless; the story is too sad. Unterweger spent his childhood in orphanages, without his mother; he never knew his father. He grew up mostly in the company of prostitutes and crooks. He slugged his way—in the truest sense of the word—through life. Today he writes his story. Jack Unterweger has spent twenty years of his life in prisons. For over a year he has been free, and now reckons with his past and his brutal youth in the underworld milieu.*

The program, which covered Jack's "lifelong" story (*lebenslang*, denoting "life sentence") was broadcast on July 22, 1991. Jack gave the interview a few days after his return from L.A., but he said nothing about his trip or about any project he was working on at the time. The program was mostly a recounting of *Purgatory*, which had been published nine years earlier. Quotes from the autobiographical novel were interspersed between Jack's ruminations about his life and Elisabeth's commentary. Even his parole the year before was old news, which might have prompted listeners to ask, Why the retelling of Jack Unterweger's sad past?

Critics of the ORF have characterized the state broadcasting company as a clique of trendy left-wingers who use their monopoly of the

Austrian airwaves to air their ideological obsessions. To what degree that's true is a matter of debate, but this much is indisputable: starting with its broadcasts of Jack's children's stories in the late seventies, the ORF had regularly given the "murderer and writer" a powerful forum. In the summer of 1991, twenty-two-year-old Elisabeth Scharang was the latest in a series of ORF journalists and producers to embrace his story.

Of his murder in 1974, Jack explained: "Today one can only say the same. The entire thing, as hard as it sounds, just happened. It wasn't a planned event, and therein lies a major difference. And after it happened, I could no longer take it back. And in the moment in which I can no longer take it back, I can only live with it."

The program quoted passages from *Purgatory*, including his account of his feelings for his grandfather:

> *In my dreams I slit open Grandfather's body with glowing fire pokers . . . Then I wouldn't have to run away anymore, into the woods . . . I wanted to throw Grandfather in the cesspool as he did the rats. I caught the rats with my bare hands, and on them I trained my thoughts of revenge. I pushed them . . . strangled through the outhouse hole . . .*

Another intriguing passage quoted on the program was his account of how he read in a newspaper about the murder of his Aunt Anna, a prostitute in Salzburg.

> *I thumbed through it to pages 4 and 5, where a headline across both tore the moment apart . . .*
>   HER LAST CUSTOMER WAS HER MURDERER!
> *Underneath were photos of her and the murderer . . .*

Early in the program, Elisabeth touched on the key to the Jack Unterweger story: "The tragedy. The murder of an eighteen-year-old in December 1974 and the to this day unanswered question: Did Unterweger commit the crime for 150 Marks and a fur coat, or was it a sudden blackout in which his pent-up aggression against his mother was released, as

Unterweger tries to claim? The verdict was spoken by the jury on June 1, 1976: *Murder, Life Sentence.*" An attentive listener might have wondered why the motive for Jack's 1974 murder remained unclear. Did that mean that Elisabeth and the other journalists who'd taken an interest in him hadn't examined the testimony at his 1976 trial?

On August 4, two weeks after the *Zick Zack* program on "Jack Unterweger, murderer and writer," a couple strolling in the woods near the village of Wolfsgraben, five miles from Vienna, discovered a decomposed body lying on its belly, covered with a thin layer of soil and a few tree branches. No clothing or handbag was present, but two small earrings and the victim's dental work identified her as Silvia Zagler, who'd disappeared on the night of April 8, 1991.

CHAPTER 15

A TRIP TO VIENNA

CAROLINA DRIFTED BACK into consciousness, becoming aware of the steady throb of the jet engines. It was after midnight over the Atlantic, August 8, 1991. Her final destination was Munich, where Jack wanted to introduce her to his mother before they drove to Vienna.

Carolina didn't know what to expect of Austria. It seemed so far away and foreign. Her father had known something about the Austrians; ethnically speaking, he was one. Born to German parents in Moravia (the eastern part of what is now the Czech Republic) in 1899, he was a subject of the Hapsburg imperial monarchy for the first nineteen years of his life. With the breakup of the empire at the end of the Great War, Moravia became part of the new state of Czechoslovakia. In the mid-1930s he moved to Central America to seek his fortune in emerald mining. By the time he fathered Carolina, he was sixty-two years old, had no connection with Austria, and never spoke his native German to her. And then, when she was sixteen, he died.

Life had always seemed more secure when he was there, with his understanding of things. Even as a girl she'd sensed that Guatemala was a troubled country, but as long as her father was there, she'd never worried. His death set her family adrift in a land without a bright-looking future. In 1980 her mother moved the family to Los Angeles, where some of her relatives were already living.

Despite her Moravian paternity, Carolina was a Latin girl. Her native language, her habits of thinking, her attitudes about men and family—all came from her mother's country. Central European culture was a mystery. In L.A. her social network remained Hispanic, and though she learned English, she still spoke Spanish most of the time.

Now she was flying across the Atlantic to be with an Austrian, and she thought about what was compelling her to go so far away from home. Jack said Vienna was a beautiful city without the chaos and pollution of L.A. In his own country he was famous and had made a lot of money from his books. And he seemed to care about her more than any of the other boys she'd dated. He'd pursued her with such persistence, and had been so excited when she finally met him outside the Hotel Cecil. He said he loved her and that they could make a life together in Vienna.

She felt strongly for him, but she wasn't confident that she really knew him. Their common language was English, but neither of them spoke it well enough to convey complex thoughts and feelings. There was also his foreignness. True, that was part of what made him intriguing. He was funny in a weird kind of way. She smiled, thinking of the outfit he'd put on for his departure back to Austria, like some crazy cowboy taking off into the sunset. But instinctively she felt she knew little more about Jack Unterweger than she did about Austria. She was flying to a strange land to live with a strange man. Maybe it was just an adventure. If she didn't get along with Jack, she could always get on a plane and go home.

In Munich she had to clear customs, but her luggage never rolled onto the carousel. She was one of the last passengers to emerge in the waiting area, and was surprised that Jack wasn't there. When he arrived half an hour later, it was a happy reunion, but she'd never felt so exhausted in her life. It had been a grueling trip and the change of nine time zones was playing havoc with her body and mind.

"I can't wait to get some sleep," she said.

"It'll be a while. You must stay awake until late tonight so you'll be on the same schedule as me."

"Okay, I'll try."

She told him her bags hadn't made it, and they walked over to the luggage department, where Jack spoke to a woman in German. The girl typed on the computer and said something about Paris, and Jack exploded. The girl was terrified and kept repeating a phrase that Carolina took to mean "I'm sorry."

Finally he spoke to Carolina in English: "They lost your luggage in Paris. She says they'll deliver it to Vienna."

"When?"

"Maybe tomorrow." His anger was alarming, but so was no fresh underwear or toiletries. She was having her period and needed her pads, but as she began to tell Jack, he started walking toward the exit, still furious.

He changed his mind about visiting his mother and got on the highway to Vienna. It was a four-hour drive, and trying to stay awake was torture. Every time she started to nod off, he reached over, shook her shoulder, and shouted, "Can't fall asleep!" At times she noticed the beauty of the Bavarian and later the Austrian countryside, but most of the drive was a blur of distorted perceptions and halting conversation.

They arrived in Vienna and parked in the courtyard of a building more modern than the surrounding ones. Though Carolina didn't know it, she was standing on the site where an Allied bomb had landed forty-five years earlier. They went into Jack's apartment, which looked spacious and comfortable. The walls were decorated mostly with nude female paintings and drawings. They didn't bother her, though it was kind of weird to be surrounded by so many naked women. She didn't know that Jack had developed his taste in graphic art in prison.

That afternoon they went to a café next door. It was an elegant place with a cozy atmosphere. People sat at dark wood tables, drinking coffee, smoking, chatting, reading the newspapers. Many recognized Jack and greeted him as they walked in.

Carolina couldn't imagine a city less like Los Angeles. She was amazed at how orderly everything was. There was no traffic and honking horns, no loud and aggressive people on the streets. In Jack's café she occasionally saw people chatting animatedly or laughing, but for the most part the Viennese were quiet and reserved. Walking down the sidewalk, she sometimes studied their faces and thought them impenetrable.

They would have been more discernible if she understood German. Much of Jack's sweet talk sounded like English. *Honig*, honey. *Ich liebe dich*, I love you. *Du bist so süss*, You are so sweet. *Gib mir einen Küss*, Give me a kiss. But phrases were one thing, conversation another. She started taking German lessons with a woman in the neighborhood, a friend of Jack who never said a word about payment. She had a cool manner, and Carolina wondered if her feelings for Jack ran deeper than friendship. All of his friends were women, and they were all polite but distant. A few of them took her out sightseeing, but Carolina sensed they did it only as a favor to Jack, who said he needed time alone to work.

The most self-assured was Susanna, the beautiful girl from the photo he'd showed her in L.A. In person she was even more beautiful. Carolina liked her the most. She was friendly and didn't seem concerned about her position with Jack. She had the biggest breasts, even though her body was slender.

"I once saw her breasts and laughed at them," he said. "They are like cow's tits."

The most sophisticated of his friends was Margit Haas. She was a rich girl with beautiful clothes and jewelry, and she lived in a palace with her parents. What sort of relationship did she want with Jack?

"You want to know about Miss Goat?"

"Miss who?"

"Miss Goat." He laughed. "*Haas* means goat in German."

"Really?" Carolina asked, giggling as well.

"Yes. Miss Goat is just a friend. Sometimes we meet for a coffee or dinner, and talk on the phone, nothing more."

Had Carolina looked it up in a German-English dictionary, she would have seen that Haas (a proper name) doesn't mean goat. But it didn't occur to her to look it up. It didn't occur to her that Jack made things up.

Sometimes she went into his study while he was working and sat down in a chair next to the window. One day, about a week after her arrival, he rotated in his desk chair and looked at her with a pensive expression.

"You know, I was once in prison," he said.

She laughed, thinking he was being silly.

"I'm not joking. I really was in prison."

"Prison! Tell me what for!"

"I robbed a bank with a couple of guys. I got caught, they got away. I could have gotten a shorter sentence, but I refused to rat on them."

She was stunned by the confession; Jack seemed so well known and respected in Vienna. To think that he'd once been a bank robber! "But why did you rob a bank?"

"It happened a long time ago. I was poor, I needed the money. You have to understand how much my life has changed since then."

"Tell me about your life back then."

"My mother abandoned me when I was little. She was a prostitute," he told her, "and when I was just a baby she left me with her father. He was an alcoholic and he beat me. When I was a teenager I went out on my own and I got jobs working as a waiter and at gas stations, but I never had enough money. One day I met some guys who said they were going to rob a bank, and they asked me to join them. I didn't really think about it. I figured it was my way out of being poor. I learned how to write when I was in prison; my books became popular, and that changed everything."

The next day, Carolina asked Margit to lunch.

"There's something I've been wondering about," she asked.

"What's that?"

"Why did Jack go to prison?"

An alarmed expression appeared on Margit's face. "I think that's something you should ask him," she replied. Her tone sounded vehement, and Carolina lost her nerve to pursue it any further.

That afternoon, Jack left Vienna, saying he was the guest of honor at an event in his hometown, and was going to read from his books. He explained that because everyone would be speaking German, it wouldn't be fun for her, but that he would be back in a few days. If she got lonely, she could call Margit or Susanna; otherwise she should stay at home and not answer the intercom if anyone buzzed.

CHAPTER 16

MYTHOLOGY

CHARLOTTE AUER HEARD that Jack was coming to the Wimitz Valley to give a reading on his birthday, August 16, and she planned to attend. But unlike the locals who intended to celebrate the occasion, she intended to confront him with his lies.

Malicious lies, she'd thought as she'd read *Purgatory*. Jack's grandfather, whom he depicted as a cruel cretin whose abuse had shaped him into the criminal he became, was her stepfather. His name was Ferdinand Wieser. Charlotte's mother, Maria Springer, had lived with him for twenty years. Charlotte and her brother, Fritz, had grown up with him in a cottage on the same site where Jack spent his childhood. The original hut in which she lived from 1936 to 1940 was much more primitive than the one in which Jack grew up.

Ferdinand Wieser, born in 1900, had spent most of his life in the Wimitz Valley—an isolated cut of land in the Carinthian Alps, Carinthia being the southernmost state of Austria, bordering Italy and Slovenia. During Habsburg times, the valley was known as "the end of civilization, a place of outlaws and Protestants."

Ferdinand had almost no book learning, but he could do anything with his hands. During the war, he, along with a few other Austrians and a team of British and French POWs, built an eighteen-kilometer road through the valley, connecting St. Veit at the base to Pisweg at the top.

In 1940, Ferdinand built the cottage that became the mythical site of Jack's childhood in *Purgatory*. To earn a little extra money, he wove baskets out of hazelnut branches, a skill he taught Charlotte. Many in the valley called him "Körbler" (basket weaver) instead of by his family name.

Charlotte believed that, despite his roughness, her stepfather was a decent man. When she had her own children, she let them spend their summer breaks with him and her mother. Her daughter Gertrude, born in 1952, was Jack's closest playmate. She grew up to earn doctorates in psychology and political science. In *Purgatory* Jack depicted his grandfather as a hateful man, but in reality, Ferdinand loved and spoiled him. Whenever Jack wanted a new toy, he got to work building a wooden truck, cart, airplane, or sled.

The journalists in Vienna wrote about how hard life had been for Jack in Wimitz. With astonishment Charlotte read that he'd grown up in a cottage with no electricity or heating appliances, only kerosene lamps and firewood. No one in Wimitz had electricity or appliances. At night, without a full moon directly overhead, the valley is pitch black. Though a child who grew up in the cottage would grow accustomed to going outside at night, a city dweller might be seized by a primal fear of the surrounding woods that envelop the cottage in darkness.

Charlotte was incensed by Jack's claim in *Purgatory* that there was no steady woman in the cottage. Her mother, Maria Springer, was his stepgrandmother; from 1952 to 1958, she looked after him, and for the first four years he lived in the cottage, she also loved him. The trouble began in the winter of 1957, during his first year of school. It was then that he became so strong-willed for a boy of six, and equally clever at getting what he wanted. As Charlotte saw it, Jack became like his biological mother, Theresia.

Theresia Unterweger lived in the cottage with her stepsiblings, Charlotte and Fritz, for about a year and a half during the war. Like Jack, she was pretty and bright. The adults in the valley found her adorable, which, according to Charlotte, enabled her to carry out her nefarious schemes without falling under suspicion. The year she attended school in Pisweg, things started disappearing from the schoolhouse, and no one but Charlotte knew that Theresia was the thief.

At the age of eleven she got into the black market of rationed goods. Because the gigantic German military was consuming so much leather and wool, the Nazi administration controlled the civilian market for clothing and shoes through ration tickets. Theresia went to the rationing office and said she was there to pick up tickets for elderly people in the valley who were too feeble to make the long walk on their own (few owned a horse, no one owned a car). Naturally the civil servant didn't suspect that the little girl was a fraudster who planned to sell the tickets to a black marketer.

In 1942, Theresia left to live with her mother in a different village, and in her late teens she moved out on her own. After she had Jack, she kept him for a year and a half, but when she was jailed for fraud, the children's welfare office placed the baby with his grandfather and step-grandmother. After Theresia's release from jail she married the G.I. who had probably fathered Jack, and she never returned to Wimitz to pick up her baby.

A year after Jack became such a difficult child, his stepgrandmother, Maria Springer, left the cottage and moved to Linz to live with her daughter Charlotte. Jack was left alone with his grandfather for two months, after which the children's welfare office placed him in the cus-tody of Ferdinand's sister. Charlotte figured that Jack's two months alone with his grandfather were the kernel of the myth of his awful childhood. During that time, Ferdinand probably was bossy and often drunk. False was Jack's oft-repeated claim in *Purgatory* that he'd slept in the same bed with his grandfather and whatever women were around. He had his own bedroom on the second floor, above the kitchen.

In 1976, Charlotte read in a newspaper that Jack was convicted of murder and sentenced to life in prison. Six years later, *Purgatory* was published and he became a celebrity. By then Charlotte and her hus-band had retired and moved back to Wimitz. One day in 1985 an ORF reporter called and invited her to give a radio interview about her famous nephew. She didn't conceal her anger.

"His grandfather was my stepfather. I lived with the man for eight years—two years longer than he did—and I'm no robber or murderer, nor is my brother, Fritz." Six years later, on the first anniversary of Jack's release from prison, she made similar remarks to a journalist from *Viennese* magazine.

The day before Jack's reading in Wimitz, she was working in her garden when she heard a big engine rumbling down the narrow lane of her village. She looked up just as a Ford Mustang was pulling in front of her yard. Behind the wheel sat Jack. He stared at her for what seemed like a long time, and something about his look caused her to remain silent. Finally she said, "Hello, Hansi" (Jack's nickname), but he didn't return her greeting. He pulled forward, turned around, and slowly passed by.

For his reading the next day she gathered photos of him between the ages of two and eight—as a toddler standing in the garden, his grandfather Ferdinand reaching down to hold his hand, playing with her daughter Gertrude in a wooden truck, and playing with a sled (Ferdinand had carved both toys for him). Finally there was a picture of him as an eight-year-old about to attend his first communion, wearing a navy blue suit that Ferdinand had bought for him. She put the pictures in an envelope and headed down to the Wimitzwirt restaurant.

She walked in to find Jack sitting at a table with a group of women.

"Hansi, I'm here to tell you that what you wrote about your grandfather is a malicious lie. He—"

"I'm sorry, but I don't think I know you," he said in an icy tone.

"Of course you know me; I'm your aunt Lotte!"

"No, I don't, and I'm trying to enjoy my birthday, so would you please leave us."

"You listen to me—"

He rose from his seat and turned his back to the people at the table so they couldn't hear his voice over the chatter in the guest house.

"Be quiet or something may happen to you," he hissed.

At that moment her anger turned to fear, and her mind flashed back to him cruising by her garden in his Mustang. She'd felt uneasy, but not scared that he would come after her—his old aunt who'd loved him when he was a child. The ferocity in his eyes and the hatred in his voice told her he would.

CHAPTER 17

A BATH

CAROLINA LIKED THE PARK a few blocks from Jack's apartment, a pleasant place to sit on hot August afternoons. One day (after Jack returned from Carinthia) a man sitting at a neighboring bench said something, and realizing she didn't understand, he asked if she spoke English. His English was excellent, and they ended up having a friendly chat. Later she told Jack about him.

"Where did you talk with the man?"

"I told you, in the park."

"Which park?"

"The one down the street."

"Which direction?"

"The one right down the street, toward the center of town."

"Don't ever talk to strange men. You never know what they want."

"He was a nice guy, he just wanted to talk."

"You know nothing about the men here. Something could happen to you."

That evening he took her for a drive.

"I'm going to show you the bad parts of Vienna—the parts where you should never go." He drove to the street next to the West Train Station and pointed at hookers standing on the sidewalk.

"This is where the bad people are. Never come here. If you ever come here I will find out and be angry. Okay?"

"Yes, of course. I don't want to come here."

———

Jack was in some ways the opposite of some of the macho Latinos she'd
known. He liked to cook, and she found it soothing to watch him prepare dinner. In the kitchen he was tranquil, methodically peeling and
mashing the potatoes, flipping the steaks in the frying pan with a grace-
ful movement. At such times he seemed content, happy to have her
there. A few times he spoke of marriage, of getting a house together and
raising kids.

He sometimes played practical jokes, like dumping water on her
from the window over the courtyard when she took out the trash. The
first time the shock of the cold water slapping down on her head made
her angry, but then it became a game. She would tie off the trash and
sneak out so that he wouldn't hear her from his study. As she approached
the Dumpster, she would look up at the window to see if he was there,
lurking in the shadow with a pot of water (he always was). She would
then make a dash for the Dumpster and try to get the bag in it before he
could pour the water at the right time. It always made them laugh.

On other occasions he did things that weren't funny. One day she
walked into his study to find him sitting at his desk, flipping through her
address book.

"What are you doing?"

"Just looking," he said, apparently relishing his violation of her privacy while she watched. And then his expression changed from amuse-
ment to anger.

"What is my mother doing here?" he shouted.

"You told me to write down her number in Munich in case we didn't
find each other at the airport." He slashed the book with a pen.

"Forget about my mother! She's a bad woman." Looking at the book
later, Carolina saw FORGET! printed below the crossed-out entry for his
mother.

A couple of days later she washed a load of laundry and hung it up
to dry. The summer heat and the steamy clothes bathed her in sweat,
and Jack offered to draw a bath for her.

"Sounds good," she said, and went into the kitchen for a glass of water. She was sitting at the kitchen table trying to read a German magazine when he yelled, "Bath is ready!" She walked into the bathroom, where he was standing next to the sink.

"Time to get in the bath, crazy chicken." "Crazy chicken" was his new pet name for her, which struck her as weird but sort of funny. She undressed and started to get into the tub, but jerked her foot back.

"It's too hot! The point was to cool off."

"Get in slowly and you'll get used to it." Getting into the hot bath was an example of her increasingly compliant way with him. He stood there watching.

"See how nice it feels."

She did get used to it, and after a while she began to relax. Jack left, and she closed her eyes. A few minutes later she sensed him walk back in. He was noiseless; maybe she felt his body displacing the damp air. She kept her eyes closed, waiting for him to speak, and felt his hands on her shoulders. She thought he was going to give her a massage, but instead he pushed her under. The shock of the water running into her sinuses caused her to exhale most of her air. She tried to push with her feet on the back wall of the tub, but to no avail. Reaching back and grabbing his forearms, she felt the taut tendons and muscles holding her down.

CHAPTER 18

DEATH BY DROWNING

TWO HUNDRED MILES to the west, in the city of Salzburg, the retired police inspector August Schenner was wondering why the Vienna police had not acted on the tip he'd given them on May 31, almost three months earlier. During the last week of May, Schenner had read in the papers about

the "Vienna Woods Killer," and it reminded him of a case he had investigated exactly eighteen years earlier—the case of a murdered woman
found in the Salzach Lake.

The lake, which lies just north of Salzburg next to the Salzach River,
is surrounded by woods that give it a peaceful and isolated atmosphere.
On Sunday, April 1, 1973, a thirty-four-year-old man was standing on
the bank, fishing with his son, when he heard shouts and looked over to
see a couple of boys running toward him.

"Look over there!" The fisherman saw it about twenty feet from
shore, floating just below the glassy surface like an apparition, its dark
upper body contrasting eerily with the ghostly white of the lower half.

A patrol officer arrived and tried to pull the body in with a tree
branch, but he couldn't get a good purchase. The fisherman proposed
snagging his hook on the corpse's clothing, and soon he was reeling it
into shore. It was a young woman, naked from the waist down.

The Salzburg investigators arrived at 11:10 and found the body lying
on her side on the pebbly shoreline with her lower legs still in the water.
She was twenty-five to thirty years old, with long dark hair and the features of a pretty Yugoslavian girl. Her upper body was clothed in a brown
jacket and a ribbed white turtleneck sweater, but whatever she'd been
wearing on her lower body was missing, as were her shoes. On her left
ring finger was a large gold signet ring stamped with the head of Nefertiti.

Rolling her over slightly, the inspectors examined the binding on her
wrists—a red necktie with black-and-silver checkered stripes. Her killer
had started with a knot around one wrist, leaving both ends free. He'd
then taken the longer end and tied another knot around the other wrist,
again leaving the end free, and then tied the remaining ends together in
between her wrists. Plainly visible on one end of the tie was the label
MODEN-STEINER, WELS. The town of Wels lies about sixty miles east of
Salzburg.

Photographs were taken and the body was hauled completely out of
the water. Though she was now lying on her back, rigor mortis froze her
in a semi-fetal position. The gag was composed of bandage tape, presumably from a car's first-aid kit, which the killer had wrapped around
her head and over her mouth nine and a half times without pulling her

hair out of the way, so that locks of hair were taped to her face. The forensic doctor pulled them aside to reveal her black, swollen eyes. Her killer had hit her repeatedly with his fists. Her legs were bound tightly together just above the ankles with a pair of brown panty hose.

Other than the blunt-force trauma to her face, no other injuries were apparent. Though the forensic doctor considered the possibility she'd been knocked unconscious, he could tell that the blows to her face hadn't been lethal. In other words, she'd been dragged into the lake alive and drowned.

Fresh tire tracks between the shoreline and the woods had likely been made by the killer's car, because everyone else who'd visited the lake that morning had parked in the lot next to the paved road. The tracks were recorded.

An autopsy revealed that the cause of death had indeed been drowning, between 12:00 and 2:00 a.m. Though it contained semen, her vagina showed no signs of trauma, indicating that her killer might have had normal sexual intercourse with her before he beat her and tied her legs together. At 5'2", barely over 100 pounds, she would have been easily overpowered, and once her hands and legs were bound, she would have been helpless. Her gold dental fillings (as distinct from the other metals used in Austria since the war) were another indication that she was a Yugoslavian.

In Salzburg, the idyllic birthplace of Mozart and the setting of *The Sound of Music*, a city with one of the lowest murder rates in the world, no resources were spared in trying to catch the killer. Officers combed through the apartment complexes of the city's Yugoslav community, questioning people, trying to identify the dead girl.

The next morning a Yugoslav guest worker named Mato Horvath, a resident of a neighboring village, appeared at the police station to report his wife, Marica, missing. She'd gone into the city on Saturday evening, March 31, and had never come home. He described her to the police and showed them her passport photo. They took him to the Institute of Forensic Medicine, where he identified the body as his wife's.

Twenty-five-year-old Marica Horvath was born near Zagreb, Croatia. After meeting each other in 1970, the young couple married and moved to Austria to find work. She found a job as a maid; he as a truck driver. On Saturday afternoon, March 31, 1973, Mato had gone into the city to watch a movie and had returned home early that evening to find his wife gone. A neighbor said she'd left around 6:00 p.m. to take the bus into the city. She didn't come home that night, and when she still didn't come home the following Sunday afternoon, Mato began to worry. The next morning he went to the police.

On April 3, a policeman working a dog along the Salzach River found one of Marica's shoes. It was easy to reconstruct what had happened. After dragging her into the lake, the killer had driven back to the road along the river and tossed her shoes over the bank. One of them landed in the water, the other just shy of it. A fisherman downstream snagged a woman's purse, which contained only Marica Horvath's wedding ring. The killer had apparently taken everything else with him, as well as her underwear.

Inspector Schenner had never seen such a cold-blooded crime. He imagined the girl's terror and pain as her tormentor beat her, gagged her, and tied her up. Then to have dragged her into the icy pond, where she struggled and drowned—what kind of man would do that? And why? Though he'd taken a bracelet and a small amount of cash, robbery didn't appear his prime motive for murdering her. All signs indicated an exceptionally sadistic sexual murder.

Schenner's best lead was the necktie with which her killer had bound her hands—one of a kind. Manufactured by Maestro clothing in Vienna, it had been delivered, along with 199 ties of the same pattern but different coloration, to the shop Moden-Steiner in Wels on March 8, 1973. Examining her records, the shop owner determined that the tie had been sold on either March 10, 16, or 17, but no one could remember to whom it had been sold. Mrs. Steiner vaguely remembered a young man with a swatch of suit material for which he was looking for a matching tie.

Had the killer bought the tie himself, received it as a gift, or stolen it from the original purchaser? What was certain was that he'd acquired it during the two to three weeks preceding his murder of Marica Horvath. Notices with a photograph of the tie were put up in Wels and Salzburg, with an explanation that it had been used in a murder, but they didn't produce any leads.

After months of investigating the crime, Schenner marveled that no one remembered seeing anyone or anything suspicious. It was as though Marica's killer had suddenly appeared, phantomlike, murdered her, and then disappeared without a trace.

It wasn't until the spring of 1975—two years after the brutal murder of Marica Horvath—that Inspector Schenner got his first promising lead. He heard that the Salzburg D.A. was about to prosecute a young man for assaulting various young women. His crime spree had culminated in the murder of a girl in Germany in December 1974. The man had recently been transferred to the Salzburg jail, where he was awaiting trial for the offenses he'd committed in Austria. Schenner obtained copies of his files.

Twenty-four-year-old Jack Unterweger, an itinerant waiter and disc jockey, had a long criminal record. Starting with minor theft at the age of sixteen, he'd graduated to robbery, car theft, burglary, and fraud. He committed his first offense against life and limb in 1970, when he abducted a sixteen-year-old girl and tried to coerce her into prostitution. A series of jail sentences had had no corrective effect.

In the years 1973–74, numerous girls in various towns had made complaints against him. Schenner was most interested in the complaint of a Salzburg girl named Daphne. On the night of May 13, 1974, a young man offered to give her a lift from a bar near the Salzburg train station. He was good-looking and nicely dressed, and his Ford Mustang was parked across the street (in those days an American sports car was a potent status symbol). Instead of taking her home, the man drove beyond the city limits to a meadow surrounded by tall bushes, where the car got stuck in the mud. When she "got a funny feeling" and tried to walk away, he knocked her to the ground and sexually assaulted her.

Reading Daphne's statement to the police (guided by their questioning), Schenner marked the following passage:

As I tried to scream, he hit me on the head with his fists, and pushed my face down into the mud. Then he pulled off my shoes

and ripped my stockings from my body. He then turned my wrist
behind my back and wrapped the stocking around it, and then did
the same with the other wrist, and then tied it off with a large knot
in the middle, so that my hands were bound behind my back with
a few centimeters of play room between each wrist.

He then pushed her back into the car and raped her with a steel rod
while he masturbated. Afterward he cut the stockings and asked her if
she was going to turn him in. She said she wouldn't, and right then another car appeared on the meadow. The young man got out, feigned distress, and asked for help. While he was talking to the driver, she ran over
to the car and asked the man in the passenger seat for a lift, and then
went to the police.

When Daphne's story checked out, the young man, who was identified as Jack Unterweger, was arrested and put in jail. However, shortly
thereafter he swallowed a large dose of prescription pain killers he'd smug-
gled into his cell, and because of this suicide attempt, he was placed in a
Salzburg psychiatric clinic, from which he was—with tragic consequences
for the German girl he murdered a few months later—soon released.

Schenner read Unterweger's statement to the police, concentrating
on his account of his movements in the years 1973–74:

From October 1971 to January 1973 I was in the Wels jail. After my
release I traveled to Italy, where I vagabonded around until I reached
southern Italy. I traveled back north to Switzerland, and then later,
as I tried to cross over into Germany at the Three Country Corner
near Basel, I was arrested by the German authorities. That was at the
end of February or the beginning of March 1973. I remained in Ger-
man custody until August 25, 1973, at which point I was transferred
back to Salzburg, where I was released. I then moved to Tyrol, where
I worked in various places as a waiter and a filling-station attendant.
Since January 8, 1974, I have been employed as a disc jockey.

So Jack was released from the Wels jail in January 1973. The tie
used to bind Marica Horvath's hands was purchased in a Wels shirt shop

two months later. On June 11, 1975, Schenner interrogated Jack in the Salzburg jail.

"Where were you on the night of March 31–April 1, 1973?" he asked.

"I was arrested by the Germans when I tried to cross their border at the end of February or the beginning of March. I was in German custody until August."

"I've spoken with my colleagues in Germany, and their records show that you were arrested for violating their immigration laws on April 4. So once again, where were you on the night of March 31–April 1, 1974?"

"Well, if I wasn't already in Germany, I must have still been in Switzerland. After wandering around Italy for a few weeks in January, I headed back north and lived in Basel for a while."

Checking with the Swiss, Schenner determined that Jack had moved into an apartment in Basel on January 24, 1973. Additionally, the unknown killer had used a car to transport Marica Horvath to the Salzach Lake, and Schenner could find no record of Jack owning one at the time. He claimed he'd traveled by train and hitchhiking, which seemed plausible, given his small, irregular income. Though the suspect couldn't demonstrate that he was not in Salzburg on the night of March 31– April 1, Schenner could find no records or witnesses placing him in the city in the year 1973 prior to August 25.

In July 1975 Schenner attended the trial of Jack Unterweger for violent offenses against four girls. He was convicted on all counts and sentenced to three years in prison. By treaty with Germany, the Austrians assumed responsibility for trying Unterweger for the murder of the German girl Margret Schäfer. The following year he was convicted and sentenced to life in prison. Time passed and everyone forgot about the officially unsolved murder of the poor Yugoslavian girl down at the lake—everyone but her family, friends, and Inspector Schenner.

Ten years later, on the night of February 1, 1983, a fifty-two-year-old man was arrested in the town of Wels for walking out on a bar tab. The police checked his identity and released him, but as he was leaving, he said, "You know, you police have an unsolved murder. I know something about it, but I don't want to say anything because it could mean trouble for a family member." After some prodding, he said he was talking about the murder of a Yugoslavian girl in Salzburg, but at that point he clammed up. The police concluded he'd drunk too much and was trying to make himself important.

At around midnight the man dodged another check and was again detained. Noticeably drunker, he spoke again about the murder in Salzburg.

"It doesn't matter anyway, now I'm gonna tell you how it really was," he said, and proceeded to tell the following story:

This murder happened many years ago, I'm not sure when exactly. My daughter, who is now twenty-seven years old and lives here in Wels, had a friend back then—a blond-headed boy, about twenty-two-years old. This boy, whose name I can't remember, was the son of an Ami [American]. His mother lived in Munich and ran a filling station. Years ago he did some time in the Wels jail, where he was the cellmate of . . . an acquaintance of mine. Back then I owned an Opel Record, but as I was also in jail, no one was using it. This boy, who was released before I was, went for a drive in the car with [Manu]. He was apparently a karate fighter, or at any rate was interested in it, and while he was in prison he often trained with dumbbells. When he and [Manu] were in a pretzel bakery in Salzburg, he punched the Yugoslavian girl in the throat and killed her. He then drove her body to Waller Lake. My daughter was herself a witness but has never said anything out of fear.

The boy tied the girl's hands with a tie from the Steiner shirt shop in Wels, in the Kaiser Josef Square. At the time he bought it, he had my dog with him, a husky with gray fur. Later he was put on a publicized trial in Salzburg and is apparently still in prison.

The Wels police didn't know what to make of the man's story, though some remembered a notice displaying the image of a necktie. They contacted the Salzburg police, and a copy of the report soon landed on Schenner's desk.

The part about the boy punching the girl in the throat was wrong.

She had no throat injury, and she definitely died of drowning. Being a "karate fighter" was the sort of thing Jack might have boasted about (in *Purgatory* he boasted about being a featherweight boxing champion), while at the same time implying he'd hit the girl without intending to kill her. Waller Lake instead of Salzach Lake was also inaccurate, but the rest of the man's story, though secondhand, rang true.

Shortly before Schenner departed for Wels, he heard that the informant had just died of a heart attack. It had taken ten years for a witness to emerge in the murder of Marica Horvath; maybe he'd made the confession because he sensed his end was near.

Frustrated but not deterred, Schenner tracked down the man's daughter, Manu, who remembered her relationship with Jack Unterweger.

> I was a chambermaid at [a hotel] in Wels. Sometime around the beginning of 1973 I met Jack Unterweger, but I never learned anything definite about his past. I didn't know—I've just heard it for the first time today—that he was an inmate in the Wels jail. He said he worked as a waiter in Switzerland and that he could get a job for me as well, but before we went to Switzerland, we went on holiday in Italy.

She then told Schenner about their trip to Italy and then back north to Basel, where Jack worked as a waiter and kept her cloistered at home. When he caught her venturing out alone, he flew into a rage and beat her up. He told her he'd become distraught out of fear that something had happened to her.

One day he said he was having trouble with the police, so they returned to Wels, where Jack bought an old Opel from Manu's mother. Shortly thereafter they drove to Salzburg.

> We stayed in a place near the train station and had dinner in its restaurant. Afterward we went up to the room, and he said he was going out for a while to meet a friend from Germany about a money matter. The evening wore on and I fell asleep. Later I was awakened by sirens and blue lights flashing through the window. I looked out

*and saw that a car had skidded into the neighboring storefront. It
was then that I noticed that Jack was back in the room. He'd also
gotten out of bed and was looking out the window. When he returned to the room I can't say; I didn't hear him come in.*

*The next morning we drove back to Wels, where he dropped me
at home and, without explanation, drove off. A couple of days later
he sent a telegram from Basel saying he'd again found work in the
city, but had fallen ill and needed me. I took the train to Basel, and
when I met him, he said he wasn't sick, nor did he have a job. Yet
somehow he had money.*

*Neither during nor after our visit to Salzburg did it cross my
mind that he might have murdered a woman that night, but I remember that in the hotel room in Basel he'd collected newspaper
reports about a murder in Salzburg. When I asked about them, he
said it was none of my business and threw them away.*

Manu's story checked out. A follow-up with Swiss immigration revealed that Jack had resided and worked without a permit until March 14,
1973, when he was confronted about his illegal status. That put the
couple back in Wels around the fifteenth, and the necktie used to
bind Marica Horvath was purchased from the Steiner shop on either
March 10, 16, or 17. A follow-up with the Basel police revealed that Jack
had checked into the Hotel Bernerhof on April 2.

Yet there was still the problem of *proving* he was in Salzburg on the
night of March 31–April 1. Though Manu knew it was sometime in the
spring of 1973, she couldn't remember the date, nor could she remember
the name of the hotel. Schenner drove her around Salzburg and she recognized it. Guest House Dietmann was located about a mile from the train
station, on the opposite side of the river, and a couple of miles south of
Salzach Lake. Schenner asked to see the registration forms from the night
of March 31–April 1, 1973, but the owner had already destroyed them.

At that point he hung his hope on one detail from Manu's recollection—the car accident. The shop owner remembered the accident, but
not the particular night it happened. Going through the shop records, he

found an insurance claim for damage to the storefront from a car accident in the early morning of April 1, 1973. Schenner cross-referenced it
with the log of the Salzburg traffic accident squad, and there it was—at
12:45 a.m. to be precise.

Schenner reviewed the transcripts of Jack's interrogations in 1974 and
1975, and noticed how carefully he'd avoided mentioning anything about
being in Austria between his release from the Wels jail in January 1973
and his deportation from Germany in August 1973. He said nothing about
his Austrian girlfriend Manu, and nothing about having a car in March
1973, though he spoke freely about being in the country *after* the relevant
time. In an interrogation with another Salzburg inspector, he said, "During
my stay in Kitzbühel, I owned an Opel Coupe, painted bottle green. That
was in October 1973, though I only owned it for three weeks." He didn't
mention that he'd driven an Opel Record in March and April of the same
year. Had the car been found, it probably would have had the same tires
and first-aid kit (containing the tape used to gag the victim). By volunteer-
ing benign facts that could be verified, Jack gave the impression of candor
and distracted attention away from where the guilt lay. Schenner had studied the suspect for long enough. It was time to confront him again.

On Good Friday, April 1, 1983, exactly ten years after Marica Horvath was murdered in Salzburg, Schenner visited the prime suspect in
prison. Stein prison, built around a former convent in the village of Stein
(a suburb of Krems), probably has the most idyllic setting of any prison
in the world, situated in a stretch of the Danube Valley known as the
Wachau. The surrounding hills, covered with vines and dotted with the
occasional castle, comprise a premier white wine region. Just west of
Stein is the town of Durnstein, where, legend has it, Richard the Lion-
heart was held for ransom after an Austrian duke captured him on his
way home from a crusade.

"Inspector Schenner, so good to see you!" Jack exclaimed as his interrogator entered the visitors' room. His recognition was too quick;
eight years had passed since he'd met Schenner, who was just one of
many policemen with whom he'd crossed paths. Someone had told him
who was coming.

Schenner learned from the prison's deputy director that Jack held a "special position" in the prison and was also a rising star in the literary scene.

"Forget about the preliminaries and get to the point, or else I'll go back to my cell," Jack said.

"Your alibi in connection with the April 1, 1973, murder of Marica Horvath in Salzburg—the alibi you offered to me on June 11, 1975—is no longer tenable," Schenner said.

"Why not?"

"Because you were in Salzburg."

"No way; maybe before or after, but not on that night."

Schenner halted the interrogation because the prisoners entering and leaving the visitors' room were a distraction. His irritation mounted when the guard took them to an unheated cell that was very uncomfortable on that unseasonably cold day. Schenner was reminded of Jack's "special position."

"I was told in writing I'd have a proper interrogation room," Schenner told the guard. They were taken to a conference room, at which point the prison director, Karl Schreiner, tried to join them. To Schenner's astonishment, Jack curtly asked him to leave the room, which he did. It was as though Jack, and not Dr. Schreiner, was running the prison.

"I don't want to discuss this," Jack said to Schenner. "Among the six hundred prisoners here, seventy of which have life sentences, I hold the second-highest position, and I have no intention of losing it. I live in safety and with a number of advantages; why should I risk them? And by the way, I'm certain that, in no more than twelve years, I will be free. It's senseless for me to discuss unsolved crimes with you. I've already received one life sentence and I can't receive a second."

Jack knew the Austrian criminal code, which has no provision for multiple life sentences, and no condition for a life sentence without the possibility of parole. During the entire interrogation, he paced around and refused the lunch that was offered him.

"There may be something to Manu's story," he finally conceded. "It's all very gray, but I have a vague memory of spending a night with her at a guest house in the city. And I have some recollection of a car accident nearby. But that was certainly before the night of March 31, 1973. Or perhaps it was afterward."

"The car accident happened at 12:45 a.m. on the morning of April 1, 1973," Schenner said.

"If you keep this up, I'll go back to my cell and hang myself," Jack said, bursting into tears.

Schenner backed off and let Jack talk some more about his "special status."

"A few days from now I will present here at Stein my latest book of poetry, *Raving I*. You should also know that numerous writers are working for my early release. I have corresponded with the president [Rudolf Kirchschläger], who wrote to me that I am not yet mature enough to be released. I have also made amends with the parents of Margret Schäfer, the girl I murdered in Germany. Thanks to them I have been able to pursue my education in prison. Before, I needed a proofreader for my poems, plays, and novels, but now I can manage on my own."

That the parents of Jack's victim had financed his education didn't seem credible, but Schenner was beginning to appreciate the convict's talent for turning the world on its head.

The conversation continued aimlessly, and then Schenner tried to return to the false alibi.

Jack relaxed and softened his tone. "I really can't understand why you are trying to hang two life sentences on me. We both know that I can only be given one. But I admit that I spent a night with Manu in a guest house in Salzburg, from which I observed the car accident. And I did leave her alone in the room to loaf around the neighborhood near the train station and to meet some old friends. You ask me why I didn't wake her up when I returned to the room, to which I say, I didn't see any reason to wake her. As for returning to Basel the next day, all I can say is that I liked it there. As for the newspapers that Manu saw in my hotel room, I admit, I was interested in the case, just like a lot of other people. As for why I didn't tell you that I owned a car in March and April, it was because I didn't have a driver's license at the time, and I didn't want to get into trouble."

He regained his confidence, and Schenner understood why. The inspector had focused exclusively on the issue of Jack's false alibi. Manu aside, he'd said nothing about other witnesses and nothing about a recovered car, tires, or a first-aid kit. And so Jack placed his bet—namely, that the false alibi was the only card Schenner had to play. Was that enough to persuade the D.A. to prosecute?

Schenner tried to approach it from other angles—the striking similarities between Jack's sexual assault of Daphne in Salzburg in May 1974 and the murder of Marica Horvath just one year before. But by then he'd lost his leverage and Jack knew it. There was no way he was going to confess that he'd murdered the girl.

On his way out, Schenner stopped by Dr. Schreiner's office and asked him why he tolerated Jack's insolent behavior.

"Unterweger has many powerful advocates, and I have no desire to be called to the Justice Ministry to explain myself," Schreiner replied.

Schenner continued investigating for a while, and then presented his case to the Salzburg district attorney.

"He already has a life sentence," the D.A. said. "He can only be given one." To Schenner, the D.A.'s decision was a blatant injustice. Even if Jack couldn't receive a second life sentence, a second murder conviction would have gone on his record and lengthened the amount of time he would have to serve before being considered for parole.

Schenner believed it was obvious that Jack had murdered Marica Horvath. To begin with, if he didn't murder the girl, how had Manu's father come up with the story that contained several verifiable facts? His drunken account of the murder, ten years after it was committed, didn't seem calculated or rehearsed, and if he had a motive for slandering Jack, why hadn't he told the story earlier?

Then there was Jack's false alibi and his other deceptive statements to the police, the tie purchased in Wels on one of three days when he was in the city, his going out alone in Salzburg on the night the murder happened and sneaking back into the room, his trip to Switzerland the next day, his collection of newspaper reports on the murder, his record of assault against other girls in the Salzburg area using an identical modus and identical method of binding the victims' hands behind their backs, his psychiatric evaluations at his trials in 1975 and 1976—it all added up in a way that would have almost certainly persuaded a jury of his guilt. Though it was conceivable that a good defender could have won on the grounds that Schenner's case was circumstantial, the evidence was still strong enough to warrant putting Jack on trial. So why wasn't he prosecuted?

CHAPTER 19

JUST PLAYING

JACK TURNED CAROLINA LOOSE. She gasped for breath and coughed and tried to clear her sinuses, and as she recovered from the shock, she heard Jack, somewhere in the apartment, laughing. She got out of the tub, put on a bathrobe, and found him sitting in the living room.

"Jack, you're crazy. I almost drowned."

"No, you didn't, not even close. I was just playing."

"How can you say that? You held me under for a long time!"

"Oh, don't be so dramatic! I was just playing." Was it just another practical joke, like pouring water on her when she took out the trash? It didn't seem as if he was just playing.

A couple of days passed without incident, and her bathtub scare began to fade. And then Jack said he wanted to leave Vienna.

"Today we are going for a drive. I'm thinking about renting a little house outside the city, and we have a meeting with the owner." They drove a while, and after passing through a village in the Vienna Woods, they turned onto a dirt road that ended in a clearing with a cottage. A middle-aged couple came out and greeted them. Jack introduced Carolina in English, but as soon as they sat down to talk business, he switched to German. Carolina needed to go to the bathroom, but felt shy about interrupting to ask if she could use it. She waited for a break in the conversation, but it never came. After ten minutes or so, Jack stood up to leave, and she decided to wait till they got on the road.

The couple walked them to the car, and as Carolina was about to get in, the woman gave her a hug.

"It was nice to meet you, take care," she said with a look of distress on her face. Something was worrying her.

"It's a nice house," Carolina said, trying not to act perturbed as they drove off.

"That's not the one they're renting. It's another place. It sounds perfect, but it's expensive. I told them I'd think about it."

"When would you move in if you decide to take it?"

"It's not just for me, it's for both of us. I was thinking the beginning of September."

They reached the end of the dirt road and turned onto the pavement.

"I need to go to the bathroom. Can we stop at the next filling station?"

"Sure," he said, but he didn't slow down as they approached it.

"Hey, there it is!"

"There's what?"

"The gas station. I need to go to the bathroom, remember?"

"Oh, sorry about that. I'll stop at the next one."

They drove through another little town with a gas station, but once again, Jack didn't stop to let her go to the bathroom.

"Jack, why didn't you stop? I really need to go." He smiled and kept driving, and as they entered an outer district of Vienna, they approached another station. He signaled and took his foot off the gas, but then, with a laugh, kept driving.

"It isn't funny," she said, which made him laugh harder. She wondered why he thought it was funny. Why did Jack—a man who could be so tender—sometimes seem to take pleasure in tormenting her? She thought about telling him that she wanted to go home to America, even though she was still attached to him. Her general feeling was confusion, though of one thing she was certain—she did not want to move with him to a place outside the city, where she would be even more isolated.

CHAPTER 20

HOT TIP

HOT TIP IN THE SEARCH FOR THE PROSTITUTE MURDERER was the headline of a report in the September 1 edition of the Viennese *Kurier*.

> *The investigation of the Vienna Woods prostitute killer is on the back burner. Other murders and almost daily bank robberies have diverted the attention of the investigators, but they still have a hot tip.*
>
> *The man they are looking for could be a murderer already known to the authorities. The crime for which he was sentenced to life, in the meantime paroled, bears striking parallels to the crimes in the Vienna Woods.*
>
> *The police have already given the eerie Vienna Woods prostitute killer the apt nickname "Jack the Struggler," or the "Strangler of Penzing."*

The crime reporter Peter Grolig was the best in Vienna, though he might have consulted a German-English dictionary before writing "Jack the Struggler." An article on the murders in the journal of the Association of Police Investigators earlier that summer had also referred to the unknown killer as "Jack the Struggler." Originally the nickname had been a play on "Jack the Ripper," but as it turned out, the police had a suspect who really was named Jack, an extraordinary coincidence, given that Jack Unterweger may have been the only native Austrian who bore the Anglo-American name.

Grolig learned about Schenner's tip through a contact at headquarters shortly after it was received at the end of May, and he went to work studying the life and crimes of Jack Unterweger. To him, Jack's murder in 1974 did indeed resemble the Vienna Woods murders in 1991. Grolig knew that some investigators felt the same way, and yet, three months after headquarters received the tip, the investigation of Jack Unterweger was still barely creeping along, with little more than sporadic surveillance.

Grolig wondered if the slowness to pursue the paroled convict had something to do with his special status among writers, intellectuals, and officials at the Justice Ministry. Was Edelbacher worried he would have a public relations problem if Unterweger cried "police harassment"?

In every case of murder without witnesses or physical evidence, the police could only pursue whoever appeared to be the most probable suspect. They had to recognize that the suspect was presumed innocent until proven guilty, but they still had to pursue him. Grolig believed it was time for Chief Edelbacher to take a harder look at Unterweger, and so, on September 1—three months after the police received Schenner's "hot tip"—the reporter disclosed the tip (in a very diplomatic way) to the public, though he stopped short of revealing the suspect's full name. Most readers would still think that "Jack the Struggler" was a play on Jack the Ripper. Only a well-informed and highly attentive reader would recognize the identity of the man to whom the moniker referred.

When September 1 came, Jack made an announcement, but it wasn't that he and Carolina were moving. Instead, he said they were going for a bicycle ride along the Danube. What sounded like a pleasant idea became a trial of endurance, because he rode fast; every time they stopped at a signal light, she noticed he wasn't even winded. When they reached the Danube, the beginning of the ride, she was already exhausted. After a few miles of misery on the bike path, they finally stopped for a rest. Sitting on a grassy area, watching the great river flow by, Jack started to cry. She noticed his tears, and for a moment she forgot her concern for herself.

"What's wrong?"

He started to say something, but was choked by a sob.

"What is it? Tell me why you're crying."

"Something has happened; you must go back to America."

"What's happened?"

"Some trouble. Something I have to deal with. You can come back to Vienna after everything has cleared up." With that he stood, got on his bike, and rode back in the direction from which they had come, far too fast for her to keep up. She did her best to remember how they'd come, and somehow found her way back to his apartment.

"Hey, crazy chicken!" she heard him shout as she entered the courtyard. She looked up to see him in the window, a goofy grin on his face, and she marveled at how his mood had swung so dramatically. He booked her ticket the next day, and on September 5 she flew back to L.A.

CHAPTER 21

CONFRONTATION

THE DAY AFTER he took Carolina to the airport, Jack popped by Chief Edelbacher's office to tell him about his trip to Los Angeles. He was relaxed and cheerful as he laid out the photos from his trip and told a few anecdotes. He'd taken the pictures while riding around with LAPD patrol officers, and had learned a lot about crime in the great American city. The chief thanked him for sharing his experiences.

The timing of Jack's visit, just four days after Grolig's report about the "hot tip," seemed suspect, but to be fair, he had said he would come by after his return from L.A. True, he'd returned from his trip in mid-July, but the chief had been on vacation for most of August. How to proceed? Edelbacher believed it was best to continue playing dumb and to put him back under surveillance.

On September 16, eleven days after Jack visited Chief Edelbacher, the ORF youth program *Zick Zack* broadcast his story on "The Dark Side of Los Angeles." The host, Elisabeth Scharang, gave the introduction:

*The heat is on and the sun is shining. It makes California. It keeps
the dream of California alive. Every day it fights its way through
filth and smog to cast light onto the scenes of the dream factory.
The shady side—just a few kilometers away from Beverly Hills, in
downtown Los Angeles—remains in darkness. Jack Unterweger
spoke with young prostitutes, with homeless people, and with policemen about life and the struggle to survive behind the scenes of
Hollywood.*

The most gripping part of Jack's story about L.A.'s dark side was his
conversation with a street prostitute. While much of Elisabeth Scharang's narration sounded exaggerated and contrived to appeal to leftist
sentiment about heartless, capitalist America, the shaky voice of the
drug-addicted woman telling her story sounded very real.

JACK: You are working in L.A. as a prostitute?

PROSTITUTE: Yes, because I'm disabled. I cannot work a normal job. [*An inter-
pretation in German takes over, and when the voice of the prostitute returns, she is describing her job, presumably in response to Jack's question.*]

PROSTITUTE: It's ugly, it's dirty, it's scary. Every time you walk out on the
street you take your life in your hands. You could die every time you
get in a car. Every time you drive away, you don't know this person,
you don't know if he's gonna kill you, if he's gonna be nice to you, if
he's gonna beat you up, if he's gonna hurt you. And you're scared
every single time you get in a car. It's scary.

On October 7, three weeks after the *Zick Zack* broadcast, Jack again
appeared at headquarters to tell Edelbacher about a story he was writing
on homelessness in Los Angeles and Vienna. At that moment, the chief
decided to go ahead.

"Mr. Unterweger, there's something I'd like to talk with you about. It
pertains to the women who were murdered last spring—the murders
that you reported on for the ORF."

"Have you found a suspect?" Jack asked calmly.

"We've looked at about 130 possible suspects. What I want to tell you is that in our discussions about suspects, your name has come up."

"I'm not surprised, given my past. I also know where the tip came from. I know that a retired inspector in Salzburg has got it in his head that I'm the killer, which is obviously absurd. After all those years in Stein, there's no way I would commit a crime. Not only would I lose my freedom, it would be a terrible disappointment and embarrassment for everyone who has helped me."

"I understand," said Edelbacher. "It would still help us to clear your name from our list of suspects if you could tell us where you were on the nights the four women disappeared." Jack said he'd try to reconstruct his whereabouts on the nights of April 8, 16, and 28, and May 7. Edelbacher gave him two weeks to think about it and to go over his records.

CHAPTER 22

CRANK CALL

THE NEXT NIGHT, October 8, Rudolf Prem, the husband of the still missing Regina Prem, got another round of crank calls. Since he'd made his dramatic appeal in *Kurier* at the end of May, he'd occasionally been awakened by anonymous callers. The voice on the night of October 8 sounded familiar. Rudolf figured it was the same man who had called at the beginning of July and said, "At the Vienna Woods lake go left and follow the path that steeply ascends and forks. A few are lying there. When the figure eight at the zenith stands, then I'll tell you where your wife lies."

On August 4, a month after Rudolf got the call, the body of Silvia Zagler was found in the Vienna Woods, and it was notable that the route from Vienna to the crime scene was similar to the route described by the anonymous caller. The second part of what the anonymous caller said in July sounded like rhyming verse:

Wenn der Achter im Zenith steht,
Dann sage ich Dir wo deine Frau liegt.
When the figure eight at the zenith stands,
Then I'll tell you where your wife lies.

Rudolf believed it was the same voice that called him three months later, on the night of October 8 at 11:45, and said, "I am an executioner, on Tulbinger Hill lies Gerda. God commanded me to do it. Tonight I have completed my work. To eleven I have carried out the just punishment."

At 5:00 a.m. the same voice called back and said, "They lie in the place of atonement, facing downward, toward Hades, because otherwise it would have been an outrage."

CHAPTER 23

ALIBIS

TWO WEEKS AFTER Edelbacher told him he was under suspicion, Jack returned to headquarters to present his alibis for the nights of April 8, 16, and 28, and May 7.

For the entire months of April and May, I must confess that I cannot offer any alibis. I began keeping a record of my activities on September 3, 1991, when I first learned that I was under suspicion [from the September 1 Kurier report]. From November 11, 1990, to March 25, 1991, I worked intensively as an actor and director of two theater pieces. In the months of April and May I stayed in Vienna, mostly working at home, though I did make a trip to Munich to visit my mother, as well as to East Germany, though I cannot say when exactly.

A car is registered under my name, a VW Passat with the license plate W JACK 1. *I don't have a driver's license, but I have attended classes at a driving school and will obtain a driver's license in February 1992. I myself don't drive the car, but I have friends who chauffeur me. To prepare for my radio story on the prostitute murders, I spent four evenings in June in the milieu conducting research and was questioned by police officers. That was on the day before I came to headquarters to conduct the interview here. Otherwise I've had no contact with the milieu of prostitutes and pimps.*

One cannot accuse me of committing an offense such as the murder of a prostitute. I am psychologically stable, and have changed so much from my earlier life that I would never again commit such a crime. I am entirely happy with my occupation; I consume no drugs, and I even abstain from alcohol.

I understand that one would suspect me based on the experiences of a retired Salzburg inspector, but his perceptions in no way correspond to the reality of my life. I know the tip came from him; he has threatened me, told me he will give me no rest. His suspicions have no basis in fact whatsoever. I have no need to pick up a prostitute. I am fully integrated in society—there's plenty of evidence of that. I grant permission to take two Polaroid pictures of me.

After Jack left, Edelbacher studied his statement. The part about not driving himself revealed that he was capable of lying poker-faced to the chief of police, but it also revealed he didn't know he was being watched. Or did it? Maybe he avoided cruising around the milieu because he knew he was being watched but wanted to give the impression he didn't know.

Edelbacher figured that an apartment search was pointless. When Jack learned he was under suspicion at the beginning of September, he would have disposed of anything connected with the crimes (if he really was the killer). Maybe the investigators would find prostitutes who recognized him from the Polaroids.

A few days later, an unusual teletype appeared at headquarters. Inspectors in Graz were investigating the murders of two prostitutes, and they were wondering if the Vienna police could assist.

CHAPTER 24

GRAZ

THE GRAZ POLICE had renewed their search for the killer after the second body was found in the woods on October 5, 1991. The trouble had started a year earlier, when the first woman had disappeared. Thirty-nine-year-old Brunhilde Masser had worked in the Graz red-light district for over a decade. If she looked north from her corner, she could see the illuminated clock tower on Graz Castle Mountain, about half a mile away. Since medieval times the castle had been one of the most impregnable fortresses in Europe. Neither the Ottoman Turks nor Napoleon's Grand Army had managed to take it.

Brunhilde probably glanced up at the tower for the last time around midnight on October 26, 1990. At 12:15 a.m. a taxi driver who knew her stopped and asked why she was working so late, as most of her colleagues had already gone home. She said she was hoping for one last customer, as she planned to take her children on an outing that day (National Celebration Day) and needed the money. Shortly thereafter, her last customer must have appeared.

He picked her up, drove her out of the city and onto the main road that runs parallel to the Mur River as it bends to the northeast. Just north of the village of Gratkorn he turned off onto a forest road that ascends into the wooded hills. The entrance to the lane isn't lit; he'd seen it before and knew when to slow down for the hard right turn.

Two months later, on January 5, 1991, children playing in the woods found her corpse lying facedown in a small brook, partly covered with a couple of tree branches. She was naked except for her jewelry; her clothing and purse were missing. An animal had devoured part of her buttock, and it appeared he'd started at the site of a stab wound. The forensic pathologist deduced that she'd been strangled with a wide strip of fabric, but because of the advanced state of decomposition, he couldn't make a definite determination.

Because her body was found five miles outside Graz, inspectors of the gendarmerie (the law-enforcement agency of the countryside) were the first to work on the case. When they discovered that the victim had been picked up in the city, they began working with the Graz police. At first suspicion fell on one of Brunhilde's regular customers, a prominent member of Graz society, known among prostitutes for his kinky tastes. He was into bondage, and liked to drive girls into the woods and masturbate in the car while they danced naked in front of the headlights. On the other hand, no girl had ever complained of being assaulted by him, and the inspectors could find no evidence linking him to the murders. Under questioning by the examining magistrate, Wolfgang Wladkowski, he offered multiple alibis.

Two months later, on the night of March 7, 1991, the Graz hooker Elfriede Schrempf disappeared from where she stood on the sidewalk next to the Volksgarten (a public park not far from where Brunhilde Masser was last seen). Though officially she was a missing person, the Graz police figured she'd met the same fate as Masser. A fellow prostitute stated that she had seen Elfriede, at around 10:15 p.m. on March 7, get into a VW Golf that looked like a police cruiser. She told a reporter the same, and the notion that the killer was a cop created a media sensation that haunted the Graz police for months.

Investigators tracked down and interviewed about a thousand VW Golf drivers, including patrol officers, but none was a plausible suspect. However, in October 1991, investigators interrogated the owner of a light yellow VW Golf. He stated that he had, on the night of March 7, 1991, at around 10:00, parked next to the Volksgarten, talked with El-friede Schrempf, and then gone with her into the park for a sexual favor. He had then returned to his car and driven away.

After closely examining the man, the investigators concluded that he wasn't the killer. During further questioning of the woman who'd given the VW Golf tip, she reiterated that the car "bore a striking resemblance to a police car" and that she was certain that "it was white with red stripes." However, she also said that the car did not have a police license plate. As she had recalled in her first interview, the car's identification "began with *St* and consisted of six digits"—an accurate description of the light yellow Golf's license plate.

In May 1991, *Viennese* magazine published a report about the murder of Brunhilde Masser and the probable murder of Elfriede Schrempf, and suggested they were the work of the same killer—possibly the same killer who'd murdered two women in their apartments in January and October 1989. Because prostitutes were seldom murdered in Graz prior to 1989, the four murders in 1989–91 appeared to be serial, but Hans Breitegger, the chief crime reporter of the Graz *Kleine Zeitung*, cautioned against jumping to conclusions: "At the beginning of the eighties we had two prostitute murders. Everyone believed it was just one killer, but it turned out to be two."

What would compel a man to murder prostitutes? *Viennese* magazine consulted Austria's most eminent scientist in the field of human sexuality, Dr. Ernest Borneman. "Prostitute murder almost always goes back to a hatred of women," he explained. A couple of years earlier, Dr. Borneman had added his authority to the campaign for Jack's parole in a letter to the then–justice minister, Egmont Forreger:

> *I write to you about the issue of the prison inmate Jack Unterweger . . . I don't know him personally, but I have read his autobiographical novel* Purgatory *. . .*
>
> *The man has intelligence and would, freed from prison, doubtless be able to make a living from his literary work. He has written numerous theater pieces that have been successfully produced, and he edits his own literary magazine . . .*
>
> *The man committed a serious act, is remorseful, understands the motive of his actions at the time, and has the means never to have a relapse. As a sexual researcher, I can evaluate his act better than many psychiatrists, and therefore I am convinced that this act will never be committed again. I therefore support his attempt to obtain an early release from prison.*

On May 28, 1991 (three days before he spoke with Schenner about Jack Unterweger), a Viennese inspector traveled to Graz to assess the possibility that the Graz murders were connected with the Vienna murders, and he concluded there weren't enough parallels. The most glaring difference was that two of the three women in Graz were murdered in their apartments, while all the women in Vienna had been picked up and driven out of the city and into the woods.

Three months after the Viennese inspector's assessment, on October 5, 1991, Elfriede Schrempf's skeleton was found in the woods about fourteen miles south of Graz. Except for her jewelry and a pair of wine red socks, it was completely bare. The rest of her clothing and her handbag were missing. The skeleton was found about 400 yards from the nearest road, indicating that her killer had forced her to walk to the place of her death, though there were indications that he had dragged her the final stretch. As only a skeleton remained, the forensic pathologist was unable to determine the cause of death, though her skull and bones had no bullet, knife, or blunt-force trauma marks, which suggested she'd been strangled.

After Elfriede Schrempf was found, the Graz inspectors concluded that she'd indeed been murdered by the same man who'd murdered Brunhilde Masser, yet months of investigating both murders hadn't yielded a strong suspect, and while the police were ready to give up the search for the unknown killer, the crime reporter Hans Breitegger had just begun.

As long as a bigger story didn't hit, he could take all the time he wanted to work on it, and he had more freedom than the inspectors of any particular police agency. At thirty-seven he'd been a reporter for fifteen years and had cultivated contacts with cops and court officials all over the country. A cheerful and entertaining companion, he was someone with whom cops liked to drink beer and talk.

He'd already figured it was a mistake to assume that all four Graz murders in 1989–91 were committed by the same killer. The discovery in October 1991 of the fourth victim *in the woods* strengthened his conviction that the killer of 1989, who preferred apartments, wasn't the same as the killer of 1990–91, who preferred the woods.

The latter two murders resembled the murders that began in Vienna a month after the last Graz victim disappeared. Hans's hypothesis: The Vienna Woods Killer had started in Graz, and getting away with those two murders emboldened him to kill with the same modus operandi and with greater frequency in Vienna.

A few days later, while reporting a case near the Czech border, Hans bumped into a Viennese inspector he knew.

"How's the investigation of the prostitute killer going?" he asked.

"A while back we got a tip from Salzburg that the murders bear the signature of Jack Unterweger."

Jack Unterweger. Hans had heard of the ex-con who'd written books in prison, but knew little about him. He spent the following days in the archives, learning everything he could about the author in Vienna, and then plotted a timeline:

JANUARY 10, 1989: Gertrude Seger murdered in her Graz apartment.

OCTOBER 27, 1989: Gerlinde Rosenkranz murdered in her Graz apartment.

MAY 23, 1990: Jack Unterweger released from prison, settled in Vienna.

OCTOBER 26, 1990: Brunhilde Masser murdered in the woods near Graz.

MARCH 7, 1991: Elfriede Schrempf murdered in the woods near Graz.

APRIL 8, 1991: Silvia Zagler murdered in the Vienna Woods.

APRIL 16, 1991: Sabine Moitzi murdered in the Vienna Woods.

APRIL 28, 1991: Regina Prem probably murdered in the Vienna Woods.

MAY 7, 1991: Karin Eroglu murdered in the Vienna Woods.

In other words, Unterweger was released after the Graz apartment murders in 1989 but before the Graz woods murders in 1990–91. Hans shared his hypothesis with the head of the gendarmerie Homicide section, Adolf Steger, and his deputy Helmut Golds. Golds found it compelling.

"You're right. This is damned hot," he said. The tip made its way to the chief of the gendarmerie, who decided to let the Viennese handle it. A teletype was sent to Vienna headquarters on November 5, 1991, and a couple of weeks later, Hans heard their reply: Negative. They could find no evidence linking Jack Unterweger to the murders.

"Was I really so wrong about this?" he asked.

Inspector Golds didn't think so. "The parallels are there," he said. "I'm gonna keep working on it."

CHAPTER 25

BIANCA

IN THE AUTUMN of 1991, Take Five was the "in club" of the Vienna *Schikeria*—the rich and trendy. Owned by a couple of aristocrats, it was popular among bluebloods whose families hadn't lost everything with the downfall of the Austro-Hungarian Empire—smooth men educated at elite schools (some could speak English with almost an Oxford accent). A few still owned old castles in the countryside; none had much to do in Vienna. On a big night at Take Five one might see the Formula 1 champion Niki Lauda or the pop star Falco at the bar.

Though Bianca Mrak had only just turned eighteen, Take Five had long been her favorite nightclub. With her curvy figure, her face made up, and her long chestnut hair, she didn't look like a teenager. Her mother, the caretaker of an apartment building, had named her after Mick Jagger's first wife: Bianca, the Italian word for "white," contrasted with her family name, Mrak, the Slovenian word for "darkness." Her names were an apt expression of her character, still relatively innocent, but curious about the murky side of human nature.

Sitting at the bar on the night of November 16, 1991, she noticed a fortysomething sitting a few stools down, gazing at her. He was an attractive man, the gray above his temples contrasting with his boyish face, his slender frame dressed in a white silk suit and red bow tie. It was a wacky outfit, especially for the time of year, but he carried himself with such confidence that he seemed to pull it off. As he sipped his glass of champagne, she saw his gold lion's-head ring. So he's a Leo, she thought.

They made eye contact and smiled, and he raised his glass, toasting her from afar. He was in no hurry, though, and seemed equally absorbed in his conversation with a woman to his left. When Bianca caught his glance again, she made a gesture that had never failed: looking into his eyes, she motioned for him to come to her with her index finger. He smiled and turned to resume his conversation with the other woman. Bianca hadn't felt so small in a while, but as she was about to retreat to a table in the corner, he motioned her to come to him with his index and middle fingers. She didn't hesitate.

When he introduced himself as Jack Unterweger, she felt the thrill of meeting someone whose name she'd seen in print. The previous spring she'd seen notices for his play at the Tribunes Theater in Café Landtmann, which happened to be around the corner from her apartment. They chatted for a while, and he mentioned that he lived in the 8th District, near Café Florianihof. His apartment in a stylish neighborhood was one of many things he volunteered about himself, but he didn't do all the talking, and when Bianca spoke, she noticed he listened, his facial expressions registering the effect her words were having on him: a knit brow of consternation when she mentioned an insult, a bright smile when she said something witty. He was really interested in her world.

Listening to her wasn't the only thing he wanted, but she didn't want to go home with him. After a while she told him she was meeting someone at Montevideo, the club next door.

"I'll escort you," he said. He walked her to the entrance and said good night, but when she walked back out a few minutes later, he was still standing there.

"I knew you weren't meeting anyone in there," he said reproachfully.

"Excuse me, but I didn't say I wanted to spend the rest of my night with you."

"Very well," he said, and handed her his phone number. "Call me if you change your mind." He turned and walked in the direction of the

State Opera, the click of his heels on the stone pavement echoing off the Baroque façades of the Annagasse.

Bianca thought there was something fascinating about the guy at Take Five. Partly it was the fascination of all men who've stepped out of the anonymity in which most live onto the stage of public recognition . . . or notoriety. To describe Jack Unterweger as "famous" wasn't accurate, because "famous" wasn't the same as "well known." She knew he wasn't a famous writer like Peter Handke (though he'd once told a journalist that he started writing after reading Handke and realizing he knew better stories). She sensed the man himself was more compelling than his literature: Jack the bastard child of an American soldier and Austrian prostitute, the "prison poet" who wrote a critically acclaimed autobiography that was made into a movie.

"Mad, bad, and dangerous to know," as Lady Caroline Lamb once wrote of Lord Byron, suggesting that he was exciting *because* he was dangerous to know. Likewise, that Jack Unterweger had murdered a woman held a mysterious fascination for many women. Though Bianca appreciated his bad-boy aura, she had no knowledge of the murder he'd committed in 1974, when she was only one year old. One of her teachers told her about all the writers and artists who'd advocated Jack's release after he published *Purgatory*. Her school didn't include the novel on any of its reading lists, but others did. Jack's life story was taught as a triumph of the individual over all the social and political pathologies into which he'd been born.

Still, Bianca knew that the idea of Jack being "rehabilitated" was bloodless compared to the idea of him being a "murderer"—that in the minds of ordinary people, the stain of his crime hadn't washed away. She figured her mother would have a stroke if she knew her daughter was entertaining the thought of calling him. Bianca was tired of her mother, always nagging her for staying out late and going to clubs full of predatory men. She called him on Wednesday.

———

They met at the public library near his apartment, and she was amused by the funky outfit he was wearing. With his white snakeskin boots, tight jeans, black leather jacket over a tight-fitting T-shirt, rings on his fingers, and a chain around his neck, he looked like a pimp from the early seventies. They went to the Café Florianihof and chatted for a while, and then he offered to show her his apartment next door. Most notable was its size: 1,400 square feet was large by Viennese standards. She was impressed, and imagined he was earning a fat living from his books.

He said he didn't need so much space and was thinking about renting the spare bedroom. If she wanted to leave her mother's place, she was welcome to take it. Bianca didn't ponder it for long, and a few days later she moved her stuff into his spare room. Soon she was sleeping in his bed, and when December 1 came, she didn't pay her share of the rent.

Quickly she discovered that living with a well-known author wasn't as she'd imagined. Jack didn't take her out with smart people, but cloistered her at home, controlling her life more than her mother ever had. The days followed a strict routine—up at six, eat breakfast, drive to school with Jack, get picked up and brought home by Jack. No hanging out with friends after school. Her friends, he explained, "have nothing in their heads."

She didn't understand how he enslaved her, but there was nothing unusual about it. Since his youth, Jack had been a master of bondage in theory and practice. In Stein he wrote a story titled "Bondage Without a Person: A Woman's Fate," and he probably studied psychological literature on the dependency that might develop in an erotic relationship.

It began with his selection: find a girl unsure about herself, going through a tough time. Just as a wolf can spot a wounded or sick animal from afar, he could spot a troubled woman. What was making her dissatisfied? Most men never figured it out because they didn't care. The easiest targets were girls on the threshold of adulthood and women on the threshold of menopause, as both were going through a period of instability. The former were often frustrated because it seemed no one took them seriously; the latter because no one seemed to desire them anymore. Shortly after his arrest in 1975, while in jail awaiting trial, he wrote the following reflection, cribbing the first sentence from a Nietzsche aphorism.

No theme is more poetic than the death of a beautiful woman. Women are like cheese soufflé; when they are fresh from the oven they are crisp and fresh outside, but the filling isn't yet mature and hard to digest. When they become older, the crust may not be so pretty, but then the filling develops. There is an age at which a woman must be beautiful in order to be loved, and there is an age in which a woman must be loved in order to be beautiful.

That Bianca wanted to break free of her mother played into his hands. The first step was to obscure the abnormality of her relationship with him by isolating her from normal relations with others. He justified his extreme control by saying it was because he loved her, and that he— an older and wiser man—knew more about the dangers of the world. He was like a protective father who also gave her sexual intimacy. He was good in bed and creative about keeping it exciting. Like many Austrian girls, she was crazy about American movies, and once she suggested they enact erotic scenes from 9½ *Weeks*. Jack played his role well.

One day he told her his income was going through a lull, and he suggested she do some part-time work to help pay the bills. An upscale escort service was hiring, and he reckoned she'd be a good hostess, showing tourists and foreign businessmen around. Bianca had a notion of what an escort does, but it wasn't altogether clear, and so she agreed to talk to the manager about it.

Jack drove her into the city center and told her to come to the Reiss Bar after her meeting. The escort service was located in an elegant apartment a few blocks from St. Stephen's Cathedral. A man around thirty welcomed her, and his courtly manners were as false as the euphemisms he used to describe his trade.

"Most of our clients are very polite gentlemen."

"So what am I supposed to do if I get an assignment?"

"Be nice."

"What do you mean 'be nice'?"

"First you go with him to the opera or cinema, and then afterward to a bar."

"And then what?"

"And then you accompany him back to his place."

"Will I have to sleep with him?"

"Well, actually, yes."

"And if I refuse?"

"You won't get any more assignments."

So "escort" was just another word for prostitute. The opera and cinema, showing the client around, being "nice" to him—all were just preliminaries to the real deal. Bianca left the upscale pimp and marched toward the Reiss Bar. Her anger became fury as she entered to find Jack sitting at the bar, drinking a glass of champagne with two middle-aged women, laughing.

"You were going to put me to work for a pimp!" she yelled at him.

He left money for his drink and hustled her out.

He'd overestimated her pliability; he'd have to take smaller steps. It hadn't worked out with the American girl Carolina, despite her tendency to become dependent on men. When Carolina told him about the guy in the park, he assumed the man might also be trying to get into the business.

He'd driven her to the red-light district to test her reaction, watching her as he condemned the trade, looking for some expression that she didn't think it was really so bad. Hadn't the thought crossed her mind that turning a trick would be easier money than working in that dreadful hotel? But instead of saying, "I don't think it's such a bad job," she'd acted confused.

Bianca also balked. His escort service attempt had enraged her, but it didn't send her home to mama. He decided to take smaller steps. A few days later, he found her a job as a barmaid at Piccadilly, a nightclub on the fringe of the red-light district.

Advent is a time of enchantment in Vienna, regardless of one's religion. An atmosphere of happy expectation pushes out the November gloom, and the streets fill with shoppers who congregate at punch stands, keeping warm with steaming cups spiked with schnapps. Parties are thrown every night in candle-lit apartments, the smell of hot spiced wine drifting out of the kitchen. During the month leading up to Christmas, the envy and gossip that are prevalent in Viennese society ebb a little, giving way to feelings of reconciliation and desire.

Bianca was as vulnerable to the good feeling as anyone, but then Jack went to an Advent party hosted by *Success* magazine without bringing her along. It was in keeping with his habit of not introducing her to his writer and journalist friends. So far the only friend she'd met was a shady character named Rio. No, the party "was sure to be stiff"; Jack would "make an appearance out of courtesy to the editor, and come home early."

He didn't. Around 6:00 a.m. he entered the bedroom and tried to slide into bed without waking her.

"I guess it wasn't so stiff after all," she said angrily.

The party had concluded at Take Five. Sitting at the same bar where, as he noted in his diary, he'd made Bianca's acquaintance the month before, he continued his conversation with Elisabeth, a young assistant at *Success*, until she invited him home.

Just before Christmas Jack and Bianca drove to Munich to visit his mother. Out for a stroll, they passed a jewelry store, and Jack stopped to look at the rings in the window.

"I think that one would look good on you," he said. "Will you marry me?"

Bianca was thunderstruck. All she could think to say was "Yes."

The following day, Christmas Eve, they returned to Vienna, where Bianca's mother was hosting a party—the perfect opportunity to break the news. That afternoon he managed to get away to spend an intimate hour with his other girlfriend, Elisabeth, and he suggested they go skiing together on Christmas Day (when Bianca was scheduled to return to work at Piccadilly for the rest of the holiday). He told Elisabeth he couldn't spend Christmas Eve with her because he was working at a homeless shelter soup kitchen.

That night at the party, Bianca and Jack announced their engagement, and the next day he told his fiancée he was giving up his apartment in Tarvisio, Italy, and that to avoid paying January's rent, he needed to vacate it.

CHAPTER 26

BREAK

NINETEEN-YEAR-OLD JOANNA was standing on her corner when a BMW pulled up; through the window she saw the driver staring at her. As he parked under a street lamp, she saw the license plate: W JACK 1. A small man wearing a white jacket and a red bow tie got out and walked up to her.

"How much to do it in the car?" he asked.

"Three hundred Schillings [$30]."

"Okay, let's go." They walked over to the car and got in, but before he started the engine, he turned to her.

"I'm a well-known journalist and I can't be seen doing this. I'll give you another two hundred if you'll drive out of the city with me."

"Another two hundred?"

"Yeah. It's not far, and I'll bring you right back."

"Okay." He seemed like a nice man, well-dressed and well-groomed. He started the engine and off they went. After 10:00 p.m. there was little traffic, and within a few minutes they'd cut across town and were driving past the university.

"You're from Vienna?"

"How did you know?"

"I saw your license plate."

"Yeah, I live in Vienna, but I'm often in Graz to do stories. Right now I'm reporting on your milieu. This evening I made the rounds with the cops. You probably know them—Hütter and Prettenthaler." She did.

"I've gotten to know a prostitute who lives here," he continued.

"We've become friends and I often take her out to dinner, but she's not available tonight."

From the university he drove through the northeast suburb and into the countryside, along Mary Consolation Brook. About five miles outside the city he made a hard left onto Dominion of Heaven Way, a narrow lane that ascended into the hills. Looking out the window to the right, she could see the illuminated façade of the Mary Consolation Church, perched on the opposite side of the valley. The road ran through a field and then entered a dense forest. Darkness. He switched on his high beams, which reflected eerily off the trunks of the spruce trees. A little farther on he parked in a side lane and killed the engine.

"I play a game with my friend here in Graz. She lets me tie her up. Maybe it's silly, but I think it's exciting." He handed her eight 100-Schilling notes.

"Will you let me tie you up?"

"Yeah, okay."

"Let's start by getting you naked."

"Completely naked?"

"Yeah, why not?"

"Okay." She took off her clothes and laid them on the back seat of the car. He reached over and pulled the lever that reclined the passenger seat.

"Now lie on your belly and put your hands behind your back," he said.

She rolled over, and as she was getting her body situated, lying face down on the seat, he locked her wrists tightly behind her back with a pair of handcuffs. He then undressed.

"Are you afraid?" he asked.

"No, why should I be afraid?"

"I want you to act as though you are afraid. I want you to show me fear." His jocular tone had turned somber, and she really was afraid. Until then she'd been so fixated on the money that she hadn't thought about her safety. Now that it was too late to do anything about it, she realized the dangerousness of her situation. The steel bit into her wrists, and the pain intensified by the second. He finished undressing, leaving only his undershirt on. He put on a condom, moved behind her, and mounted her from behind with a forceful thrust.

She began to cry, which seemed to spur him on to ever more violent pounding. With each jolt to her body, the small of her back pushed on the handcuffs, driving the edges into her wrists. She screamed with pain and fear, and the louder she screamed, the more he moaned. Then he started saying things, but not in a normal speaking voice—weird phrases that he repeated, sometimes mumbling, sometimes exclaiming . . .

"And then?" asked the Graz inspector.

"After about five minutes, I screamed really loud and he was unable to copulate with me anymore," she explained. "He then took off the handcuffs and drove me back into town."

The incident had happened in October 1990, nine days before Brunhilde Masser disappeared a block away from Joanna's corner. When the Graz investigators approached Joanna on the evening of January 11, 1992, and showed her a picture of Jack Unterweger (which they'd gotten from the Culture Section of *Kleine Zeitung*), she recognized him as the man who'd driven her into the woods. She still remembered it vividly because it had happened shortly after she'd started working as a hooker, and it had scared the hell out of her.

When the reporter Hans Breitegger heard Joanna's story, he knew the Unterweger story was about to get hot, and he wanted photos (which would also be useful to the Graz investigators) and an interview before it boiled over. He needed someone bookish to help him with the ruse.

Twenty-nine-year-old Bernd Melichar was temperamentally the opposite of Hans. Whereas Hans liked to hang out with cops and had an investigator's ability to obtain and analyze information about crime, Bernd was interested in its psychosocial background. He had a talent for turning up the family histories, sufferings, and motives of criminals, and he tended to think of them as characters in books. He was a voracious reader; his favorite author was Philip Roth. On January 16 he looked up from his desk to see Hans standing in his doorway.

"What do you know about Jack Unterweger?" he asked.

"The usual story. Killed a girl in his youth, became a writer in prison. I read *Purgatory*; I thought it was a fascinating book."

"What do you think about him murdering a bunch more women since he got out?"

"No way," said Bernd.

"Yes, way," Hans replied, and told the story of Jack Unterweger the traveling playwright, poet, and prostitute killer.

"I can't believe it," said Bernd.

"Believe it or not, he's probably about to be arrested, and I want to get a final interview and photos before it blows up." And so the plan was hatched. Hans and Bernd would pose as journalists from the Culture section trying to get a scoop on Jack's latest book (whatever that was). Because Bernd knew the literary scene, it was his job to get Jack on the phone and to lure him into an interview.

The next day he came into Hans's office.

"I keep getting Unterweger's answering machine. See, check it out." He picked up the phone on Hans's desk (a new one, just installed the day before), dialed the number, and hit the speaker button. It rang a few times, and when the answering machine came on, Bernd said, "Hello, Mr. Unterweger, this is Bernd Melichar from *Kleine Zeitung* calling again, please call me back." He then put the receiver back on the cradle and turned to Hans.

"Hütter [the editor of the Culture section] told me this morning that Unterweger has many influential friends—that we and the gendarmerie should be careful with him."

A couple of hours later, Bernd heard back from Jack.

"You're working with the police," he said angrily.

"No, we're just journalists. We were hoping to interview you about your latest book." They agreed to meet the next day at the Turks' Hole, an old student pub in Graz in the cellar of a Baroque palace near police headquarters.

Jack knew the Graz journalists were working with the cops, trying to gather information about him. He called Graz headquarters and asked to speak with Officer Hütter. In September 1990, Jack had gone on patrol with him, doing research for an article on the Graz red-light district.

"What may I do for you?" Hütter said.

"Some journalists left a message on my answering machine. They said something about my influential friends and the gendarmerie. A lot of it is garbled, but I could clearly hear your name mentioned."

"I'd be happy to listen to the tape," said Hütter.

"I'm meeting these guys tomorrow afternoon at the Turks' Hole. I'll pass by the police station on my way and drop off the tape."

"Very good."

"And something else. I've heard that I'm a suspect for the murders of some prostitutes in Graz, and I'd like to talk to the head of your Homicide section about it."

Once again he was a step ahead of the police. Inspector Brandstätter wanted to investigate further before he confronted the suspect, but Jack was forcing his hand. After giving Hütter the answering-machine tape, he went to Brandstätter's office and asked what the rumors were about. The inspector recounted the two murders in Graz and explained that his name had come up as a possible suspect.

"Maybe you can tell me where you were on the nights of October 25, 1990, and of March 7, 1991. I'd also like to hear about your contact with Graz prostitutes in general."

Jack replied with the following statement:

In September 1990, for my reportage for the magazine Basta, *I went on patrol in the red-light milieu with Hütter. I received permission to ride with him from the press service of the Interior Ministry.*

After I went on patrol, I visited the nightclubs Eve, Haiti, and the Sauna Bar, where I took a few photos. That is the only contact I've ever had with the Graz prostitution milieu.

At the end of November I was interrogated at Vienna police headquarters by officers under the direction of Court Counselor Edelbacher about the prostitutes who were murdered in Graz in October 1990 and March 1991. I was asked for my alibis, and I stated that on the day of the first murder I was directing a rehearsal at the Tribunes Theater in Vienna.

Regarding the second case, I drove with my theater group to the Graz Minoriten Center on March 5, 1991. That evening we produced the theater piece and then drove back to Vienna at 10:30. On

March 6 we drove back to Graz in the afternoon. After that production we had to break down the stage, and then I left to drive back to Vienna between 10:30 and 11:00. I arrived in Vienna around 1:00 or 2:00 a.m. I used the south Autobahn and drove alone.

As for what I did on the following day, March 7, 1991: I spent the afternoon with my girlfriend Katharina in my apartment. As I recall, I took her home between 6:00 and 7:00 p.m., and I'm certain that afterward I drove into the city and visited a few bars. I can't remember exactly when I returned to my apartment, but it's my habit to go home around midnight.

As for whether I met any of my actor friends during the day of March 7, 1991, I'm certain I didn't. No production was scheduled. I can't name anyone I was with in the evening hours of March 7, 1991.

Brandstätter explained to Jack that the first part of his statement—the part about having no contact with Graz prostitutes outside of his *Basta* reportage—had been contradicted by a witness. Would he like to revise his statement?

"What do you mean a witness?" he asked.

"A prostitute you picked up. She identified you from your picture. She says you drove her outside the city, got her naked, and put handcuffs on her."

Jack replied:

Two or three weeks after my reportage, I picked up a prostitute in Graz near a large intersection. The street runs by the university, and a little farther along, in a side street, we screwed. At the time I was driving a BMW with the license plate W JACK 1. We drove to the side street and I gave her 400 Schillings. She pulled down her stockings and hitched up her skirt. I had to pay her an extra 100 Schillings to lift up her T-shirt. Certainly she didn't take off all her clothes. We had normal intercourse without a condom, and as my shirt was open, she saw my tattoos and asked me if I'd been in prison. Afterward she wanted to smoke a cigarette and needed a light. I don't smoke, but I thought there might be a lighter in the glove compartment. In it was a pair of black metal handcuffs, a gift from a friend on my birthday, August 16, 1990. I still have them in a glass case in my apartment in Vienna. She was sitting next to me and I told her to give me her hands. She asked me if I intended to do something to her, and I said I would never do anything that would send me back to prison. I cuffed her hands together in front of her, she rolled over on her side, and I took her from behind. After I removed the cuffs, she demanded 1,000 Schillings, which I refused. Instead, I gave her another 400 Schillings, for a total of 800. She wasn't satisfied and wanted more. I didn't give her any more money, but I did offer to take her back to her corner. She wanted me to take her home, and so I drove her to her apartment south of Graz and let her out. I haven't seen her since.

The girl's story made him look bad, but three details were particularly damning: (a) he drove her outside town, into the woods; (b) he got her completely naked; (c) he cuffed her hands *behind her back.*

He omitted these details from his version of the story, but as Brandstätter recited the girl's statement, Jack apparently realized that it would be difficult to contest them. Her memory of the episode was vivid, and he'd already been caught lying about having no contact with Graz hookers. And so he admitted the truth of her story. The cops were looking for a killer, not a guy with a fetish for forest roads and handcuffs. He denied only her claims that she'd cried during the sex and that he'd worn a condom.

"For what purpose did you keep the handcuffs in your car?" Brandstätter asked.

"Since I received them as a gift, I kept them in my glove compartment. For a while I hung them on the rearview mirror as a reminder to stay out of trouble. In my apartment I have never put them on a woman. Once, with her consent, I tied up my ex-girlfriend Katharina with her bathrobe belt."

The episode had happened on the night of October 17, 1990. As Jack noted in his diary, earlier that evening he'd gone to the Graz Casino,

where the actress Marisa Mell, a native of the city, presented her memoirs titled *Coverlove*. In her youth she'd been a brunette of heartbreaking
beauty, immortalized by her performance as Eva Kant in the cult film *Di-
abolik*. She met Jack shortly after his release from prison. Alfred Kolleritsch, editor of the literary magazine *Manuskripte*, saw her with him at
the Frankfurt Book Fair, infatuated. Jack said he was going to cast her,
along with Helmut Berger, in his movie *Love Till Insanity*. If Berger
pulled out, Jack could always play the lead role himself.

But that night at the Graz Casino, Marisa, and not he, was the center of attention. Many who attended weren't interested in him, and after
her presentation Marisa mingled with all her guests without showing
any special interest in him. At 10:00 he left the party alone.

From the casino it was a five-minute drive across the river to where the
prostitute Joanna was standing. He'd probably scoped out the Dominion of
Heaven Way in advance, as the entrance to it off the main road is small and
unlit. The lane, which ascends the hill and into a patch of forest, appears
isolated at first glance, but is actually a thoroughfare for residents farther up
the hill. Because Joanna was lying facedown, she couldn't have seen the
headlights of an approaching car, but Jack could have.

Hans and Bernd were sitting in the Turks' Hole when Hans's mobile
phone rang.

"Listen, boys, I've gotten held up here," Jack said. "There's a girl in
the pub waiting for me; she's got long curly blond hair. Would you mind
keeping her company?" Hans looked around and noticed a pretty girl sitting by herself. Yes, she was Jack Unterweger's friend. Her name was Elisabeth (Bianca was in Vienna, unaware of Jack's trip to Graz with his other
girlfriend). Hans and Bernd talked with her and realized she had no idea
her boyfriend was talking with the cops. Hans went to the bathroom, and
when he returned, Jack was sitting at the table, cursing the Graz police.

"And I know you guys are working with them!" he said angrily.

"We don't work with the cops," Hans said, acting insulted. "We invited
you here to talk about your latest book. I think it's good publicity, but if you
keep up this cop stuff, you can forget about it, because I'm leaving."

Jack softened. He knew Hans was lying about being a culture reporter, because he'd read his stories on the Graz prostitute murders in the
spring of 1991, but there was no sense in making an issue out of it. Instead, he tried to win some sympathy. *Kleine Zeitung* had the biggest circulation in Styria; it was an excellent opportunity to charm the residents
of the state—a state whose law officers might soon be coming after him.

Hans was taken aback by Jack's presentation. The small man with the
neatly trimmed hair graying around the temples was wearing a jacket and
tie, though his tie, made out of a roll of 35-millimeter film, might have said
something about his strange interior life. He had a disarmingly boyish face,
and he spoke softly in a high tenor voice. After he backed off about the police informant business, he became warm and polite. He was very articulate, and his countenance and gestures underscored his sincere tone.

"After twenty years in prison, I've not lost my sense of humor. I drove
down here from Vienna voluntarily. I knew I was going to be interrogated
about the Graz prostitute murders, but why should I murder prostitutes?
I've always lived from them. On the other hand, I don't have a bad relationship with the cops. They received a tip and it's their job to check it out, but
I don't think they appreciate how hard I've tried to become a better man.
Do you know many people who worked at the homeless shelters during
Advent? When I was in L.A. last summer, I met a black woman with a sick
child running a high fever. Like so many poor blacks in America, she had no
health insurance, so none of the hospitals would treat her baby. They just
turned her away. Amazingly heartless, isn't it? So I took her and her child in
my rented car and drove all over L.A., from one hospital to the next, until
we finally found an emergency room that would give her treatment."

"Generally speaking, how's your life been since your release from
prison?" Hans asked.

"Wonderful. I'm not stuck in the past, and I'm always ready for spon-
taneity. The reality, though, is that one doesn't only have friends. There
are also the envious out there who say you don't deserve what you have.
For example, the cop who has dragged up this old story from Salzburg.
He can't let go of the idea that he was right but just couldn't prove it.
That's his problem, though, because I know I didn't do anything."

Hans asked him more about the "old story" from Salzburg, but felt

Bernd kick him under the table, reminding him to stay in the culture-reporter character.

"What are you working on now?"

"A book called *The Power of the Pigs*. It's about the men who exercise power without legitimately possessing it. It's about a man who observed the world through the media for sixteen years and how he returned to society. It's about what he sees has changed in human development."

"What has changed?"

"I'm struck by the indifference, the egotism in love. People are simply incapable of loving each other anymore."

"I don't think it's him," said Bernd after Jack and his girl left just before midnight.

"Why not?" Hans asked.

"It doesn't make sense. He's obviously not the guy he was in his early twenties. He's a middle-aged author. I don't see how it could be him."

"The facts speak for themselves," said Hans. He knew that Jack had tried to use the interview for PR—not for his book, but for protesting his innocence to the public before Brandstätter built his case. And so Hans held off on publishing it.

CHAPTER 27

KATHARINA

AS THE SCHOOLGIRL KATHARINA (Jack's alibi for the night of May 7, 1991) recalled, she was strolling with her parents one day in October 1990 when a German shepherd bounded up to them. As his master was nowhere in sight, they took him home, and through the animal protection society, they were connected with Mrs. Müller.

Joy belonged to Jack Unterweger, but the dog had been staying with Mrs. Müller while his master was at the Frankfurt Book Fair. Katharina's family loved Joy and was happy to keep him until Mr. Unterweger returned to Vienna. When Jack showed up a few days later, Katharina and her mother found him engaging and they invited him for a stroll. He said he was a writer and was often on the road for book promotions and theater productions. They said he was welcome to leave Joy with them anytime.

Jack mentioned nothing about his past, but Katharina's parents soon learned about it, and her father forbid her to be alone with him. A few weeks later, Jack started picking her up from school and taking her back to his place. He was never violent in bed, nor did he ever ask for anything too unusual.

There was the time they were walking Joy, when he turned the leash around Katharina's wrist and said, "I'd like to tie you up." She thought he was kidding, but once, at a restaurant near his apartment, she got drunk on red wine and must have passed out, because when she awoke, she found herself in his bed and didn't remember how she got there. She sensed that he might have done something to her while she was unconscious.

"Did you tie me up?" she asked.

"No," he said, but his grin told otherwise.

At a New Year's Eve party she met a boy her age and began to pull away from Jack, and she quit seeing him altogether when his play *Scream of Fear* went on tour at the end of February 1991. As a souvenir she'd saved the tour schedule. On March 5–6 the play was performed in Graz, and she vaguely remembered him saying something about a reading in Graz the following night.

She received a postcard from him from Los Angeles, and a few months later, in November, he called her.

"Why did you cut your hair so short?" he said.

"How do you know that?"

"I know everything about you." Katharina demanded that he quit spying on her and leave her alone, and after an acrimonious exchange, he hung up. That was the last she'd heard about him until the police called.

When they interviewed her on January 28, 1992, they were most interested in whether she was with Jack on the afternoon of March 7,

1991. It was easy to determine that she wasn't, because she'd saved her desk calendar. At 2:00 p.m. she'd attended a Green Party function at Parliament, and afterward had gone home.

"I definitely wasn't with him on March 7, 1991. I'd already broken up with him."

After taking Katharina's statement, Brandstätter called Hans Breitegger.

"The girl here in Vienna says she definitely wasn't with Unterweger on the afternoon of March 7. She thinks he may have given a reading in Graz that night."

"I'll see what I can find," said Hans. He hung up and called the editor of the culture section.

"Can you tell me if Jack Unterweger gave a reading in Graz on the evening of March 7, 1991?" The editor said he'd check it out and get back to him. And then Hans remembered a detail he'd seen in the press about the prostitute murders. The gendarmerie in Vorarlberg—the westernmost state of Austria, near the Swiss border—had an unsolved murder from December 1990. Hans checked his file of reports on the murders and found it: Heidemarie Hammerer had disappeared from her corner near the train station in Bregenz, the capital of Vorarlberg, around 11:00 p.m. on December 5, 1990. Her body was found on New Year's Eve in a wooded area south of the city, near the village of Lustenau, strangled.

Hans called a contact at the *New Vorarlberg Daily*. "Check the events notices around December 5, 1990, and see if Jack Unterweger produced a play or gave a reading around Bregenz."

He heard back from *Kleine Zeitung*'s culture editor first. On the night of March 7, 1991, Jack gave a reading in the town of Köflach, twenty miles west of Graz. A few hours later he heard back from the *New Vorarlberg Daily*. On the morning of December 6, 1990, Jack recorded a performance of his play *Dungeon* at the ORF studio in the town of Dornbirn, eight miles south of Bregenz and three miles from the village of Lustenau.

CHAPTER 28

A FLASH OF RECOGNITION

"IT'S HIM," said Inspector Leopold Etz of the Lower Austrian police to Werner Windisch, head of the department's Homicide section. "He was near Graz on the night of March 7, and he was near Bregenz on December 6, the morning after their girl disappeared."

Etz and Windisch were working on the case because two of the Vienna prostitutes were found in the woods far outside the city, within the state of Lower Austria. Etz would always remember the date the first of the two girls was found, May 23, because it was the same day his daughter, his first child, was born. He'd spent the morning at the maternity ward, the afternoon at the crime scene.

The cold-bloodedness of it had shocked him. The distance between the crime scene and the forest road suggested that the killer had coerced the woman to walk into the darkness of the woods. The blows to her face, including a particularly savage one that tore her ear, indicated he'd terrorized her.

There was something conspicuous about the way her arms were lying on the ground, her hands immediately adjacent to her upper legs. The lower arms were rotated clockwise, and her wrists were facing upward. Etz had a flash of recognition. He'd seen arms in that position before. *Yes, of course*. As a police officer he'd seen arms in that position hundreds of times because it was the position they take when they are handcuffed behind the back.

That was how he did it. First he put the woman in handcuffs, and then he made the strangulation instrument out of her leotard, probably tying the elaborate noose in front of her to heighten her terror. He then marched her into the woods, and at the spot he selected for her death, he pushed her to the ground and then strangled her. After she became lifeless, he removed the handcuffs, which he could do only with her lying on her belly.

Etz imagined her at the moment she was handcuffed and helpless. Once he started marching her from the car into the woods, she had to have known she was going to die. She must have felt a primal terror as she was prodded into the landscape that has always symbolized the despair of being alone, away from the familiarity and safety of civilization.

"Our hypothetical m.o. perfectly matches the story of that woman he took out into the woods near Graz," Etz said.

"It sure does," said Windisch. "But she lived to tell about it."

"Maybe he was going to kill her but then had second thoughts for some reason."

"Maybe, but that's conjecture. That's what he and his attorney will say."

Windisch was just playing devil's advocate. He too believed that Jack was the killer. The trouble was proving it.

CHAPTER 29

A JOB IN SWITZERLAND

AROUND THE TIME THE COPS were checking Jack's alibi with Katharina, he showed Bianca a notice for a waitress job in a Swiss bar during Carnival season. For the three weeks leading up to Mardi Gras, the Catholic cantons of Switzerland "let the pig out," and to handle the surge of drinkers, the bars hire additional waitresses who heighten the excitement by going topless or scantily clad.

"You could earn as much in three weeks in a Swiss bar during Carnival as you could in three months working in a Vienna disco," Jack explained. He said he could also use the time alone to research an "underworld story" that he figured he could sell for a lot of money.

Jack was indeed working on an "underworld story," the story of the prostitute murders in the spring of 1991. His research involved speaking with various contacts in the government, press, and Vienna police about the investigation. From his informants he learned about the arrival of the Graz investigators in Vienna to check his alibi for the night of March 7, 1991. He'd offered Katharina because, as he would later claim, he remembered regularly picking her up from school around that time.

Three months earlier, on October 28, 1991—six days after he talked with Edelbacher about his alibis (or lack thereof)—he'd purchased a mobile phone. The service contract was not with a telecom provider but with a private individual, and the price of the device, $1,300, was a fortune for any Austrian in 1991 (Jack couldn't even pay his own rent). Yet with the mobile phone he could be reached by anyone with information, at anytime, even near the borders of Italy and Switzerland.

Jack and Bianca left Vienna on February 2, 1992, and drove to Gossau, in the Swiss canton of St. Gallen. At the pub Nazionale she met her new boss and was shown her quarters, a grim little room near the grim little bar where she would earn her wages until Ash Wednesday.

PART II

CHAPTER 30

SPECIAL COMMISSION

SO SCHENNER WAS RIGHT, Geiger thought. The notion that Jack Unterweger was the killer had seemed improbable, but damn it if it wasn't him. After Geiger heard the Graz woman's story, he launched a massive search for Vienna hookers who'd had encounters with the suspect. His investigators set up in the Health Office, and over five days, as the city's eight hundred registered prostitutes came in for their weekly checkup, they were shown photographs of Jack and asked if they'd ever seen him. Three girls claimed he'd been their customer, quick encounters in his car. Another claimed she'd lived with him for five days in the autumn of 1991, and that he'd tried to put her to work for him. In other words, contrary to what he'd told Chief Edelbacher, Jack had had plenty of contact with Vienna prostitutes.

How bizarre that he'd thrown away such a glorious second chance. Or had he? Geiger had only just begun to study the suspect, and he already understood the lesson of Schenner's experience with him. Getting on Jack's trail was one thing; persuading the D.A. to prosecute him was something else. Schenner had failed in 1983. Would Geiger have better luck in 1992?

On February 10, 1992, he submitted a report to the Vienna D.A. listing the grounds for suspecting Jack Unterweger of murdering seven women in the cities of Vienna, Graz, and Bregenz. The investigators hadn't found a smoking gun, but an abundance of clues that pointed to Jack Unterweger. Still, when the D.A. read Geiger's report, he concluded that it didn't present enough evidence to warrant arresting Jack.

Following the D.A.'s decision, the Interior Ministry created a Special Commission to further investigate Jack, assembling inspectors from

Vienna, Lower Austria, Graz, and Vorarlberg into one working unit, thereby eliminating (at least in theory) the spirit of independence and competition that had so far prevailed between them. Thenceforth they would share all their information. Geiger was appointed its head; its first meeting was scheduled to convene in Vienna on Friday, February 14, 1992.

CHAPTER 31

ONCE A MURDERER, ALWAYS A MURDERER

TWO DAYS BEFORE the first meeting of the Special Commission, Jack went to the studio of Thomas Raab, a photographer for *Viennese* magazine, for a photo shoot. Thomas, who knew only the outlines of Jack's story, was impressed by the nicely dressed, engaging man. His rural background was evident in his accent, but only slightly, and it was a reminder of how high he'd risen.

Talkative sitters were the best because they revealed something about their character, but after chatting for twenty minutes, Thomas still didn't have a sense of how to portray Jack.

"I'm trying to figure out how to shoot you," he said. "I know a lot of other photographers have done portraits of you and I want to do something new." What could that be? Since his parole a year and a half earlier, Jack the Writer, the Dandy, the Hangman, the Pimp, the Convict, had posed as everyone and everything.

Margit Haas, who had made the introduction, arrived at the studio, and Thomas asked her what would be a good occasion for doing a story and photo spread.

"How about the second anniversary of his parole?" she said.

"All right," said Thomas, "Your second anniversary of freedom. What is your identity now?"

"How about 'Once a Murderer, Always a Murderer,'" said Margit.

"Why do you say that?" said Jack.

"I heard rumors the police think you may be the prostitute killer."

"Where did you hear that?"

"In a bar in the milieu I overheard a cop mention to the owner that they are checking you out."

"Which bar, and what was the name of the cop?"

"I don't remember, some place I checked out for my erotic guide." Margit and Thomas were doing an "erotic guide" to the brothels and swinger clubs of Vienna.

"Why didn't you tell me before?"

"I figured you knew they were checking you out. About a week later I was at a press conference at the Flamingo Bar to discuss some new regulations of the red-light district and I heard a reporter mention it."

"Well, isn't this just super!"

"Calm down, Jack. They're just checking you out because of your past. When they don't find anything, the investigation will run into the sand." He walked over to a cabinet where Thomas stored his gear and grabbed a pair of handcuffs hanging from the knob (while traveling, Thomas prevented his camera case from being stolen by cuffing it to things). Jack turned around, grabbed Margit by the wrist, and before she realized what was happening, her hands were cuffed behind her back. For a moment she just sat there, stunned at how swiftly he'd done it.

"You feel helpless, don't you?" he said.

"Yes, I do. Please take them off."

"It's exactly how I was when the Swiss handed me over; the whole drive from Basel I sat in the back of the van, just like that," he said, his mouth twisting into a bitter expression.

"I'm sorry to hear that, and now would you please take them off?"

While Thomas fetched the key, Jack said they'd have to do the shoot some other time and hurried out.

Peter Grolig at *Kurier* got a call.

"Hello, it's me, the mass murderer," the voice announced.

Grolig recognized it. "Hello, Mr. Unterweger. How are you?"

"Not well. I hear my name came up at the hooker press conference a few weeks ago, and that I'm under suspicion."

Grolig said he hadn't heard of any new developments.

Jack insisted that the whole thing was the fantasy of a retired Salzburg inspector. "Since the press conference in the Flamingo bar I've lived in constant fear. I traded in my old license plate, W JACK 1, for a regular plate; otherwise someone will demolish my car. Also, a relative of one of the murdered prostitutes recently attacked me with a knife. If this keeps up, I'm going to have to leave Vienna."

When Margit returned to the office, the receptionist gave her an exasperated look. "Call Jack Unterweger. He's called thirteen times."

"You called," she said.

"Listen, Margit, I've called police headquarters, the Interior Ministry, the papers, and no one can tell me what's going on. Please try to remember where you heard that cop say I'm under suspicion. It's very important to me."

"Why are you stirring this up? Just let it die."

"Please, Margit, try to remember."

"Just some bar in the red-light district—one of many I visited that day for my erotic guide."

The next day, February 13, 1992, the Graz district attorney Karl Wenzl petitioned the Graz Criminal Court to issue an arrest warrant for Jack Unterweger. While Vienna hesitated, Graz decided to go for it. The examining magistrate assigned to the case was Wolfgang Wladkowski, but he was vacationing in Cuba, so his deputy wrote the warrant. He reasoned that Unterweger's false alibi for the night of March 7, 1991, was grounds enough. Inspector Brandstätter sent a teletype to Vienna headquarters, stating that he'd obtained a warrant and would arrive the next morning to make the arrest.

Hans Breitegger was informed about the warrant. The deal was simple: he got the scoop on condition he didn't run the story until the Saturday, February 15, edition. By then Jack would be in custody.

When Brandstätter arrived in Vienna, he learned that the surveillance team had lost Jack in traffic. The team wasn't concerned, as they figured he wouldn't go far. While the inspectors waited for Jack to return, they convened the first meeting of the Special Commission.

Dinnertime came and went, and Jack still hadn't returned. And then the news broke that probably explained why. The Friday-evening distribution of the Saturday, February 15, edition of the Graz *Kleine Zeitung* had hit the streets, and on the front page was the headline: MURDER SERIES: AN ARREST WARRANT FOR JACK UNTERWEGER.

That evening in Gossau, Switzerland, Bianca was working her tenth day of fourteen-hour shifts and was about to fall apart. The pain in her legs and lower back from standing on high heels for so long was becoming unbearable, and the thick clouds that had hung over Switzerland since her arrival were giving her a case of the blues.

Jack called and she cried into the receiver. She was at the end of her tether and didn't think she could hang on much longer. Just as she began to unburden her sorrow, she felt a tap on her shoulder and turned to find Jack standing there holding his mobile phone, a grin on his face. He'd been sitting in a corner for half an hour watching her. He said he'd missed her so much that he'd decided to make the long drive out, though it would be a brief visit. He had to return to Vienna the next day.

Back in Vienna, the first meeting of the Special Commission almost turned into a brawl. Suspicion for leaking the information about the arrest warrant fell on a police officer who was known to have a working relationship with Hans Breitegger.

"I'm gonna slap you all the way back across the Semmering," said Alfonse Tranninger of the Lower Austrian police to the officer, referring to the mountains that separate Vienna and Graz. The Graz team countered that Jack had slipped Vienna surveillance hours before the paper was distributed. To them it appeared that Vienna headquarters was leaking (they wondered if a secretary had seen a teletype from the day before and passed on the information). A while later they received a copy of Breitegger's article. It was thorough; when Jack read it, he would know the grounds for the arrest warrant (which were entirely circumstantial).

The next day, Saturday, February 15, Jack didn't return, and the investigators searched his apartment. In a glass case in his living room they found three pairs of handcuffs; in his closet a can of mace, a switchblade knife, and a pump-action 12-gauge shotgun, none of which a convicted felon was allowed to possess.

That afternoon the entire Austrian media picked up the story, and many wondered how Jack had managed to ditch surveillance and disappear on the day he was to be arrested. The reality was that the police had seen no reason to chase him down, because they believed he didn't know he was about to be arrested and would therefore return to his apartment. What exactly did Jack know when he left Vienna on February 14?

He knew a lot about how the Viennese investigators were proceeding. On February 10—the day Geiger requested a warrant for his arrest—Jack spoke with his probation officer (who'd been in contact with the police) about the investigation. The following day he went to the Justice Ministry to visit an official with whom he'd discussed his difficulties in 1983, when Inspector Schenner was investigating him for the murder of Marica Horvath.

Thus he was already, to some degree, monitoring the investigation when Margit told him about overhearing the cop. Her words caused him to panic, possibly from the thought that his informants had not given him a full account of what was going on. And so he started calling various newspapers and ministries, trying to glean information. His conversation with Peter Grolig on February 12, in which he claimed that he "lived in constant fear and would have to leave Vienna if this keeps up," indicated that he was already—the day before the arrest warrant was issued in Graz—thinking about getting out of town.

Since his youth it had been his habit to go to Switzerland whenever it appeared that an investigation against him was about to get under way

or intensify. He arrived in the town of Gossau, where Bianca was working, on Friday night. On Saturday, after lunch and a stroll, he told her
that he had to return to Vienna. The brevity of his stay—fewer waking
hours than the drive from and back to Vienna—is a further indication
that visiting Bianca was a pretense for leaving Austria during the first
meeting of the Special Commission. After departing Gossau, he spoke
with an informant on his mobile phone and learned about the Graz arrest warrant. But why would the Graz police allow Hans Breitegger to
run the report *before* they took him into custody? It looked like a trap.

At 4:50 p.m., Saturday, February 15, Graz headquarters got a call from
Jack, asking to speak with Officer Hütter, with whom he'd cruised
around in the red-light district in September 1990.

"Why are the Graz police persecuting me? They have no evidence, so
what is the meaning of this arrest warrant?" Hütter couldn't tell him about
the investigation, only that it would go better for him if he cooperated.

"You'll be detained for a couple of weeks, and when everything is
cleared up, you'll rise like a phoenix from the ashes."

"No, I won't. I cannot bear going back into a cell, and this news has
already destroyed me socially. There's no sense in my staying in Austria."
At about 5:00 p.m. he called Vienna headquarters and asked to speak
with Inspector Hoffmann, who'd been present at the meeting in Edelbacher's office when he'd presented his alibis (or lack thereof).

"I can't believe how unfair this is," Jack said. "You have no evidence
against me, so what is the meaning of this arrest warrant?"

"Why don't you come in and talk to us about it?" said Hoffmann.

"I'm not going to turn myself in until the warrant is rescinded. I've
spent twenty years of my life in a cell, and I'm not going back."

"I'm sure we can clear everything up, but you need to cooperate
with us."

"No, I won't do it. I know you are a decent investigator, but there are
others like Schenner and Brandstätter who want to destroy me."

"I don't think that's the case," said Hoffmann.

"Then why did they get a warrant for my arrest?"

"Really, Mr. Unterweger, the thing to do is to come in and talk to us."
After Jack hung up, Hoffmann and Geiger discussed the call.

"He's trying to figure out what we know," said Geiger. "The warrant from Graz took him by surprise, and now he's trying to figure out what, exactly, they found."

A couple of hours later, Jack called Peter Grolig at the *Kurier* and proclaimed that the police had no evidence—that the arrest warrant was part of a carefully aimed campaign from Graz, directed by a cop who'd set his sights on him.

"What do you intend to do?" asked Grolig.

"Get myself a pump gun and do myself in."

The first clue about his whereabouts came when a woman named Mrs. Mrak contacted headquarters and explained that her eighteen-year-old daughter, Bianca, had run off with the fugitive Jack Unterweger. When Mrs. Mrak heard about the warrant for his arrest, she'd called the pub in Switzerland where her daughter was working and was told Bianca had left with her boyfriend. Swiss investigators soon arrived at the Nazionale pub and were informed that Bianca had gotten her final wages and returned to Austria because her father was on his deathbed. Her boyfriend had picked her up.

CHAPTER 32

THE MISSING DIARIES

LIKE MANY ARTISTS in Vienna, Jack had received generous subsidies from the Ministry of Arts and Education. To document his expenses for his readings and theater tours, he had saved receipts for gasoline, car repairs, and hotel bills. These could be analyzed to reconstruct his movements during the period the prostitutes disappeared—a task Geiger delegated to Inspectors Windisch and Etz. A handheld electronic address book was found containing about eighty contacts, as well as a list of forty women, both first and last names, with whom he'd had sex since his parole a year and a half earlier, replete with notes on their performance. A few were married, one was recently divorced from a well-known politician. Neither they nor their husbands were going to be happy when they received a summons from an examining magistrate. After the women he listed by name, he listed dozens of others by their profession, or by the place where he had picked them up, such as "Seven bimbos from Reiss Bar and Take Five, first names only, one-night stands."

Most interesting to Geiger were Jack's diaries. He had a mania for recording the events, people, and places of his daily life, both in a diary and in a separate desk calendar. The diaries and calendars started in 1975, ended at the time he was released from prison, and then began again on September 3, 1991. One of his last diary entries for 1990 was on April 30. In large letters he had written: "Transfer to Free Leave Status!!! End of this Diary! From today onward my own diary! (only more sexualis . . .)"

The word *sexualis*—Latin: "of sex"—was notable. The expression is never used in written or spoken German. To encounter a Latin phrase in German literature, one would have to go back to the scholarly writings of the nineteenth century. Had Jack been reading Krafft-Ebing's *Pyschopathia Sexualis*?

On April 30, 1990, he made a similar entry in his desk calendar, concluding with: "From today onward my own Diary/Calendar!!" So where was his "own Diary/Calendar" for the period between May 23, 1990 (his release from prison) and September 3, 1991 (two days after Peter Grolig's "hot tip" report appeared in *Kurier*)?

Geiger thought of two conspicuous things. The first was Jack's statement to Edelbacher in October 1991 that he couldn't remember what he was doing, or whom he was with, on the nights the prostitutes had disappeared in Vienna, and that he hadn't saved any records from the time. Yet he was clearly addicted to recording the daily events of his life. The idea that he'd just stopped altogether seemed extremely unlikely.

Then there was Jack's entry for the day he committed the murder for which he'd received his life sentence. Investigators had seized the diary when Jack was arrested in January 1975, but its contents were noted in the file on the murder, which Geiger had recently been studying. Under the date December 11, 1974, Jack had written: "Murder of Margret Schäfer."

It seemed that Jack had hidden or destroyed his diaries from May 1990 to September 1991—the period during which the women were murdered—because he'd made incriminating entries. Getting rid of the diaries also enabled him to claim that he had no idea where he was or whom he was with on the nights the murdered women disappeared.

CHAPTER 33

JACK ENTERS HADES

TWO DAYS AFTER JACK FLED ARREST, the Graz examining magistrate Wolfgang Wladkowski returned from a family holiday in Cuba. Having arrived that morning from Vienna via Brussels, the plane was provisioned with copies of Vienna newspapers. Wladkowski saw the report about Jack Unterweger's flight from arrest. He couldn't wait to get home for an update.

"No material evidence, but a lot of clues," said Inspector Brandstätter, who also explained what a political mess the case was turning out to be. Already press reports were appearing about the irregular way Jack had been paroled—so irregular that it might result in some heads rolling. The Freedom Party, a nationalist-populist party that some critics describe as extreme right wing, was making a stink in Parliament about how the Ministry of Arts and Education (under Socialist Party leadership) had not only given Unterweger a small fortune for his works "of doubtful literary quality" but had also either approved or tolerated a number of occasions when he'd been invited to talk to schoolchildren. Hans Breitegger was reporting on the officially unsolved murder of Marica Horvath in Salzburg in 1973, and how odd it was that Unterweger hadn't been prosecuted for it.

"The ministries are afraid they've got a major scandal brewing," said Brandstätter.

If Jack was convicted for murdering the seven women, and if his early release turned out to be the result of political patronage instead of an impartial psychiatric evaluation, the Justice Ministry was definitely going to have a scandal on its hands. The idea that the poster boy for rehabilitation cruised around the country strangling hookers, paying for gas, food, and lodging with state subsidies, was too embarrassing to contemplate.

A week after Jack fled, the investigators still didn't know where he was. Theories abounded that he was hiding in Switzerland or Italy. In his novels he'd written about his adventures in both countries. For a while he'd kept an apartment in the Italian city of Tarvisio, just across the border, and on a few occasions he'd gone on road trips in Italy. He'd also mentioned to a couple of his girlfriends that he'd abandoned his beloved Mustang Mach I somewhere in Italy, which made no sense unless he'd had reason to think the car was a liability.

Street prostitution was a major occupation in Italy. Vienna headquarters sent a query to the Interpol office in Rome, and after the news broke about the arrest warrant for Jack, pimps in Vienna called their contacts in Italy and told them to be on the lookout for him.

"Jack will probably try to enter Italy near Lake Como," explained a Viennese pimp to a reporter. "There are many unwatched points along that stretch of the border used by smugglers to run their money into Switzerland. He may try to cross there, but he'll have no chance of hiding among the Italians or the Austrians who work with them in the prostitution scene."

Rudolf Prem, the husband of the still missing Regina Prem, had connections in Rimini, where Regina had, like many Austrian prostitutes, occasionally worked.

"We all knew Regina well," said a Rimini pimp to the same reporter. "Jack has no chance of hiding among us. If he shows himself in our domain, we will grab him. We won't kill him, but we'll haul him back to Austria." Geiger had heard that Jack wasn't popular with his fellow pimps. Some believed that he'd served as an informant for the guards at Stein, but his greatest offense in the eyes of the underworld was that he'd murdered a defenseless girl. "Milk the cow but never slaughter it" was an unwritten law of the milieu. It was repugnant, and if Jack's victim in 1974 had been a prostitute, it would have destroyed another man's capital. When Regina Prem disappeared, apparently murdered, her husband, Rudolf, lost not only his wife and the mother of his child but also Regina's income.

On February 10, 1992, Inspectors Windisch and Etz interviewed Regina's colleagues and friends, as well as Rudolf, asking them if they'd ever seen or heard of Jack Unterweger cruising around in the milieu. During their interview with Rudolf, they reviewed the crank calls he'd received on various nights the previous October and July, and made a note of the phrases: "When the figure eight at the zenith stands, then I'll tell you where your wife lies." And: "To eleven I have carried out the just punishment. They all lie in the place of atonement, facing downward, toward Hades, because otherwise it would have been an outrage."

It was noteworthy that the caller spoke words almost never used in spoken German—*Sühne* (atonement) and the archaic word for "outrage" (*Frevel*). Maybe it was just an educated crank caller who'd watched a lot of horror films. On the other hand, when the caller had phoned at the beginning of July, he'd given a rough description of the route from Vienna to where the body of Silvia Zagler was later found. It was also notable that he'd claimed to have carried out the "just punishment" to *eleven*. So far the investigators had only found *six* bodies that seemed to bear the signature of the same killer, plus the officially missing but probably dead Regina Prem.

A week later, while sifting through documents found in Jack's apartment, one of the investigators came across a newspaper article with the headline JACK ENTERS HADES. At that point they began combing through Jack's documents for other phrases spoken by the anonymous caller. In Jack's library they found a copy of the novel *The Golden Hades*, by the British crime thriller writer Edgar Wallace, as well as a scholarly book about Greek mythology with a chapter on Hades (the Greek god of the underworld and the underworld itself).

A conspicuous feature of the Greek mythology book was that it was missing the bottom third of pages 17 and 18 and all of pages 19 and 20. As the book was out of print and relatively rare, the investigators were unable to find another copy to see what was written on the missing pages. Had they found another copy, they would have seen that the pages torn out of Jack's copy told the story of Oedipus. Abandoned as a child, Oedipus didn't know the identity of his parents, and when he grew up, he unwittingly murdered his father and wed his mother, the Queen of Thebes, thereby becoming King. At the bottom of page 19 is written: "The Atonement (*Die Sühne*): After a long and blessed reign, the gods sent as a punishment for Oedipus'—unknowingly committed—outrage (*Frevel*) a plague over the land."

According to Rudolf Prem, the anonymous caller also spoke the phrase "When the figure eight at the zenith stands." In another manuscript found in Jack's apartment titled *The Burial*, the investigators found the sentence "With a stick he drew a figure eight in the air, and with his entire body in the air, and his feet on the ground he formed an eight." Had the investigators read Jack's novel *Mare Adriatico*, they would have also seen his repeated use of the word "zenith." "When the figure eight at the zenith stands" suggested an astronomical or astrological event, and also found in Jack's apartment was what appeared to be a chart for making celestial calculations.

CHAPTER 34

COUNTEROFFENSIVE

WHEN THE NEWS BROKE of the arrest warrant for Jack Unterweger, Geiger braced for a media Blitzkrieg from his supporters, but during the week following his disappearance, it didn't happen. The initial reports by

Hans Breitegger and Peter Grolig indicated that the police had good reason to suspect Jack. Fleeing arrest also made him look bad.

But then on Thursday, February 20, Jack launched a counteroffensive. Shortly after 9:00 p.m. he called the ORF from wherever he was hiding and announced he would call the following day at 5:00 p.m. to give a live interview. The next day, the Interior Minister went on the ORF *Midday Journal* program and warned him that the police would trace his call. Jack called the studio in spite of the warning, and all over the country people tuned in to hear his conversation with the radio announcer Johannes Fischer, who opened the interview by asking Jack to state his position.

UNTERWEGER: . . . From the moment I fell under suspicion as a result of an anonymous tip from a retired Salzburg investigator, I have always made myself available to the police . . . All of them were of the unanimous opinion; there is no evidence . . . But then a cop named Toth Christian went around the milieu with my photo saying, "Hey, did you know this is Unterweger, who we'd gladly have as the hooker murderer . . ."

The other issue is this: the police are under pressure. Over the last years there have been a number of unsolved prostitute murders and sexual murders of children, old women, and whores. Because I am free, they can try to hang these murders on me . . .

FISCHER: Mr. Unterweger, why then have you fled when you feel yourself to be so innocent?

UNTERWEGER: Because I won't go back into a cell. I will give myself up to any authority, any lawyer, any cop; it makes no difference to me, but not in a cell. I have made twenty trips abroad, and I always returned to Austria. I made no preparations to flee. I have always been in contact with my neighborhood police station, because I knew what would happen if something went wrong and the media caught wind of it. I am, factually speaking, not fleeing as a result of any feeling of guilt but because my first intention was to commit suicide . . . Now I won't do that. Now I will begin to fight back. I can only do that when I am able to speak with whom I'd like to speak. First the arrest warrant must be rescinded. I am ready to clear up these unanswered questions.

FISCHER: Mr. Unterweger, a final question . . . Can you tell us if [your companion Bianca] is in danger . . . or even still with you? Can you tell her to call her mother?

UNTERWEGER: Ask Bianca yourself.

FISCHER: I can't ask her.

UNTERWEGER: I'll put the question to her. I must hang up now . . . Both of us would prefer to be in Vienna to fight this. But because of the arrest warrant, that is impossible. The way the police are dealing with the people who have helped me and continue to help me is madness, and I'm not prepared to subject more people to their treatment . . .

FISCHER: Would you grant us a television interview, Mr. Unterweger?

UNTERWEGER: Certainly. But I must call you sometime next week . . .

Geiger listened to the interview, marveling at the boldness of the counteroffensive. Jack was a great storyteller, and few of his listeners knew how leniently the justice system had always treated him. If he was innocent of the murders in 1990–91, he had no reason to think he wouldn't receive due process, with many supporters in Vienna pulling for him. As Geiger listened to Jack's story, he knew he would hear it again soon.

Three days later, the February 24 edition of *profil* magazine hit the stands with a long report on the Unterweger affair. The title was indicative of its overall tone: "The Grotesque Murder Witch Hunt: Mishaps, Malice, and Lust for Character Assassination. In the hunt for the 'prison poet,' the justice system, police, and press show what they are capable of." The lead writer was the political affairs journalist Robert Buchacher, and the first page of the report had a marked pro-Jack slant. Unlike Breitegger and Grolig, Buchacher had not been studying Jack for the previous months. The gist of his report: the police were incompetent, they didn't have any solid evidence against Jack, but because they were under pressure to catch the killer, they were focusing their investigation on him because of his past. Because they knew they didn't have evidence, it appeared they had intentionally leaked the arrest warrant to the press to frighten him, thereby "inviting him to flee."

The notion that the police were under pressure to catch the killer and were desperate to find a suspect soon gained currency among people who were inclined to sympathize with Jack. It was an alternative explanation for why he'd fled—not because he was guilty, but because he was afraid the police would hang the murders on him no matter what.

Jack's "police under pressure" hypothesis sounded convincing when he stated it during his live radio interview, and Buchacher lent it further credibility by reiterating it in his highly respected magazine. But was it true? Buchacher was the same journalist who had, in early June 1991, written a report on the prostitute murders titled "Streetwalkers Die," and as he himself stated in the sub-headline: "The chances of catching the killer are next to zero." The implication was clear: no one should *expect* the police to catch the killer.

No one did, and when the murders in Austria stopped (a few weeks before Jack departed for Los Angeles), public awareness of them faded. When the arrest warrant for Jack was issued nine months after the last victim in Austria disappeared, neither the public nor the government was pressuring the police to solve the murders.

CHAPTER 35

MIAMI VICE

SOMETIMES IT SEEMED as if they were on vacation. Bianca loved the mornings on the beach, with the sun rising over the Atlantic, warming her skin while the sea breeze kept her cool. Then there were the pastel-colored buildings, the terrace restaurants, and the people-watching on Collins Avenue. While the poor devils back in Vienna were slogging through the slush, she and Jack were relaxing in Miami Beach.

The adventure had begun in Switzerland on February 15. After they'd lunched and strolled around Gossau, Jack had departed around 5:00 p.m. About a half hour after he left, a call came to the bar for her. It was Jack, hysterical, saying something about prostitute murders and a retired Salzburg policeman. She told him to calm down and come back to the pub.

In his car in the back parking lot, weeping, he told her that his world had just collapsed, all because of a retired Salzburg inspector on a mission to send him back to prison.

"He was enraged by my release, and now he's trying to frame me for some prostitute murders last year. He's made the whole thing up, but the cops in Graz and Vienna are happy to listen to him because they're under pressure to catch the killer."

"But they can't send you to back to prison if you didn't do it," said Bianca.

"Oh yes, they can. You don't know the police. Even without evidence they'll put me in a cell. The only thing for me to do is drive into the woods and put a bullet through my brain." He pulled out his little automatic to show he meant business. (She didn't know it had a broken slide and couldn't chamber a cartridge.)

"No, Jack. No, you're not."

"It's the only thing left for me to do. You will return to Vienna and I will kill myself."

"No, I won't let you. Either you go with me to Vienna or I go with you."

They drove west. Jack felt at home in Switzerland; on a few occasions in his youth he had lain low in Zurich and Basel after committing crimes in Austria. But after picking up Bianca at the pub, he knew it was just a matter of time before her mother (who knew where she worked) contacted the Vienna police, who would in turn contact their Swiss colleagues. And so he decided to press on to France.

After they crossed the border, both were overtaken by fatigue, and Jack announced that he would find a road into the woods where they could catch a few hours' sleep in the car. Bianca didn't like the idea, but Jack insisted, and soon found what he was looking for.

They woke early, drove to a filling station for croissants and coffee, and discussed where they should go. Jack considered Spain, which had no extradition treaty with Austria, but then decided that America was the better choice. It was easy to disappear in a big American city, and the *Amis* were so friendly and trusting. They drove to Orly, near Paris, went into the terminal, and learned that American Airlines Flight 99 was soon departing for New York with a connecting flight to Miami.

Miami. The name had a magical sound. It was the city of Crockett and Tubbs. Bianca was a huge *Miami Vice* fan; she thought Don Johnson was the sexiest man alive. It was the perfect escape from cold and gray Europe.

They had no choice but to travel on their own passports and to book the tickets on Jack's Visa card—clear records of their flight to the United States, which the Austrian police would eventually discover. On the other hand, they had to get away from Jack's car, and at that moment they had no means of assessing the risk of being arrested in France. Even with the paper trail, going to the States still seemed better than staying in Europe.

After they booked their tickets, Jack moved his car out of the terminal parking lot, ditched it somewhere away from the airport, removed and hid the license plates, and then somehow made his way back to the terminal before the flight departed.

When they stepped out of the Miami terminal into the warm air, Bianca's excitement overcame the stress of the previous forty-eight hours. Jack in his cowboy boots, blue jeans, and fur coat seemed so incongruous with the atmosphere. Her excitement mounted as their taxi drove over the causeway. For the first time in her life she was going to see the ocean.

Then the letdown of the "historic" Franklin Hotel. The grimness of the place reminded her of how little money they had. Lying on the bed while Jack showered, she saw a cockroach crawling on the wall. Huge, chocolate brown with a tan spot on his back, his giant feelers swiveling back and forth. Never had she seen such a dreadful insect, and he seemed to symbolize the wretchedness of the place. If they were going to do any better, they'd need a lot more money than the $1,200 she'd earned at the Nazionale pub.

The next morning over breakfast Jack perused a newspaper employment section. Miami Gold was seeking go-go dancers—a perfect position for Bianca. He scheduled an interview for that afternoon, and they spent the morning looking for an apartment. On Euclid Avenue, behind the Miami Beach police station, they saw an APARTMENT FOR RENT sign in front of a two-story Art Deco building. Jack introduced himself as Jacques Onderweger. Thank goodness, the landlord, a man named John Schnarch, didn't ask to see their passports. A one-bedroom apartment was available for $315 per month. All they had to do was fill out a one-page lease, pay a security deposit of two months' rent, and the place was theirs.

That afternoon they went to Miami Gold for her interview. It didn't bother her prospective employers that she'd never go-go danced before. Her nubile body was the only asset required; the "dancing" consisted of wiggling her bottom and swinging around on a brass pole—skills she could learn on the job.

The next morning they hit the beach. Bianca was enthralled by the Atlantic, Jack by the sunbathing girls. Lying on a towel, she drifted off into a peaceful sleep, and when she awoke, he was gone. A bit dazed, she looked around and saw him sitting a few yards away, looking between the legs of another sleeping girl. He could be such a pervert.

"What are you doing?"

"Just checking out the scenery," he said. "By the way, did you see those red flags on the lifeguard stands?"

"What do they mean?" she asked.

"It's a shark warning."

Bianca was getting used to the stories of wildlife in America. On the plane a tourist had told her about "fifteen-foot man-eating alligators" and "swamp rats as big as dogs" that lived in the Everglades.

That afternoon they found a secondhand furniture shop where they bought a bed, a dresser, and a folding table. As her first evening of work drew near, she took the bus from South Beach across the causeway. Looking out the window, she marveled at the waterscape—private islands with magnificent houses of all different styles, drawbridges, pelicans standing on pilings. Then there were the boats. Sailing yachts, power yachts, a cruise ship, freighters and tankers of all sizes, a whole other bustling city on water. She couldn't imagine a place less like old, landlocked Vienna.

On the mainland she transferred to a bus that took her north on Biscayne Boulevard. Her final stop was a half-mile from Miami Gold, and a stretch of the road ran next to a marshy, wooded area (East Greynolds Park). She walked along, occasionally glancing into the trees, making sure there wasn't a fifteen-foot alligator about to lunge out and drag her to its nest.

When she arrived, the manager introduced her to some of the other girls, as well as the cook, a middle-aged Mexican named Miguel. He had a warm, gentle way that put her at ease. He gave her an orientation, and in the dressing room he showed her how to operate the tanning booth.

"You should try to keep a tan, but always wear your bikini. The guys here like the innocent look—pale bottom and breasts."

She felt the butterflies in her belly grow as the time to go-go dance drew near. As a novice she'd gotten the early shift, before the crowd arrived. A few lonely looking characters sat at the bar. The dj asked if she had any requests.

"I don't know, an oldie of some sort," she said.

"And now please welcome Bianca the German girl!" the disc jockey announced, and out of the loudspeaker blared an Elvis song. As she walked out on stage, all she could think to do was curse Jack. She tried spinning around the brass pole and swinging her hips to the rhythm of the bass, but she couldn't overcome her self-consciousness. When the song ended, she hurried off stage, put on a robe, went into the kitchen, and burst into tears.

Miguel put his arm around her. "It's nothing to be upset about; you'll get used to it." He had a tip for her: "Have a shot of rum."

Miguel was right: she did get used to it. The shot of rum also helped, and with each successive number she felt herself thinking more about the music and less about herself. As her shyness diminished, the audience grew, as did the number of dollars stuck in her garters. Her shift ended at 11:00 p.m. and she arrived at the apartment around midnight, sleepy but buoyed by the feeling that she'd worked and earned well.

"How much did you make?" Jack asked.

"Just over $150," she said proudly.

"Give it to me."

"The whole sum?"

"I'm going to have to talk several hours long distance with my lawyer and my informants."

He made the first of his calls the next day just before lunch. While he talked in a phone booth at the USA Money Exchange, she sat in a diner around the corner eating a burger, fries, and a milkshake. Such terrific junk food; no wonder the Americans were fat.

Jack came storming up. "My informants tell me that the media are exploiting my story. Enough running. Today I start to fight back."

"What are you going to do?"

"Call the ORF and go live."

"You're going to do what!"

"I'm going live to tell the country how it really is." She thought about it for a moment and realized that, as crazy as it sounded, it was actually a brilliant idea.

"When will you do it?"

"In a few days. First I must work on my written defense."

Bianca arrived at Miami Gold for her second night of work. Another evening of dancing, another late-night arrival at the apartment to find Jack still awake. But this time he didn't ask straightaway for her money, as he was absorbed in his defense.

"As soon as I finish writing it, I'm going to send copies to everyone— the President, the ministries, the mayor of Vienna, the newspapers."

"But won't they see the Miami postmark?"

"No. I'm going to send all the copies to a confidant in Vienna."

"And then your confidant will distribute them."

"Exactly."

They had arrived on Sunday, February 16, and by that Thursday were settled into a routine. Mornings at the beach, with Jack taking an hour before lunch to phone Vienna; afternoons strolling around South Beach, people-watching and window-shopping; evenings dancing at Miami Gold while Jack worked on his defense. Thursday, February 20, was their three-month anniversary. They celebrated with a "super morning on the beach and lunch at Burger King," as Jack noted in his diary. That afternoon he called the ORF studio in Vienna and announced he would call the next day during the 5:00 p.m. (Vienna time) broadcast of *Inland Report* to give a live interview. He hoped the word would spread and the whole country would tune in for his reckoning with the police.

The following day he called and spoke well. He noted in his diary that the interview had lasted seven minutes, long enough to trace the call. He wasn't too worried, though. The next day they passed a newsstand near the beach with European papers, including the German *Bild*, and on the front page was a picture of Bianca when she was fifteen pounds heavier! God I look awful, she thought.

"Bianca Mrak: Her Life in Danger!" Wearing a baseball cap and sunglasses, she bought the newspaper, walked a few feet, and began reading it. Such sensationalist crap, she thought. Jack didn't tell her that in his live interview the day before, the host had asked that she call her worried mother. His rush to get off the phone when the interviewer asked about Bianca's safety had sounded ominous.

"I'm suing *Bild* as well," he said. Bianca knew her life wasn't in danger, but the report made her realize that her family and friends back home didn't know that. She hadn't spoken with any of them since she'd fled with Jack the week before.

"I need to call my mother," she said.

"You know the police are set up to trace the call."

"I'll take just a second to tell her I'm okay."

"No, you can't. It's too risky." After a heated argument, she relented, but the next morning she thought about how cruel it was to let her mother worry herself to death.

"I really *have* to call my mother."

Again he tried to talk her out of it, but this time she was determined. She got up from the beach and began to walk toward the USA Money Exchange. He followed her, telling her that it was a terrible idea, pleading with her not to do it, but the farther she walked, the more resolved she became.

"Mama, hello, it's me," she said, and burst into tears. Her mother started to speak and also began crying.

"It's all right, Mama. Don't worry. I'm okay." Just as her mother started to speak, the connection was broken. Stunned, Bianca turned around to see where Jack was standing. For a second it crossed her mind that *he* had somehow ended the call.

"What did she say?" he asked.

"I don't know; I lost the connection," she said.

"Did you at least tell her you're all right?"

"Yeah."

They headed back to the apartment, stopping at McDonald's to pick up a Coke. Strolling along, she pondered why Jack talked for hours every day with his lawyer, informants, and "confidant" in Vienna, but tried to hinder her from having a five-minute conversation with her mother. Who were his informants, and why wasn't he worried about the police tracing his calls to them? Who was his "confidant"? To Bianca, the word had a feminine ring. An informant conveys information; a confidant was someone whose loyalty you could count on, and the strongest root of loyalty was affection. She felt her feminine intuition stirring, and as they approached the apartment, she had her revelation.

Since Jack had come home at 6:00 a.m. from the Advent party, she'd been pondering a few questions. Why had he switched off his cell phone when he drove down to Tarvisio to vacate his apartment? He'd done the same on a few nights when she'd tried to reach him from Switzerland. Suddenly it all fell into place. He'd met a girl at the Advent party and had, ever since, been leading a double life. He hadn't really vacated his apartment in Tarvisio just after Christmas, and he hadn't really worked on his "underworld story" while she was in Switzerland, at least not round the clock. He'd been sleeping with the other girl, who was as attached to him as she was. Just as Bianca had dropped out of school and then abandoned everything to flee with him, the other girl risked going to jail for aiding and abetting him.

She stopped on the sidewalk and turned to face him. "Your confidant is a girl you met at that Advent party, isn't it?"

A shocked look appeared on his face, and she knew she'd hit the mark. A fight ensued on the sidewalk and continued into their apartment. She'd never been so upset in her life. Already feeling sad and guilty about her mother, she was unhinged by the revelation that Jack had been deceiving her the entire time.

"I can't believe I dropped everything to run away with you."

They were in the living room, she sobbing, he standing there, his usual eloquence having abandoned him. She wanted to hurt him, and realizing that she was still holding her McDonald's Coke, she slung it in his face. As he stood there, shocked, she hurried into the bathroom and locked the door.

After a couple of minutes passed with no response, she tried to calm herself with a hot shower. As she began to relax, with the hot water massaging her, she was startled by the crash of the flimsy door giving way. Through the crack in the shower curtain she saw Jack coming at her.

Back in Vienna, Inspectors Windisch and Etz of the Lower Austrian police were busy contacting the women in Jack's electronic address book, asking if they'd heard from him. One of them, a girl named Elisabeth, admitted he'd called her a few times.

"I met him at an Advent party last November, and I found him very funny and sympathetic," she explained. "I've been seeing him ever since. He started calling me shortly after he fled." She said she didn't know where he was, but Windisch didn't believe her.

A few hours later, she got her daily call from Jack.

"The police just told me I can't help you," she said. "They're threatening to send me to prison."

He replied that the police were just bluffing and that he needed her help more than ever. He'd run out of money, was sleeping on the beach, and his life was in grave danger without his thyroid medication (like Jürgen in *Scream of Fear*, Jack had a thyroid condition). Could she send it to him and whatever money she could scrape together? She said she'd get the medicine and do her best with the money.

After Bianca had tossed her Coke on him, Jack had put her in her place with a few hefty slaps. She became more docile, but had still talked about going home. "Crisis because of Elisabeth/+ I—lied to Bia in Vienna. I'm sorry, but it's already done," he wrote in his diary.

Maybe it wasn't a bad idea for Bianca to go home, though it would mean losing his income from her dancing. He tried calling Lela, a gullible nurse. The previous spring he'd hit her up for $14,500 "to finance *Scream of Fear*." Upon his return from L.A., he told her he needed an additional $11,500, as someone had stolen his credit card and made a massive number of unauthorized charges. He hoped she would be willing to cover yet another financial emergency, but he didn't reach her. Elisabeth was his only hope.

That afternoon he accompanied Bianca to work, and on his way back to South Beach he visited the Police Hall of Fame. Afterward he went for a walk along Biscayne Bay and then headed back to the apartment. Walking east on Fifth Street, toward the beach, he saw it.

The 1967 Mustang Fastback, painted candy-apple red, was the most stylish model ever produced. He kept a portrait of it in his study in Vienna and had always wanted one, but in Europe they were too rare. This one wasn't in the best of shape, but none of its flaws were irreparable. He had to have it.

The next day passed uneventfully. After Bianca left for work, he put the final touches on his defense, made photocopies, and sent them off to Elisabeth. Bianca was still moody, but at least she wasn't furious anymore. He knew she'd forgive him.

The following day, February 26, something glorious happened. On the phone with Elisabeth, she told him that her boss at *Success* magazine would pay him $10,000 for an exclusive "on the run" interview. Jack had already written a couple of articles for her boss, who offered to wire him a small advance and to give him the rest of the payment at the time of the interview. Jack agreed, and gave him wiring instructions for the USA Money Exchange, Miami Beach.

He was overjoyed: "10,000 for interview?! Crazy!" he wrote in his diary. With that kind of money he could cover their expenses and buy the Mustang Fastback (even though Bianca was vehemently opposed to buying the old car). To celebrate the cash infusion, he took her shopping.

"We don't have the money yet," she said.

"No, but we soon will. Come on, let's have some fun."

As they browsed in a souvenir shop on Ocean Drive, a baseball cap caught her eye. It was bright yellow with a Hawaiian print, and on the front in white block letters was PANAMA JACK.

"Now that's a pretty cap!" she said.

Jack looked at it. "Hey, super! Panama Jack! Try it on." The cap fit well, but then Bianca looked at the price tag: $12.00.

"We can't afford it," she said.

"Twelve dollars is nothing for such a beautiful cap," Jack replied.

"No, I don't want it," she said, putting it back on the rack. "Let's go." She turned and walked out of the store.

Back on the street, a few yards from the shop—

"Hey, Bia baby, I've got something for you."

"Yeah?" He pulled the cap out of his shorts.

"It wasn't so expensive," he said with a laugh. How had he stolen it in that small shop, with the cashier just a few feet away? It was such an unnecessary risk for a man in his shoes to take. She liked the Panama Jack cap, but not that much.

CHAPTER 36

BETRAYAL

ON FEBRUARY 26—twelve days after Jack disappeared—Geiger got a call from Inspector Windisch of the Lower Austrian Police.

"I just talked to a guy who says he's got a big tip. He wouldn't tell me on the phone, says he wants to meet in Café Landtmann." They walked into the café and met the editor of *Success* magazine, a man named Gert Schmidt.

"Do you have any idea where Jack Unterweger is?" he asked, clearly enjoying himself. A furtive meeting in a café to deliver a message was a stock scene from Cold War Vienna, when spies from both NATO and the Warsaw Pact countries used the city as a meeting place for transmitting intelligence. Geiger would soon grow accustomed to the theatrical way with which the Viennese approached the Unterweger story.

"Maybe Italy or Spain," he said.

"No, he's in Miami." Schmidt told the story of how an assistant had fallen for Jack, who'd been calling her from South Beach, asking her to send his thyroid medication and whatever money she could scrape together. She wanted to help him, but she didn't have any money, and so she'd asked her boss. In getting to know Jack the previous autumn, Schmidt had developed a profound dislike for him and was distressed by the assistant's devotion to him. And so he'd offered a large sum for an interview without telling the girl of his true intent.

He handed Geiger a slip of paper: *USA Money Exchange, 207 11th Street, Miami Beach.*

"She's wiring the advance today. It'll be there for him to pick up tomorrow."

"The check, please," Geiger said to a passing waiter. He needed to get back to headquarters. Fast.

"We don't have time to go through Interpol," he told Hoffmann. Interpol had been founded in Vienna in 1923 by the legendary Police president Johannes Schober, but in 1992 the Vienna office had become lax. The liaison with the Americans was what the Viennese call a *gemütlicher Mensch*— easygoing, didn't get things done in a hurry.

"It'll be days before they've got people in place to arrest him. We'll try to get the Miami police to pick him up, and worry about the red tape later." Hoffmann called the Miami police, asked to speak to someone in Homicide, and was connected to Inspector José Grenado. Hoffmann introduced himself and outlined the story, explaining that they didn't know how long their suspect would stay in Miami. Maybe he intended to pick up the money and move on; they didn't want to miss the opportunity.

"We can't pick him up, but the federal marshals can," explained Grenado. "Fax me a copy of your warrant and I'll deliver it to their office here."

The next day seemed to last an eternity. At 6:30 p.m. Vienna time (12:30 p.m. Miami time) there was still no word. It's beyond my control, Geiger thought. There's no sense hanging around the office, driving myself crazy.

"I'm gonna catch the seven o'clock play at the Burg Theater," he told Hoffmann. "Page me if you hear something."

CHAPTER 37

U.S. MARSHALS

U.S. MARSHAL SHAWN CONBOY and his team of men sat on a hotel terrace on Eleventh Street near the intersection of Collins Avenue. Their orders were to watch the USA Money Exchange across the street to see if a European male— 5'6", early forties, with pale skin and tattoos on his upper arms—arrived with his girlfriend to pick up a wire transfer. It was the kind of beautiful February day that made Conboy glad he was in Miami instead of his native Boston, and he and his men were enjoying themselves, chatting, cracking jokes, soaking up the sun.

In 1992, thirty-four-year-old Conboy had been working on a fugitive task force, and there was never a shortage of fugitives in southern Florida. For men all over the country with warrants for their arrest or who'd jumped bail, Miami was the place to run. It was easy to disappear in the sprawling port, and its proximity to Caribbean islands outside U.S. jurisdiction gave comfort to people trying to avoid the law. Or maybe they just liked the warm weather.

The same attractions appealed to foreigners on the lam, but the U.S. Marshals Service was usually alerted to their presence before a U.S. warrant was issued for their arrest. "Watch him, follow him if you can, but don't arrest him" was the typical order, but what was the point of watching some shady foreigner get drunk or go to the beach?

At first glance, this Jack Unterweger was no different. The Austrians had issued a warrant, but that wasn't enough to pick him up in the United States. Authorization could come only after the State Department had reviewed it and issued a provisional U.S. warrant. It was a process that took time, and the Austrians were in a hurry. The suspect had allegedly murdered prostitutes and was considered potentially dangerous to all women. He had a girl with him, and there'd be hell to pay if something happened to her.

Their orders were to follow him and establish where he was staying. Easier said than done. Even in plainclothes it was difficult for a team of U.S. marshals, all above average size and height, to follow a guy around South Beach without giving themselves away. Conboy had little confidence in the viability or usefulness of the assignment, so he was happy to hear from the INS that Jack Unterweger had entered the country on a tourist visa without disclosing his felony conviction. It was a civil offense separate from the Austrian criminal charges, but it was enough to detain him.

To the four marshals and one ATF officer sitting on the hotel terrace wearing blue jeans, their guayabera shirts covering their service automatics, the assignment seemed like a day off, because none of them thought they'd see any action. Such tips usually came from an unreliable source, and even if the tip was solid, the suspect often changed his plans. Chances were this Unterweger character wouldn't show, but it was a beautiful day and there were a lot of pretty girls walking by.

Walking to the USA Money Exchange with Bianca to pick up a wire transfer was a scene similar to an episode in Jack's past. In January 1975, twenty-four-year-old Jack and his two girlfriends at the time—a sixteen-year-old Austrian named Maria and an eighteen-year-old German named Barbara—walked into a bank in Basel, Switzerland, to pick up a wire transfer from Austria.

The three of them had formed a little gang in Zurich in the autumn of 1974. The girls were so infatuated with Jack that they stayed with him and worked as hookers instead of returning to their middle-class families. When business slowed, Jack hatched the plan to plunder Barbara's family home in Germany, north of Frankfurt. When that didn't work out, he robbed and murdered Barbara's neighbor and friend Margret Schäfer. The three of them then robbed a jewelry store in the same town and fled back to Switzerland. In Basel he hatched the plan to ransom Maria (at only sixteen, she couldn't legally consent to staying with him). He gave her parents wiring instructions for a local bank, and as he walked in to pick up the money, he was arrested by a team of Swiss cops.

That the U.S. marshals weren't expecting him to show made it all the more strange when he turned the corner off Collins with his girlfriend. It was weird the way they all recognized him. The qualities of the description—slender, pale, tattoos on upper arms—found striking expression in the apparition that approached them. Maybe it was his ghostly white skin that made him stand out so from the sunburned tourists. No one said a word or glanced at the faxed image. They knew it was him.

Jack picked them out right away. As he turned off Collins, he was obviously looking for danger, which he spotted in the form of five large men sitting on the balcony across the street from the money exchange. The girl went in while he waited outside, occasionally glancing over at them. When she emerged a moment later, he started to walk away, and then bolted down an alley as they rose to follow him. One of them, a former tackle for the University of Miami named Darren Bruce, gave chase while Conboy radioed the Miami Beach police for assistance. Several squad cars soon arrived and blocked off a large perimeter around the intersection, at which point Bruce emerged from the entrance of a nearby hotel, holding the suspect by the back of his neck.

"Are you Jack Unterweger?" Conboy asked him.

"Yes. Why are you arresting me?"

"Why did you arrest him?" asked the Interpol officer on the phone.

"Because he tried to flee. He's wanted for murder. I couldn't just let him run off."

"But we still don't have the provisional warrant."

"Then INS will take him." It wasn't the best solution, because for lying on his visa application he could post bail and walk. Yet by the time Conboy booked him into the Metropolitan Correctional Facility, the U.S. Attorney's Office said a provisional warrant would be available for his arraignment the next day.

———

Bianca had also tried to run, but only got a few feet before one of the gi-ant men overtook her and put her in handcuffs. She yelled and cursed at him as he dumped the contents of her purse and combed through them. She saw the other men putting Jack in handcuffs into the back of a car. Another car pulled up, and she was tossed in the back seat with her hands still cuffed behind her back. As she sat down, the metal shackles bit into her wrists and she grimaced with pain.

"I promise to be good if you'll take these off," she said to the driver. Looking at his reflection in the rearview mirror, she saw him smile.

"Where are you staying?" he asked, and she gave him their address on Euclid. The men drove her to the apartment, and with her standing in the living room still in handcuffs, they did a search. The only thing of interest they found was what appeared to be a diary. One of the marshals rifled through her purse a second time, looked at her passport, and then took the handcuffs off.

"Have a nice day."

"Wait, you can't just-leave me here."

"Your visa is valid. You're free."

"But what am I supposed to do?" she said, not realizing that she, the breadwinner, could do just fine without Jack.

"Go back to the exchange and pick up your money."

"And then what?"

"Go to your consulate if you need help." Where was their sense of helping a girl in distress? The U.S. marshals weren't very chivalrous.

She went back to the money exchange to pick up the wire transfer (a measly advance for the "exclusive, on the run interview"), and then called her mother.

"It's over, Mama, they've arrested Jack."

"Good. Now get home this instant."

"It'll be a while before I get home."

"I expect you here in an hour."

"I can't get home in an hour. I'm in Miami."

"What? Miami!"

"Yes. Look, Mama, I promise to come home soon, but right now I

don't have a plane ticket or any money. Call the Vienna police and tell
them we've been arrested in Miami."

CHAPTER 38

A STAR IS BORN

HEINRICH VON KLEIST'S *Penthesilea* was a silly and boring play. Penthesilea,
Queen of the Amazons, shows up at Troy with her female warriors and
attacks both Greeks and Trojans. Why both? She wants to kill Achilles,
but she's also pretty impressed by him and probably wouldn't mind . . .
Despite the racy subject matter, the play came off as stilted. Geiger's
pager beeped at about 8:00 p.m., not a moment too soon. "They got him
and the girl," said Hoffmann.

"You need to get to Miami to talk to her before the press catches
wind of this," Geiger said. He figured there was a chance that Jack had,
in his agitation, accidentally revealed something to Bianca. They needed
to hear her story before anyone else did.

Within two hours Hoffmann and his girlfriend, who was also in the
police, were on a plane to Miami. Geiger phoned the consulate with
their flight information, and the next morning they were greeted at the
airport by a consular official.

"A funny thing happened this morning," he said. "A man walked into
the consulate and introduced himself as Inspector Ernst Hoffmann,
ready to take Miss Mrak into custody. I knew he couldn't be you, because I knew your arrival time."

Amazing. Simply amazing what journalists would do for a scoop.
And damn the leakiness of Vienna headquarters.

In Bianca's hotel room (where the Austrian Consulate had lodged
her to isolate her from the press), she told the story of her relationship

and flight with Jack, and Hoffmann sensed he hadn't revealed anything particularly incriminating to her. She seemed absolutely convinced of his innocence, which didn't surprise him. She was, after all, just a kid.

The next day, Hoffmann, his girlfriend, and Bianca departed for Vienna. Jack remained in the Metropolitan Correctional Facility, waiting for his extradition proceedings. After takeoff, Bianca went to the lavatory, and when she returned to her seat, she had a request.

"There's an Austrian journalist sitting at the back of the plane. He just offered to pay me for an interview. Would that be okay?" Hoffmann wondered whether it was the same journalist who'd tried to impersonate him at the consulate.

"It's fine with me, but I thought you said the *Kronen Zeitung* has offered to pay you for an exclusive." Hoffmann was right: the Viennese tabloid had figured out where she was staying in Miami and called her with the offer. Bianca apparently didn't understand what was at stake. She could have used an agent to help her negotiate with the press, because the press wanted to hear her story more than any other and it had no reservations about paying for it (a common practice in the Austrian media). At thirty thousand feet over the Atlantic, a star was born.

"It was my idea to flee to Miami," she told *Der Standard*.

"Why Miami?"

"Maybe it was because I like Don Johnson."

CHAPTER 39

THE TIES THAT BIND

WHILE BIANCA WAS FLYING BACK to Vienna, Geiger and Inspector Windisch prepared to interrogate her. How much did she know about Jack, and what would she be willing to tell them? One way of getting her to talk was to scare her: *We know you know something, and the only way to avoid big trouble for yourself is to tell us.* That sort of bluffing probably wouldn't work, though. In the past, girls had formed emotional attachments to Unterweger that exceeded their fear of the law.

Geiger believed the best he could do was show Bianca that he wasn't the bloody-minded cop her fiancé had made him out to be, but a decent man, just trying to do his job. If she could see that, she might begin to have doubts about Jack.

Arriving at the Vienna airport in a tight-fitting red cotton dress and a New York Yankees baseball cap, Bianca was put in an Interior Ministry limousine and shuttled to Lower Austrian police headquarters, where she met the man who'd become her fiancé's chief enemy. Ernst Geiger wasn't what she was expecting. He was young—four years younger than Jack—and handsome in a navy suit, tailored to his figure, which he'd recently slimmed down by training for the Vienna marathon. He had an open, friendly face with grayish-blue eyes, and she could tell by the way he looked at her that he thought she was cute (her suntan and little red dress helped).

She told the story, from meeting Jack at Take Five to getting arrested in Miami. Then the questioning began. They started off asking her if Jack had ever confessed any crimes to her. Absolutely not. Had she noticed anything suspicious about him, his behavior, possessions, or acquaintances?

She knew a few things that put him in a bad light, and though she didn't consider them evidence that he had murdered the women, she knew the police would consider them suspicious, and so she didn't mention them.

"You're not telling us everything," said Inspector Windisch.

"Yes, I am! I've told you everything."

"What about the car?" Geiger asked. "Do you know where he left it?"

"Just somewhere near the airport."

They broke for dinner at a nearby restaurant. Over Wiener schnitzel and a glass of wine, the atmosphere lightened. After dinner they drove to Vienna police headquarters, the Security Office, and Bianca was awed by the stateliness of it—the palace of executive authority going back to imperial times. After some more questioning in Geiger's office, they took her home to her mother's apartment.

Over the next three weeks, Bianca made frequent visits to Geiger's office. His secretary kept her door open, and she noticed that every time Bianca arrived, she first went into the ladies' room across the hall to freshen up. Just as Geiger was hoping to win information from her, she was hoping to win information from him about what he knew. He figured that Jack's attorney, Georg Zanger, was debriefing her.

Though Geiger believed she was acting as Jack's agent, he sensed that if he asked questions about simple facts, she might reflexively tell the truth. Hers was a peculiar situation. She wanted to help her fiancé evade prosecution, partly because she was attached to him and partly because she believed he was innocent. But if he were innocent, then there was no need to lie about facts. If she was concealing incriminating information about Jack, the only way to extract it from her was to loosen the emotional cords that bound her to him.

Geiger discussed the matter with Wladkowski. The examining magistrate sensed that Jack's Achilles heel was the fact that he'd two-timed Bianca with Elisabeth, so during his interrogation of Bianca, he explained to her that the other girl had stated that she'd had a sexual relationship with Jack from December 1991 till the time of Jack's flight in mid-February. In other words, he'd deceived both women, leading a double life.

On the phone with a friend, Bianca confessed that she was troubled by what Wladkowski told her. Her friend said that he was just trying to drive a wedge between her and Jack, which was true. During the first two months after Bianca returned from Miami and moved into Jack's apartment, it was the only time she expressed doubt about him on the phone. The police had tapped it and were listening to her conversations. Like the women on the outside whom Jack had known while he was sitting in Stein, Bianca was his primary helper. He called regularly from the Metropolitan Correctional Center in Miami for updates about what the police were asking her and other people he knew. He also needed money, and was hoping that she could share some of the wealth from her interviews. She couldn't help him there, as her mother had set up a trust for her income that she couldn't access until she became an adult (nineteen years old).

On one occasion he lost his cool. After chatting aimlessly, he suddenly thought of something important.

JACK: Hey, *Mausi* [little mouse], the leather jacket and that other stuff belongs to you; it all belongs to you, please.

BIANCA: They took your entire wardrobe.

JACK: Everything?

BIANCA: Yeah.

JACK: The leather jacket also?

BIANCA: The two white and the red leather jackets. I don't know why they took your things. They left mine.

JACK: [*Distressed*] Are they crazy? Maybe they're looking for traces, but they'll find nothing. Such stupidity!

BIANCA: You'll certainly get it back.

JACK: Yeah, otherwise I'll petition them to release it . . . [*Enraged*] Worst-case scenario, I get it back in the prison depot.

BIANCA: Greetings from Margit.

JACK: Pah!

Bianca also had interesting conversations with Margit Haas. Margit wasn't in love with him and she had a better sense of his character than Bianca, but she still believed in his innocence. One day she asked an astrologer to make a horoscope of his birthdate, August 16, 1950. She believed the astrologer had no way of knowing about her friendship with Jack, so she was shocked by what was written in the stars: "Sticks with old and tried patterns of behavior. Is given to ritualistic acts." Margit gave the horoscope to Bianca, who mentioned it during a phone conversation.

MARGIT: The horoscope is dangerous.

BIANCA: Why?

MARGIT: Because of the ritualistic shit.

BIANCA: I'm going to give it to Zanger.

MARGIT: Are you crazy?

Another woman named Frances Schoenberger occasionally called Bianca. From her accent they could tell she was a German, but they didn't know from where she was calling. Then she revealed that she was a *Stern* magazine correspondent who had met Jack the previous summer in Hollywood. *Stern*, she explained, wanted to do a big story about Jack and Bianca.

Who didn't? While the police regarded Jack Unterweger as the prime suspect in the largest murder investigation in Austrian history, everyone else, including his lawyer, regarded him as the protagonist in a story that could be sold for big money.

Bianca also spoke with the *profil* reporter Robert Buchacher. One day she told Jack, "Mr. Buchacher would like to provide you with an alibi. You were in Dornbirn on December 5, right?"

JACK: I don't know. I didn't make any notes of that time.

BIANCA: On December 6 you apparently told Leo Hafner at the ORF that you'd met a very dear person the evening before.

JACK: That was a nun in a convent in Lauterach [a town near Dornbirn].

Buchacher was trying to help Jack, but according to the nun, Jack visited her during the day on December 5, not that evening. She had started corresponding with him while he was in Stein, after she read one of his poems in a Catholic journal that depicted the poet's longing for freedom as he gazed through the bars of his window at a ship passing on the Danube.

Geiger knew from Bianca's phone conversations that she wasn't

close to freeing herself from Jack's spell. The media attention wasn't
helping her to see her fiancé clearly. However Jack had treated her while
they were together, her association with him was giving her the most attention she'd ever had. During the week following her return from Miami, the *Kronen Zeitung* put her up in a good hotel and did a weeklong
series on her "incurable love" for Jack. Every day on the front page was a
picture of her holding a photograph of him, or holding a telephone receiver as though she were talking with him in his cell. Above the images
were headlines such as JACK IS MY FATE! and captions like "Such tender
caressing hands could never strangle a woman."

Geiger wanted Bianca to help him find Jack's VW Passat, which he'd
abandoned "somewhere in Orly near the airport." The French police
were asking for more specific directions, and Geiger sensed that Bianca
might have a better idea of the car's whereabouts than she'd initially admitted. He wanted to find the VW because he figured Jack had picked
up the four Vienna prostitutes with it. It could contain hair and clothing
fibers, perhaps even flecks of blood.

"Are you sure Jack didn't mention where he left the car?" he asked
her one day.

"I think he said something about a junkyard near the airport."

Again Geiger marveled at Jack's resourcefulness. He'd understood the
police would search the car for trace evidence, and so he'd left it where it
would get scrapped. With his plane soon departing and no guarantee of
finding a taxi back to the airport, he'd managed to find a junkyard.

The car was found in the junkyard—not yet scrapped—and was
sent to Wiesbaden, Germany, for an interior search. It would be a few
weeks before Geiger heard the results.

Jack's attorney, Dr. Zanger, apparently understood the risk of Bianca
getting too friendly with the head of the Special Commission. One day
she told him that she and Geiger were going to the opera.

"Really, which opera?"

"He wants to see *Aïda*; I want to see *Carmen*."

Zanger told her to cancel.

CHAPTER 40

VOLUNTARY RETURN

NINETY DAYS. That's how much time the Special Commission had to make their case to a U.S. federal magistrate to extradite Jack. If they didn't succeed by the end of the period, he would walk. For two weeks they'd been working round the clock, evaluating everything they found in his apartment. Wladkowski was interrogating everyone with whom Jack had had contact since his parole—journalists, actors, writers, Justice Ministry officials, radio producers, cops, hookers, pimps, and, above all, women—dozens of them. His contacts with men were strictly business, something that struck Wladkowski and Geiger as strange. What did it say about him that he didn't have a single male friend?

A hunt was under way for all the cars he'd owned since his release. Each of the interiors would be searched for fibers, hair, and dried body fluids. The clothing found in his apartment was being analyzed for a possible match with fibers found on the body of the Bregenz prostitute Heidemarie Hammerer.

Using his receipts and a log he'd kept of long road trips, Inspectors Windisch and Etz had begun to reconstruct his movements during his nineteen months of freedom. A few of the receipts had obvious value for the investigation. One was from a filling station just south of Graz. The date, October 26, 1990, was the morning Brunhilde Masser disappeared from her corner in Graz. Then there was a receipt for a hotel room in the town of St. Veit on the Glan, in the state of Carinthia, for the night of October 25–26, 1990. Although he'd paid for the night, he hadn't checked in until the following day.

Another receipt was for work on his VW Passat on April 10, two days after the Vienna prostitute Silvia Zagler disappeared. The exhaust pipe had been repaired, as well as the passenger-side interior door handle. One could imagine Silvia Zagler, in a state of mortal panic, pulling so hard on the locked door handle that it broke.

The mechanic Mr. Koltay knew Jack as one of his bigger customers. He also remembered the repairs to the VW in April 1991.

"When he brought the car in for the exhaust, I noticed the broken door handle and I asked him if he wanted me to fix that, too. He said, 'That's nothing, and at least it keeps the bunnies from hopping out.'"

On February 28, the day after Jack was arrested in Miami, Fort Lauderdale attorney Joseph Slama got a call from a German journalist who asked him to represent Jack.

"I practice civil law," Slama explained. "I know little about criminal law."

"Mr. Unterweger just wants you to facilitate his return to Austria." The journalist had heard about Slama's practice through a contact in Munich, where the young lawyer had worked for three months during law school. Soon after he hung up with the German he got a call from a Viennese journalist who offered to pay him a couple of thousand dollars to help Mr. Unterweger.

The next day he went to the Metropolitan Correctional Center to meet his client. Slama was impressed by Jack's intelligence and intensity, as well as his English-language ability, which his journalist friends had underestimated. Also impressive was his hard-as-nails determination to return to Austria as soon as possible.

"All I want is for a lawyer to help me get home," he said.

"But you have the right to fight your extradition."

"I don't want to fight it."

"Are you sure you don't want counsel for this? I've got a buddy who is a real defender, and I think you should talk with him before you make any decisions."

"I don't need a defender. I just need someone to help me return to Austria."

Slama thought it was strange that he didn't want to contest his extradition, even though he claimed the Austrians wanted to prosecute him unjustly. Maybe there were advantages to going home and getting on with the proceedings, but there was no way for Jack to weigh them against the advantages of staying in the States. Only a proper defense attorney could help him make an informed decision. Slama repeated this counsel, but to no avail. Jack wanted to go home.

"All right," said the lawyer. "I'll see what I can do."

JACK UNTERWEGER WANTS TO RETURN was the headline in the Monday, March 2, 1992, edition of the Viennese daily *Der Standard*.

> *The writer has, against the advice of his lawyers Zanger and Josef Wegrostek, who regard the case against him for the seven prostitute murders as too thin for an extradition, resolved to take this step.*
> *Unterweger doesn't want to wait for the decision on his extradition. He has already established contact with the American lawyer Joseph Slama, who is on hand to coordinate Unterweger's return home with Vienna police headquarters . . .*
> *Georg Zanger explained his client's sudden change of mind.*
> *"Jack is sitting in the Metropolitan Correctional Center in Miami. That is a maximum security prison. He has been brought into a death cell. Exactly vis-à-vis his cell is the room for carrying out the death penalty, and he can see the electric chair. Although he is, at the moment, psychologically strong, the situation is very stressful."*

There wasn't an electric chair facing Jack's cell. "Maybe he was looking at the barber's chair," a warden joked to a journalist who visited the following week. The truth was that the Metropolitan Correctional Facility was a federal prison, softer than a state prison. It had its share of tough guys; the deposed Panamanian dictator Manuel Noriega, who sat in a neighboring cell, wasn't a gentle sort, but neither "Pineapple Face" nor any of the other inmates threatened Jack's safety.

The day after *Der Standard* reported Jack's desire to return home, it followed up with a report headlined UNTERWEGER: HOPE FOR A VOLUN-

TARY RETURN. Its message: the Austrian authorities were going to have a hell of a time extraditing Jack, and were therefore hoping he would return to Austria voluntarily. Were Unterweger to consent to his return, "all the restrictions that apply to the process of extradition would fall away."

> For an extradition, all the reasons for suspicion and all circumstantial evidence against Unterweger must be listed . . .
>
> Were such a process to be spared by his voluntary return . . . Unterweger could be questioned before he is presented with all the evidence against him . . .
>
> "We will be under heavy pressure for the next months," admitted Winfried Enge, the vice president of the [Graz] court. "Within the next ninety days we must lay solid incriminating material on the table . . . The Unterweger arrest warrant wasn't based on physical evidence, something we are working feverishly to obtain. At the moment we have only circumstantial evidence."

The cards were on the table. At the beginning of March 1992, the Austrians still had no evidence, only a basket of clues. While Vienna's journalists were comparing extradition with voluntary return, none commented on how odd it was that the suspect himself wasn't interested in weighing his options. Within twenty-four hours of his arrest he'd resolved to return to Austria. On March 2, he petitioned the U.S. Federal Court in Miami "to institute my immediate deportation."

Someone paying close attention might have sensed an urgency underlying Jack's resolve to go home—an urgency that overrode considerations of legal strategy.

CHAPTER 41

A GOOD LEAD

THREE DAYS LATER, on March 5, 1992, Detective Fred Miller of the LAPD got a message to call Linda Bryant at the Department of Justice. She had just received a report from Interpol Washington that the U.S. Marshals office in Miami had arrested one Jack Unterweger, wanted in Austria for the strangulation murder of seven prostitutes. According to the Austrian police, the suspect had been in Los Angeles from June 11 to July 16, 1991. In a search of his apartment in Vienna, they'd found photographs of him in L.A., as well as LAPD business cards, which alarmed them because they believed that part of his m.o. was to ride along with police officers as a reporter. The Austrians wanted to know if the LAPD had any unsolved cases of prostitute murder, modus ligature strangulation, from the period during which Unterweger was visiting.

Miller and his partner, James Harper, drove to LAPD Central Facilities, introduced themselves to the adjutant on duty, Sergeant Steve Staples, and asked to see the driving logs from June 11 to July 16, 1991. Staples gave them the logs, but because he no longer went on patrol, he didn't think to give them his own. They took the files into an adjoining room, and after a while he heard their voices grow testy.

"What's going on, Fred?" he asked.

"Your patrol sergeants aren't keeping proper records," Miller said.

"Whenever I had a ride-along I recorded it," he said, remembering his own log. He fetched it and opened it on the table, and one of the entries leaped off the page: *June 25, 1991, 11:00 to 14:30 hours. Austrian journalist Jack Unterweger.* Yes, Staples recalled the ride-along. Miller and Harper noted his statement and, without saying a word about what they were doing, packed their briefcases and left.

Miller figured the best way to learn about the journalist Jack Unterweger was to speak directly with the Austrians. Interpol Washington gave him a number in Vienna, and he initially spoke with Inspector Joseph Ridinger of the Lower Austrian police, who recounted the unusual murder series in Austria and the equally unusual suspect. Miller listened to the bizarre story, jotting an occasional note.

"I've got just one question," he said.

"Yes?"

"Are you *sure* this guy was here last summer?"

"His apartment was full of souvenirs from L.A., as well as a credit card statement with charges from the trip."

Miller noted the vendors and dates and hit the street.

The first was at Marathon Rent-a-Car, whose records showed Jack had rented a blue Toyota Corolla on June 11, 1991, at 17:24. He returned the car on June 20, 1991, at 10:16 with a broken windshield on the passenger side. Miller recognized the date. Funny how a case could be cold for months and then, with one solid lead, fall into place. On the damage report Jack stated that a rock had struck the windshield. Was it really a stone strike? Or was it Shannon Exley's head hitting the passenger-side glass as she thrashed for dear life?

On the rental agreement Jack stated his address in Los Angeles as the Hotel Cecil on Main Street, near the intersection of Seventh, just a few blocks from where Exley and Rodriguez had disappeared. The Cecil's records showed that he'd checked in on June 11 and out on July 2—three days after the second victim, Irene Rodriguez, disappeared from Seventh and Gladys, and one day before Sherri Long disappeared from Hollywood.

Ronnie Lancaster at the Sheriff's Department was amazed as he listened to the story. And then Miller showed him the pictures of Jack in L.A. which had just arrived by overnight air.

"Good Lord," said Lancaster, bursting into laughter. "So we've got a cowboy on our hands."

"Yeah, we can't wait to meet him," said Miller. "We're gonna fly out to Miami for a chat, but first we want to find out as much as we can about his stay in L.A. Right now we're trying to figure out where he went after he checked out of the Cecil on July 2."

"Well, you know he went to Hollywood," said Lancaster.

"That's what we're thinking."

"I'll nose around on Sunset and see if I can find him on a register."

The Sunset Orange wasn't the first cheap motel that Lancaster visited on Hollywood's prostitute promenade, but it wasn't far down his list. Its register showed that Jack had checked in on July 2 and out on July 9. He paid with cash.

Miller preferred that Jack not be given days to prepare for his interrogation in Miami, but the suspect was in regular contact with people in Austria, and on March 10, the Graz *Kleine Zeitung* broke the story of their investigation in L.A.

"He'll be expecting you," said Geiger on the phone. "We think he's more afraid of California justice than of ours. Especially your gas chamber."

CHAPTER 42

JACK'S DEFENSE

ON THE SAME DAY Detective Miller began investigating Jack's activities in L.A., Jack's girlfriend Elisabeth in Vienna received the defense document he'd composed in Miami and mailed to her shortly before he was arrested. She handed the package, which contained several photocopies, over to the police. Enclosed were instructions to distribute the document to the Graz court, police headquarters, various newspapers and magazines, the President of Austria, the Interior and Justice ministers, the mayor of Vienna, various writers and journalists, and the head of the Austrian Freedom Party, Jörg Haider. Though Haider's party was making political hay out of the Unterweger story as yet another example of Socialist Party corruption, Jack had met him one evening at the Reiss Bar and had apparently had an engaging conversation with the politician.

Jack prefaced the document, which the investigators began referring to as his "Miami Defense," with an announcement that he was suing several Austrian and German newspapers for destroying his reputation and credit.

In the foreword, he stated that the entire affair had begun with a vengeful retired inspector from Salzburg. During an interrogation in Stein prison in 1983: "Mr. Schenner reacted aggressively and angrily when he heard from a warden that I'd written a book, as he believed that a convict should spend his days carrying stones. It came to an unfriendly verbal exchange, at which point he told me he would see to it that I never saw freedom again." Schenner, he claimed, had started the witch hunt, which had been taken up by policemen in Graz and Vienna, even though "there was no, is no, and can never be any evidence."

Regarding the murder of the Graz prostitute Brunhilde Masser, last seen around 12:15 a.m. on October 26, 1990, he wrote two pages about his activities as a theater director, and then: "On the nights of the 26th and 27th of October, I had a room in the Hotel Stern [in the town of St. Veit]. On October 27 I met a former schoolmate who works for the union in St. Veit, and who is in charge of renting the conference room of the Chamber of Commerce. On the same afternoon I met Mr. Glawischnig at Town Hall, and then went to the Mayor's Office." The highway to St. Veit, a town located about four hours southwest of Vienna, passes by Graz, where Brunhilde was last seen on her corner just after midnight on the morning of October 26. The critical question was what Jack did during the night of October 25–26, but he didn't answer it in his defense.

Regarding the murder of the Graz prostitute Elfriede Schrempf on March 7, 1991, he began with a two-page account of rehearsing and promoting his "AIDS piece" (he didn't refer to it by its title, *Scream of Fear*) and visiting various women on the night of March 5. Finally he came to the day of March 6.

*That morning, at 8:30, I visited my young girlfriend [Katharina],
who on this day, March 6, 1991, skipped school. I remained with her
until 11:00 a.m., but because she was having her period, it could go
no further than petting. At midday I met a woman for lunch, and
then drove back to Graz, where I arrived at 4:00 p.m. . . .*

*I acknowledge that the woman disappeared on March 7, and we
were, as I described above, in Graz on the 5th and 6th of March to
perform, and I was on the night of the 5th and 6th of March with girlfriends in Vienna, and on the morning of March 6th with [Katha-
rina], who skipped school on March 6th. Sexually fulfilled, sleepy,
but fully satisfied with my life, feeling happy—in this moment I am
alleged by the police to have driven back to Graz to . . . Insane!*

In his interrogation with the Graz inspector Brandstätter in January,
he stated that he'd been with [Katharina] on the afternoon of March 7.
A month later, in his "Miami Defense," he claimed he met Katharina the
morning of the sixth. Still nothing about his reading near Graz on the
critical night of March 7.

The closest he came to offering an alibi was for "one of the days on
which a prostitute in Vienna disappeared. On this day I was with Martina
(last name forgotten) in a late showing at the cinema, and afterward we
went to the Café Florianihof (where I went almost daily, as it is next to my
apartment), where she met her boyfriend (the owner). I had a drink and
purchased a set of winter tires from Robert (the co-owner). Afterward I
took my German shepherd for a walk in the park and went home."

An investigator went to Café Florianihof to talk with Martina. She
remembered the cinema evening with Jack because the film *The Silence
of the Lambs* had made a vivid impression on her. Jack loved the movie;
it was the fourth time he'd seen it. Looking at her calendar for the
months of April and May 1991, she saw the entry "17:00 cinema" on the
day of Sunday, April 28. As she recalled, 17:00 (5:00 p.m.) was when she
met Jack near the cinema, at Café Diglas. The movie started a bit later.
According to the schedule at the Atelier cinema, the early-evening feature had begun at 6:15 p.m. and ended at 8:30. After the movie Martina
had gone with Jack to Café Florianihof, where he'd had a drink and

bought tires from Robert, who was able to establish from his own records that he'd sold the tires (from his wrecked car) on that Sunday.

Geiger pondered the possible alibi. In Jack's statement to Chief Edelbacher in October 1991, he hadn't mentioned his date with Martina "on the night one of the Vienna prostitutes disappeared." Four months later, in his Miami Defense, he explained that in October 1991 he'd simply forgotten about the evening at the cinema and café, but if that was true, why did he remember the evening months later, while on the lam in Miami?

Adding to the implausibility of Jack's statement was the fact that he learned he was under suspicion for the prostitute murders at the beginning of September, when he read it in the *Kurier*. In other words, in the fall of 1991 Jack had had over six weeks to think about his whereabouts and to consult his records of the previous April and May.

Geiger believed that Jack had never forgotten what he'd done on the night of April 28, 1991—that is, watched the early feature of *The Silence of the Lambs* with Martina, had a drink, bought some tires at Café Florianihof, and then murdered Regina Prem. The reason he hadn't initially offered his date with Martina as an alibi was because it wasn't one. His time with her at the cinema and café ended before 11:30 p.m., when Regina Prem was last seen walking out of the Hotel Rudolfshöhe.

But if the cinema evening with Martina wasn't an alibi, why did Jack offer it in February 1992? Geiger figured it was the same gamble he'd made in his January 1992 interrogation with Inspector Brandstätter, when he'd offered Katharina as his alibi for the night of March 7, 1991. After the passage of so many months, he figured the women would remember being with him *on* or *around* the date in question, but wouldn't remember the specific times. Unfortunately for Jack, Katharina and Martina had saved their calendars from the previous year.

Following the main body of the defense, dated Saturday, February 22, was an appendix dated Tuesday, February 25, 1992. The Monday, February 24, *profil* magazine report about Jack's flight from arrest apparently prompted him to add to his defense. In the appendix he listed his complaints against the police for their improper methods of investigating him. Most notable was the complaint:

The police know about the women with whom I've had intimate contact (no wonder, with my diary), and they have given these women the following treatment:

1. Taken jewelry from them that I gave them as gifts with the remark that it could have come from victims! This is crazy, as one has long known that this jewelry could not have come from one of the victims . . .

Geiger wondered *who* had long known that the jewelry could not have come from the victims. That all of the victims had been found with their jewelry on their bodies had never been disclosed to the press.

To Geiger, Jack's hastily composed Miami Defense was a blunder that contrasted with the skill of his live ORF interview, in which he'd made his "police under pressure" assertion. Addressing the defense to the President and to the Justice and Interior ministers wasn't, like his ORF interview, bold in a clever way, but reckless and presumptuous. If the document had been distributed, Geiger thought it comical to imagine the President and ministers reading about Jack's adventures driving all over the country, performing his state-subsidized plays in church cloisters and chambers of commerce, bedding married women, and having a morning petting session with a menstruating schoolgirl while she ditched class.

On the other hand, it wasn't the first time that Jack had submitted a written defense to high-ranking officials. When he wrote his Miami Defense, he was merely taking a course of action that had worked before.

CHAPTER 43

NOT A WORD ABOUT THE CRIME

IT HAD WORKED in the spring of 1983, during Inspector Schenner's renewed investigation of the Marica Horvath murder. At exactly that time, Jack was preparing to give his first reading at Stein prison before an audience of journalists, writers, and government officials. He knew that when they saw him—so small and boyish-looking—reading from his stories, they would think, Why, he's not a killer! He's just a wounded boy, abandoned by his mother, and now he's found his calling in literature.

On March 24, the prison director said that he would permit Jack to give a reading in the culture hall; members of the press could attend, as well as thirty-five to forty people connected with the Vienna Art Association. The following day, Jack wrote a letter to President Kirchschläger, telling him the good news. Going into Easter weekend, everything looked great. On Thursday, March 31, he received a package of Easter goodies from the journalists Dorothea Winkler and Marga Frank.

And then, the next day, Good Friday—disaster. Inspector Schenner of the Salzburg police showed up to talk about the murder of Marica Horvath exactly ten years earlier. At the moment Jack's train was pulling out of the station, Schenner threatened to derail it.

Not if Jack could do something about it. His diary from the time reveals how he went about evading prosecution for the murder of Marica Horvath. Most notably, he drafted his own eight-page version of the story and sent it to his old friend Dr. Doleisch, the former Justice Ministry Director of Penal Executions. Though Doleisch was retired, he still maintained contact with a senior official in his former section at the ministry. Six days after Schenner's visit, Jack noted that he had a conversation with the official, who arrived at Stein bearing good news: both Justice Minister Broda and President Kirchschläger had approved his reading. Jack took the opportunity to tell the official *his* version of Inspector Schenner's investigation.

On April 13, the Justice Ministry approved the reading, and the next day Jack noted in his diary that he had a conversation with the same Justice Ministry official who'd visited him the week before. The official told Jack that Dr. Doleisch had received Jack's letter of April 2 regarding his troubles with the Salzburg police, was concerned, and had visited the official to discuss the matter.

Three months later, on July 14, Jack wrote in his diary: "BMfJ. Verlangt: Kein Wort über die Tat [Federal Ministry of Justice Demands:

Not a Word about the Crime]." Though the diary entry does not specify of whom exactly the Justice Ministry demanded silence about the crime, it is notable that Jack never made another entry pertaining to his troubles with the Salzburg police. The diary for the rest of the year is filled with gleeful entries about his triumphant reading at Stein and other publishing successes, but nothing about the threat of prosecution that had weighed on him in the spring and early summer.

If he had been prosecuted and convicted for murdering Marica Horvath, it would have prevented his parole in 1990, and it probably would have kept him in prison for the rest of his life. The assertion that under Austrian law he could be given only one life sentence was a juridical formality. The conviction would have gone on his record and showed that he was a serial killer of women.

And so Jack learned that, by writing his stories—his version of reality—and submitting them to influential people, he could get away with murder.

CHAPTER 44

A CLEVER MEDIA LAWYER

IN THE MARCH 2, 1992, edition of *profil*, Georg Zanger stated that the Austrian authorities couldn't extradite Jack because they had no evidence, and because the press had prejudiced the people against him, making a fair trial in Austria impossible. The Austrian media, he explained, had completely negated Jack's right to due process.

Zanger believed in the power of the media to have a negative and positive effect on the legal process. "A clever media lawyer can be more effective than a defense attorney," he told a reporter on another occasion. After representing Jack at his parole hearing in 1990, Zanger continued giving the ex-con author counsel, and in press coverage of Jack's readings, he was referred to as "Unterweger's manager." Yet the more time Jack spent in freedom, the less Zanger managed his affairs as a writer and the more he became his defense attorney, representing him in proceedings for drunk driving and for threatening another driver. It was notable that Jack didn't consult him when he became aware he was under suspicion for murder. When he called the reporter Peter Grolig and announced he was going to shoot himself with a pump gun, Grolig said, "But you have a lawyer who has helped you before."

"He cost me a fortune and I don't have any more money."

Once word got out that Jack couldn't afford his lawyer, some of his fans began a collection, but it wasn't necessary. Zanger agreed to defend him in return for the film rights to his life story. Jack Unterweger, the ex-con dandy poet, accused of being a serial murderer, on the run with his eighteen-year-old girlfriend, was the stuff of Hollywood.

For much of his adult life, Zanger had been a member of the Austrian Communist Party and counselor for its newspaper, *The People's Page*. He also defended radical leftists, including violent Opera Ball demonstrators. Every year when the Vienna State Opera hosts an extravagant ball, hundreds of demonstrators assemble outside to protest the event, which they consider a symbol of capitalist greed, and some get arrested for throwing stones and the occasional Molotov cocktail.

Though Zanger continued representing radical leftists, he left the Communist Party before the collapse of the Soviet Union and proclaimed his adherence to the free-market economy. This was in keeping with his public image. At a time when yuppies were rare in Vienna, Zanger, with his Jaguar convertible, designer suits and eyeglasses, seemed to embody the idea. On the night of February 27, 1992, when Jack was arrested in Miami, Zanger was at the Opera Ball, reveling in the extravaganza while some of his clients protested it outside.

Zanger told *profil* that he was going to hire a private detective "to find the real murderer." Otherwise, he explained, "Unterweger will be convicted, even without evidence." After the news broke that Jack was being investigated for murder in Los Angeles, a report appeared in *Kurier* featuring an image of the American actor Stacy Keach in the television role of Mike Hammer. Dr. Zanger had "hired his own Mike Hammer, a mustached American private investigator named Nestor T.," to conduct an independent investigation of the Los Angeles murders.

"We'll make sure that Jack's rights are observed, and we'll persuade him not to return to Austria voluntarily," explained Mr. T.

Though the press never mentioned it, Zanger was also representing Bianca in discussions with a man named Nestor Tabares, who claimed to be a movie agent with contacts in Hollywood. Was "Nestor Tabares, Motion Picture Agent," the same as "Nestor T., Private Investigator"?

CHAPTER 45

A CRAZY FEELING OF TRIUMPH

IN MARCH, Geiger concluded his study of Jack's literature. He'd begun with *Purgatory*, and the further he got into the story, the more he noticed a hole at the heart of it. While Dante vividly described the sins of those in purgatory, Jack gave no account of his crime. *Purgatory* ends in 1971, when Jack is imprisoned for stealing a car—a jarring inconsistency with the fact that he received his life sentence for murdering a girl in 1974, not for stealing a car in 1971.

And while Dante depicted the punishments of purgatory as the means to redemption, Jack described his punishment as senseless. And so Geiger wondered what had caused him to change. The key to the story was missing.

After reading *Purgatory* he watched the film adaptation of the novel, directed by Willi Hengstler. Originally released in 1988 to excellent reviews in Austria, the film was shown again at the 1992 Berlinale Film Festival, which coincided with Jack's flight from justice. The Admiral cinema in Vienna was also giving it another showing (likewise a second edition of the novel was being printed).

Though Geiger didn't know it, Hengstler had also noticed the hole in the story. After he'd started working on the film, he learned the reality of Jack's crime—the reality the author had avoided mentioning. In a letter to Alfred Kolleritsch, who first published the story in the magazine *Manuskripte*, Jack wrote: "Please [publish] nothing about the killing (because of the emotions and the relatives) and the life sentence." He told Hengstler the same. The crime couldn't be depicted, for if it was it would defeat the purpose for which he'd written the book.

In co-writing the script, Jack became angry with its direction, because Hengstler refused to follow his prescriptions for purifying and aggrandizing the story's "hero." Soon Hengstler began to dread opening Jack's scolding letters from Stein prison. The closer he came to completing the movie, the more he realized that its protagonist—a convicted murderer "fighting for his freedom," as Jack put it in a letter—was suffering from a severe case of narcissism. On a visit to Stein, Hengstler asked the prison director, Dr. Schreiner, for his prognosis.

"Jack hasn't become a better man," Schreiner explained. "If he were released, he might mistreat a girl, but he's learned so much that he would never again commit a major offense, because he understands it wouldn't be worth the risk of going back to prison."

The film director found the words of the prison director reassuring.

After watching the film, Geiger watched a video of Jack's talk at the 1988 Wels Film Festival on the occasion of *Purgatory*'s premiere, which Jack was allowed to attend with a light security escort. Wearing a seventies-cut snow-white suit with black shoes, he mounted the stage in front of an audience of cheering fans. Taking his seat between the film director Hengstler and the Stein prison director Schreiner, he talked about how writing the book had forced him to analyze his childhood experiences and his destructive feelings toward his mother, enabling him to overcome the pressures they exerted on his psyche.

Jack had learned to present his transformation in Freudian terms from conversations with the renowned psychoanalyst Ernst Federn, who occasionally visited him at Stein. A concentration-camp survivor, Federn emigrated to America after the liberation of Buchenwald, but returned to his native Austria in 1972 on the invitation of Justice Minister Broda, who believed that his psychoanalytical insight could assist in formulating penal reforms.

After Jack's talk at the film festival, someone in the audience spoiled the cozy atmosphere by asking a tough question. Apparently confused about the grounds for Jack's life sentence, he asked, "With your book and now with the film you have found a kind of success. But can a rapist ever find true success?" Jack thought about it for a second and leaned forward to the microphone.

"Your question is based upon an error. I have never raped anyone. I have far too much respect for women." In an instant he'd calculated that (1) No one in the room other than Dr. Schreiner knew his criminal record, and (2) Schreiner wasn't going to spoil the occasion by calling his lie.

Jack had done a good job of concealing the reality of his past, and he was skilled at telling the arts and literature crowd what they wanted to hear, but Geiger still didn't understand why many distinguished intellectuals had been so taken by him. Shortly after Jack fled the country, two of the most prominent journalists in the country, Günther Nenning and Peter Huemer, submitted essays to *profil* magazine, explaining their involvement in the campaign for his parole.

Nenning was contrite and sharply critical of the *Literarniks* (literary intellectuals) and *Promis* (prominent persons) like himself who had sprung Jack from prison without first getting to know him. "I fear he didn't really interest us. We followed the healthy principle: Is there something to sign for a good cause—and isn't it a good cause to obtain freedom for a prisoner?—then sign it. Noble is the *Promi*, helpful and good."

Nenning also pointed out the irresponsibility of bestowing glory upon a man for whom it was destined to be taken away. "We *Literarniks* set him up. We quickly transported him from nothing to glory, and maybe the return ticket was already there." Most provocatively, Nenning pointed out that the *Literarniks* weren't attracted to Jack because they believed he'd been reformed. On the contrary: "The darkness of such a guy, that turned the intellectuals on . . . Perhaps he isn't gifted, certainly not strong, but seductive, infectious."

A week later, Peter Huemer protested Nenning's essay. He claimed he *had* gotten to know Jack through a number of conversations, a long correspondence, and a one-hour radio interview in Stein in 1989.

> . . . *But naturally we must ask ourselves if those who believe in the alterability of conditions and humans are not in danger of falling into a certain social romanticism in which wish becomes the father of thought: We long for people who overcome their sad milieu and lack of opportunity, and in this state of longing we are naturally vulnerable to being manipulated* . . .
>
> *I don't know if this applies to Unterweger, if he has deceived us all . . . Whoever wants to bring something against Unterweger must only peruse his own books, and he will find plenty of passages. To those I can add a few more from my radio conversation with him in his cell* . . .

Geiger had already listened to a recording of Huemer's radio conversation with Jack, recorded in Stein prison in 1989:

HUEMER: From the experiences of your childhood arose a second leitmotiv of your life, next to your search for your mother, namely, the constant desire for revenge . . . Am I to understand that this hatred and this desire for revenge is, so to speak, a collective condition that also seizes a child?

UNTERWEGER: It is a collective condition that also seizes children, because it is always everywhere in society . . . Many put up with it, perhaps complain. Then there are individuals who are seized by it . . . and ultimately explode.

HUEMER: That is what you describe in your second novel, *Va Banque*, as aggression, rage, impotence, and omnipotence.

UNTERWEGER: Correct. Because in the moment in which you spread fear and see another tremble with terror, you get a crazy feeling of triumph, even though you know you've done something bestial.

HUEMER: A feeling of triumph?

UNTERWEGER: Yes, because you observe how you torment the other, how the other must serve you and suffer, and you can't hold yourself back, because you don't have the mental power, even though you see your hand striking the other. But you can't hold yourself back, because you haven't found the channel. Only later in analysis was I able to work on it and become aware of it. In mental images I relived it and asked myself why I couldn't, at that moment, hold myself back. The reason is rooted in the feeling: now I will show them that we will not always serve them, and I will not let myself be constantly trampled upon by them . . .

Jack suggested that his aggression had stemmed from the broad resentment of the lower class—that his violence had been a form of striking back at the privileged. And yet, he'd never taken his violent revenge on men who held property and power, only on defenseless girls.

Geiger concluded his study of Jack's literature with his last novel, *Dungeon*, an account of his adventures following his release from the Wels jail in January 1973. On the road with his girlfriend Manu they head south into Italy. In Rome they run out of money, so (unknown to Manu) Jack poses as a male prostitute to rob a customer. A Mercedes with Munich plates pulls up, and the middle-aged driver takes him to an unlit road, at which point Jack holds a knife to his throat.

> *"What . . . what are you doing?"*
> *"Shut your mouth!"*
> *"You'll get a few years in prison for this."*
> *I laughed loud and shrill. "If they catch me! . . . Roll over onto your belly!" I tied his hands behind his back with shoelaces . . .*
> *I drove farther down the Via Casalina, until no more houses*

were visible. There was nothing around. Darkness. On a meadow obscured by bushes, I stopped the car.

"End Station!" I got out, went around the car, opened the passenger door, and jerked him out into the cool evening air. He wanted to defend himself, tried to spread his legs, but was defeated by his bound feet and hands. His cries brought my rage to a boil . . . I ripped off his pants and strewed them, like the other pieces of his clothing, in the nearby bushes. Out of me broke forth the hateful cynicism. I spat on him and kicked him, all the while cursing him with my tirades of hate.

My body felt agitated, as though filled with ants. I wanted to say so much to him, but had to suppress it so as not to betray myself. I went to work on him without seeing him. He was only an object. In an image of glaring sharpness, I observed my movements in slow motion. The swift blows of my fists were accompanied by shrill cries, and I couldn't calm myself. I heard him, but I couldn't understand what he was saying. Almost too late I sensed the pressure of my full bladder and the first wetness seeped into my pants. With the rest I played like a dog and used his naked body like a tree trunk.

Geiger was fascinated. *Dungeon* appeared in bookstores in November 1990, a couple of weeks after Jack murdered Brunhilde Masser in Graz. A serial killer gets paroled, starts murdering women again a few months later, and at the same time publishes a book with a description of his modus operandi. Posing as a street prostitute and attacking a male victim was a mirror image of the reality. The "wetness" that seeped into his pants was the ejaculation he experienced at the climax of his sadistic arousal.

CHAPTER 46

OBSESSION

I'VE LOST MY HUSBAND to a killer, Eva Geiger thought. Since the Unterweger investigation had intensified a few months earlier (in January 1992), he'd spent almost every waking hour at the office. When he came home late, she could tell by his distant expression that he was still thinking about the case. He didn't speak much, but when he did, it was about Jack Unterweger. When he wasn't reading files on him, he read the suspect's own books and plays. The only time he'd gone to the movies was to watch an adaptation of Jack's book. When he watched videos, they were recordings of Jack's interviews.

He often tossed and turned at night, thinking about Jack, and he got up every day at 5:00 a.m. to go for his morning run, during which he meditated about the same. No time for breakfast with her; he'd grab a strudel on the way to the office. When he did make it home for dinner, his pager often went off at the table—someone from headquarters with an update on . . .

He brought files home, some of them with hideous crime-scene photos, and she'd scolded him a few times for walking off and leaving them on the table while their eight-year-old daughter Katja was in the house (a well-founded fear; Katja and a couple of her friends had perused them).

Sometimes she felt sorry for him, like when journalists wrote reports favoring Jack. "Why do they write what he says without checking the facts?" he would ask, or "Why are they lying?" She didn't know, but on the other hand, why did Ernst take it so personally? He knew going into the investigation that Jack had supporters. She hoped her husband would put the evil man away forever, but how long was it going to take?

"Possibly another year," he said. Another year of living with a man obsessed with a killer—she didn't know if she could take it.

Before Jack they'd had a happy marriage, and Ernst had been interested in many things—history, literature, the theater. For their first date he'd taken her to the Burg Theater to watch Schiller's *Don Carlos*, and afterward in the café he'd talked about everything under the sun. She had inspired him.

He'd also been an entertaining host, and their friends had enjoyed coming over for dinner. Now they stayed away, unable to stand another evening of Jack Unterweger. Sometimes she thought it would have been easier if she'd lost her husband to another woman. At least that would have been normal.

CHAPTER 47

YOU DON'T HAVE ANY EVIDENCE

ON MARCH 12, 1992, Detectives Miller and Harper flew from Los Angeles to Miami to interrogate Jack. On the plane they reviewed everything they knew about the suspect. The Austrians had emphasized his cleverness and his lifetime of experience dealing with police. Miller knew not to underestimate him. They were met at the airport by Detective Dieter Thurmann of the Miami-Dade Police. A German émigré, bilingual, he served as a liaison between the American and Austrian investigators.

First they reviewed Jack's file at the U.S. Marshals office and then went to the state attorney's office to draft an affidavit for a search warrant for taking blood and hair samples. At the scene of the Irene Rodriguez murder, hair fibers were found stuck to the bumper of the trailer under which her body had been dragged. Someone had bumped his head, and the location of the hairs, near where Rodriguez's body was found, suggested it might have been her killer. Jack's blood could be compared with the sexual assault kits from Rodriguez and Exley.

The next day they obtained the warrant and proceeded to the Metropolitan Correctional Center. Jack was asked if he was willing to talk to officers from the LAPD. He consented, and at 6:00 p.m., they were led into the visitors' area.

They saw him sitting at a table, waiting for them. The old air-conditioning unit couldn't keep up with the heat and humidity, and the room was stuffy as hell. A soda machine stood next to the wall. Miller bought a Coke, walked over to where Jack was sitting, opened it, and set it down on the table in front of him.

"Have a Coke, it'll keep you cool," he said.

"Thanks," said Jack, grinning like a kid. Such a little guy, Miller thought. Did this squirt really do that to those women?

"I'm Fred Miller with the Los Angeles Police Department, this is my partner James Harper, and this is Detective Thurmann with the Miami-Dade police."

Jack rose to shake Miller's hand. "Nice to meet you, I'm Jack Unterweger," he said warmly.

"First I'm going to read you your rights," said Miller. After he recited the Miranda warning, Thurmann began to say it in German, but Jack waved at him to stop.

"I understood," he said.

"Your English is good," said Miller.

"I've been practicing it here in Miami."

"Well, tell me if you don't understand something and we'll have Detective Thurmann say it in German."

"Okay."

Harper positioned himself to watch Jack's reactions while Miller spoke.

"Jack, I know you want to go home and take your chances with your own justice system, but we're not going to let you do that. We're going to take you with us back to California and put you on trial for murdering our girls, and in California we have the death penalty."

Harper watched Jack's face. Cool. The only thing that indicated tension was his ramrod-straight posture, his head cocked forward.

"I'm going to ask you some questions about your time in Los Angeles," Miller continued. "If you are as innocent as you say you are, then you have no reason to lie to me. Just answer my questions honestly. If you lie, I promise you I will find out."

"All right," said Jack. "What do you want to know?"

"I want to know the purpose of your trip to L.A., where you stayed, who you met, what you were doing. And more than anything, I want to know why you were wearing that godawful outfit."

Jack thought for a moment, and then grinned. "You didn't like my cowboy outfit?"

"Not at all. I'm from Texas and I don't wear that shit."

Jack laughed. "I'm sorry to hear that. I paid a lot for it." He sat back in his chair, relaxing. *That's it, let your guard down a little.*

"Are you really from Texas?" he asked excitedly.

"Yes."

"Where in Texas?"

"San Antonio?"

"Did you ever ride a horse?" Something about the way he asked the question—the childlike enthusiasm and the funny accent—tickled Miller. He began to laugh and couldn't stop. It infected Harper and Thurmann, and then Jack began to laugh as well. He said something to Thurmann in German, which made him laugh even harder.

"I've ridden a few horses," Miller said, still laughing. "But that's not what we're here to talk about. Tell me about your trip to L.A."

"I went to L.A. to write stories on prostitutes and homeless people. I entered the United States through the Los Angeles airport on June 11, 1991 . . ." He gave a thorough statement of his activities in L.A., and Miller was impressed by the preciseness of his memory. On the other hand, he'd had at least three days to think about everything the police would figure out, and telling the truth about it gave the impression of honesty.

It was notable how he repeatedly mentioned that he'd sought out and interviewed hookers. On his ride-along with Sergeant Staples, he'd

mentioned nothing about his interest in them. Though Miller didn't realize it, a couple of months earlier, Jack had been caught lying about his
contact with hookers in his interview with Inspector Brandstätter. From
that experience he'd learned that it was a mistake to deny his contact
with prostitutes. The better strategy was to emphasize that he'd had
plenty of contact with them for work and sex, but not for killing. In every
encounter with a cop he learned something.

"While I was in L.A., I dated the receptionist at the Hotel Cecil, a
girl named Carolina. I also dated three prostitutes, one white, the other
two Latina. I left L.A. on July 16, 1991. Carolina came to Austria a few
weeks later to visit me. I killed no one in Los Angeles."

Miller wasn't surprised that Jack volunteered having "dated" three
prostitutes in L.A. In his electronic address book he'd recorded his sexual encounters, including: "Three black women in L.A." He knew the
police had found the address book, though it appeared he'd forgotten
having described the women as "black."

"I'm curious about the three prostitutes you dated," said Miller, not
bothering to correct Jack's inaccurate use of the American word. "How
did you meet them?"

"They climbed up the fire escape and knocked on my window."

"So they came to you."

"Yes."

"Are you that good?"

The smart-ass question puzzled Jack. He thought about it, evaluating the English words, trying to figure out if it was a trap. Then he
grinned.

"You mean, am I that good in bed? Maybe I am, but what these girls
wanted was drugs. Sex was just their way of getting them."

"And did you have sex with them?"

"Not—" He turned to Detective Thurmann: "*Wie sagt man Ge-
schlechtsverkehr?*"

"Sexual intercourse," said Thurmann.

"Yeah, not sexual intercourse. They gave me a blow job."

"I see," said Miller. "The other thing I'm curious about is that broken
windshield on your rental car. How did that happen?"

"I was driving behind a truck on Sixth Street and a rock flew into it."

"On Sixth Street?"

"That is what I remember." They continued going over the details of Jack's trip, and then he said something that struck both Miller and Harper as strange: "I am happy to answer your questions. But be honest, you don't have any evidence against me. What is the point of this?"

"The point is to bring you to justice if you are guilty, and to clear you if you are innocent," said Miller.

At the end of the interrogation, Miller served Jack the search warrant. "This authorizes us to take hair and blood samples."

"No no, you don't need that. I'm happy to give you my hair and blood." They went to the infirmary and a nurse took the samples.

"What do you think?" Miller asked Harper on their way out.

"It's him," said Harper.

"It's him, all right. What a piece of work that little guy is."

"He thinks he's pretty smart, saying we don't have any evidence. It's like he was telling us we can't prove it."

"Yeah, he seems to think the point is not whether he killed the girls but whether we can nail him for it."

CHAPTER 48

OUR SUSPECT

A MONTH LATER, on April 9, 1992, the Austrian Special Commission arrived in Los Angeles to review the three prostitute murders that were committed during Jack's visit in the summer of 1991. At their first meeting with the Los Angeles investigators, which took place in the bar of a Radisson hotel, everyone had plenty to drink. The hotel manager was an Austrian, and he invited them for a round of Long Island ice teas. After a few more, Geiger pulled out copies of the photos Jack had taken of himself in L.A.

"Our suspect," he said, and passed around the photos of Jack wearing his cowboy outfit. The booze made everyone laugh harder. A little later, one of the Austrians suggested they go somewhere for a steak.

"They may not speak very good English, but so far they seem just like Texans," Lancaster said to Miller.

The next morning they met the L.A. deputy D.A. Michael Montegna at the LAPD Parker Center. Geiger summarized the case they'd built against Jack in Austria, and enumerated the similarities between the Austrian and L.A. murders. Montegna said he was interested to hear how their investigation in Los Angeles proceeded and wished them luck.

"A little cool, isn't he," Geiger said to Miller after Montegna left.

"I should have warned you," Miller replied. "He hates smoking." All four members of the Special Commission had lit up in the little office.

They traced Jack's steps, starting at the Hotel Cecil and driving east on Seventh. Just as in Vienna, he'd targeted the bottom rung of hookers, working in an area where the traffic at night was light. He picked them up and, just as he had in Vienna, kept driving straight—in L.A. across the Los Angeles River into Hollenbeck.

"We think he scoped this spot in advance," said Miller as they stood in the empty lot behind the Girl Scout Center. "He wouldn't have just stumbled across it at night." A couple of tall eucalyptus trees stood in the lot.

"He saw the trees," said Geiger.

"It's gotta be one of the only empty lots with trees for miles around." Miller explained how he'd been perplexed by the killer's decision to drag his victim to the base of a tree.

"He had to have known it wouldn't conceal her."

They backtracked to the warehouse district where the second victim, Rodriguez, was found.

"We never figured out why he chose this spot instead of the other parking areas he passed along the way," said Miller.

Everything matched almost perfectly with the Austrian murders. Without woods around downtown L.A., he'd found a wooded lot, and then a parking lot with trailers that obscured the crime scene like trees or tall bushes. He'd gotten the women naked and strangled them with articles of their own underwear. A leotard with no bra was the fashion among Austrian hookers, and so he'd used either their leotard or their stockings. In L.A. he'd used their bras.

Driving back into downtown, Inspector Brandstätter nudged Harper's seat.

"Beer, Jimmy. Time for a beer."

"We can't stop for a beer," Harper said, laughing.

Brandstätter turned to Geiger. *"Ein Bier klingt gut, oder?"*

A beer sounded very good. The warm weather felt like summer to the Austrians.

The next day they met the Austrian consul in Los Angeles, Elizabeth Kramer, for lunch at the Beverly Wilshire Hotel, where the Hollywood Boulevard hooker Vivian Ward spent a dreamy week with the corporate raider Edward Lewis in the 1990 film *Pretty Woman*. Consul Kramer was an elegant woman; everyone was impressed—and happy she took care of the bill. After lunch they rendezvoused with an ORF camera crew that wanted to shoot some footage for *Inland Report*. They drove to the Pacific Coast Highway and stopped to look at Gladstone's restaurant. In searching Jack's apartment, the investigators had found a Gladstone's menu, which Jack had apparently taken as a souvenir.

"I showed his picture to the hostess, and she recognized him straightaway," said Lancaster. "It seems he went there a lot." He pulled out his copy of the photo of Jack wearing his cowboy outfit, standing on a terrace with the bay behind him.

"This looks like it's somewhere in Malibu. I went to the post office and showed it around, but none of the postmen recognized it." They drove along the coast, past Pepperdine University, and just beyond Solstice Bay they took a right underneath a canopy of eucalyptus trees and ascended into the chaparral.

"It seemed odd that a prostitute would drive so far out of the city with a customer," Lancaster said. "For a prostitute, time is money. Did he offer her more money to drive out here, or did he restrain her so that she couldn't jump out of the car?"

At the base of a steep, rutted fire road they parked.

"He might have parked here and hiked the rest of the way up with the girl, or he might have driven to the top. It would have been rough in a two-wheel-drive rental car, but possible."

At the top of the mesa, Lancaster pointed to where the body had been found, at the base of a laurel sumac—the only tree on the hill. The ORF cameraman took some footage of Geiger examining the area where the body was found, talking with a park ranger. He and Lancaster made a little show for the viewers back home.

"Who found the body?" Geiger asked.

"Some kids playing over there found her," said Lancaster.

"Spielende Kinder haben die Leiche gefunden," Geiger said into his recorder.

"Who does he think he is, Clint Eastwood?" Eva Geiger asked the nurse in her hospital room as they watched *Inland Report* the following evening. While her husband was in Los Angeles pretending to be Dirty Harry, she was recovering from a sinus operation. To Eva, it was yet another example of how far he'd gotten carried away with the Unterweger investigation. He'd lost sight of the reality that he was just a police lawyer in provincial Vienna, where most of the time nothing happened. Now he thinks he's like some American big-city cop.

It was true that Geiger had gotten swept up in the Unterweger investigation, and he was indeed excited to be in the middle of the high-profile case, but she could hardly blame him. It was by far the biggest of his career. A team of inspectors was working on it, but he was overseeing it, and it would ultimately be his job to pull together everything they found and organize it into a report for the Justice Minister. It was the case for which he'd trained his entire adult life.

Eva was bothered because the man she saw in the media wasn't the man she knew. In the public eye he seemed to put on a show. She didn't ask herself how he was supposed to comport himself in the limelight. Jack was always performing for the media to influence public opinion, so to some degree Geiger had to as well.

CHAPTER 49

WHEN THE FIGURE EIGHT
AT THE ZENITH STANDS

ON APRIL 19, 1992, while the Special Commission was still in Los Angeles, a retired policeman and his wife went for an afternoon stroll on the Hermannskogel, the highest hill in the Vienna Woods. Walking through the forest, he saw a dead tree branch leaning against a tree trunk, and he absentmindedly kicked it. As it flew through the air, he noticed it had a piece of fabric attached to it, and on closer inspection he saw that it wasn't a branch but a human femur in a nylon stocking. Almost exactly a year after she was last seen walking out of the Hotel Rudolfshöhe, Regina Prem was found.

A search team found most of her bones strewn over a large area by scavenging animals, though they weren't able to find her skull. Her clothing except the nylon stocking was missing, but all her gold jewelry— heavy necklace figurines of Nefertiti, a Cartier panther, and a Venetian carnival mask—was found, which, along with a denture, identified her.

The investigators bagged the jewelry as evidence and invited Rudolf to headquarters for a possible identification. After sitting him down in an office and pouring him a large schnapps, they showed him the jewelry. Everyone was surprised and a little touched when tears streamed down the rough man's face.

Rudolf had mentioned to a journalist that he wanted to recover his wife's body so that he could give her a proper burial. Following an old Viennese custom, he'd wanted a *schoene Leiche* (beautiful corpse) dressed in white, displayed to the accompaniment of her favorite Rod Stewart songs. In the end all he got was a box of bones.

———

The next day the Special Commission arrived at the Vienna airport, where they were greeted by a flock of journalists asking about the L.A. trip. Geiger couldn't linger; new developments awaited him at the office. With Hoffmann he discussed the discovery of Regina Prem's skeleton.

"Seventeen kilometers from her corner," explained Hoffmann. "He drove the same route he'd taken with Sabine Moitzi twelve days earlier but farther into the woods." He showed Geiger photos of the dirt road on the side of the Hermannskogel where the killer had parked. "Same thing; it looks like he forced her to walk from the car. It's too rocky and steep for him to have carried her, especially in the dark."

The dirt road was an interesting detail. The rain on the night Regina disappeared (April 28, 1991) would have made it muddy, and though Geiger didn't know it, the next day at 7:00 a.m., Jack washed his car and changed its tires.

Fighting jet lag, Geiger stayed at the office until, at about dinnertime, he remembered that he was supposed to have picked up Eva at the hospital four hours earlier.

He called the hospital and was told she'd taken a taxi. Because he'd been neglecting her, the agreement to pick her up upon his arrival from L.A. had become a little test of devotion, and he'd failed it. Driving home, he knew he was about to experience the first crisis of his marriage.

Walking into the silent house and seeing no one in the living or dining rooms, he braced himself for what awaited him in the bedroom. He opened the door and saw her lying in bed, little spots of blood soaking through the bandages over her nose, tears streaming out of her eyes.

What in hell did "When the figure eight at the zenith stands" mean? After the astrologer had submitted her ten pages of nonsense, Inspectors Windisch and Etz had concluded that it wasn't an astrological reference. The riddle had been kicked around Vienna and Lower Austrian police headquarters, and then, when the press caught wind of it, it had been posed to the public. Shortly thereafter some joker had called headquarters and spoken it in a raspy voice. At that point, the riddle spoken to Rudolf Prem by the anonymous caller seemed to belong in a B horror film instead of a real murder investigation.

And then Inspector Windisch thought of a solution that sounded plausible. Imagine a woman lying on her belly with her hands cuffed behind her back. The handcuffs are the figure eight. When her tormentor wants to hear her screams, he pushes the "figure eight" toward the "zenith" of the arc over her back. It was an ingenious way to subjugate her, to inflict maximum pain with minimal effort.

The riddle fit with what they knew about Jack Unterweger—a poet who'd kept handcuffs in his car and apartment, and who'd admitted to handcuffing the prostitute Joanna in Graz. It was yet another tantalizing suggestion of Jack's guilt, but not proof of it.

CHAPTER 50

THE FEAR OF DEATH

ON APRIL 29, 1992, Inspector Miller checked into the Miami Metropolitan Correctional Facility and was led to Jack's cell.

"He's expecting you," the guard said with a cryptic smile.

Miller entered and saw Jack down on his haunches, crying.

"Jack, what's wrong, man?" he said. Jack looked up at him, squinting to see through his tears.

"Is that you, Fred?"

"Yeah, it's me. What's wrong? Why are you crying?"

"They told me that men were coming to take me back to Los Angeles. They said I was going to die. That's not true, is it, Fred?"

"No. I didn't come to get you. I'm here to take blood and saliva from you."

"What for?"

"More tests."

Jack stood up and wiped his tears.

"We need to go to the infirmary," said Miller. "Are you ready?"

"Yeah, sure, Fred, let's do it."

They walked down the corridor toward the infirmary, and then suddenly Jack stopped.

"I don't know. Maybe it's not in my best interest."

"I've got a search warrant to take the samples."

"I don't want to do it."

"No choice, Jack. If I have to, I'll drag you to the infirmary and take them myself. You know I will."

Jack relented, and as Miller stood in the infirmary while the nurse drew the blood, he thought about the little drama that had just taken place. How much had the guards taunted him about getting hauled back to California and executed? Maybe Jack had staged the pitiable scene to pull his heartstrings. Staged or not, it had worked. The sight of a man locked in a cell was so awful that it was easy to forget why he was locked up. The murdered women weren't present to evoke Miller's sympathy, while the strange little man who'd almost certainly murdered them was there before his eyes, weeping like a child.

After the samples were taken, Miller conducted a follow-up interview, mostly reviewing the first interview. As he got ready to leave, a sad expression appeared on Jack's face.

"Will you come back to visit me?" he asked.

"I don't know, Jack, maybe I will," Miller replied, and started to say farewell, but then thought of something and grinned.

"Or maybe you'll visit me in Los Angeles."

On May 7, Detective Miller wrote to Geiger:

I feel that with the line of communication that was opened between our countries, we will be able to return Mr. Unterweger to prison for the rest of his life, or more hopefully, he will be sentenced to the gas chamber here in the United States.

Since your return to Austria I flew to Miami, Florida, on April 29, 1992, and obtained a Search Warrant for Blood and Saliva samples

Jack Unterweger: critically acclaimed author and poster boy of criminal rehabilitation
(*Fritz Fiedler*)

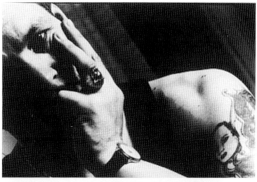

(RIGHT) With a change of clothes, the sensitive, boyish author could regain his rebellious outlaw aura (and vice versa). Many women found him fascinating. Photograph for a magazine interview with Jack, a few weeks after his parole
(*Nikolaus SIMILACHE/picturedesk.com*)

A CHILDHOOD ALBUM (*Wilhelm Schraml*)

(LEFT) "In my dreams I slit open grandfather's body with glowing fire pokers."

(CENTER) "The tramp has no time for you," Jack's grandfather tells him in *Purgatory*. Jack claimed that he'd spent his childhood years longing for his absent mother but later began to hate her for abandoning him.

(RIGHT) "I was the house and court fool, a slave, educated by grandfather to be a fraud's accomplice."

Mug shot of Jack after his arrest for murder, January 1975
(Wilhelm Schraml)

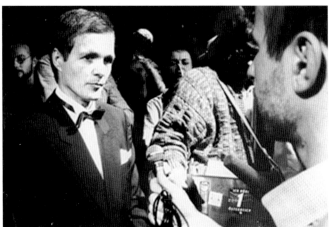

(LEFT) The murderer becomes a star: Jack at the Vienna People's Theater premiere of *Last Station Prison*, January 20, 1986
(Robert NEWALD/picturedesk.com)

Bobby Prem as Jack Unterweger in *Purgatory*, the film made from Jack's critically acclaimed "autobiographical novel" *(Willi Hengstler/epo-film)*

The celebrity: Jack at his first reading in freedom, May 23, 1990
(Foto Votava)

(LEFT) Jack at his desk, shortly after his parole *(Wilhelm Schraml)*

Jack and his German shepherd Joy at one of his favorite haunts, summer 1990. Jack played the role of writer well, seeing and being seen in Vienna's cafés, picking up girls, browsing the local newspapers for crime reports. *(Fritz Fiedler)*

The sex symbol: portrait for a women's magazine, shot in February 1991 (*www.studio-ahermann.at*)

Endless fantasizing: Jack told the photographer that he'd always wanted "to be portrayed as a dandy from the twenties." (*www.studio-ahermann.at*)

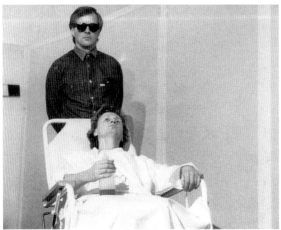

"Many lies are often the truth, just as the truth is also often regarded as lies. Who knows the difference?" Jack in a production of his play *Scream of Fear*, Graz, March 5, 1991 (*fotoatelier gert heide 1991*)

Checking Inspector Schenner's tip: a Vienna police surveillance photograph of Jack (in jogging suit) near his apartment, June 1991
(Vienna Police)

"My papa is an American who owns a ranch," Jack wrote in *Purgatory*. He was elated to be in America, the land of his father, and he asked a passerby to document his arrival at Los Angeles International Airport on June 11, 1991, with this snapshot.
(Vienna Police)

Another shot of Jack's arrival in L.A.
(Vienna Police)

"To protect and to serve": Jack at LAPD Central Facilities, June 1991
(*Vienna Police*)

(LEFT) "He was curious about everything, took lots of photos . . ." Jack took this shot while on patrol with the LAPD, June 25, 1991.
(*Vienna Police*)

At the Central Facilities squad room, Jack flirted with the female officers and took their picture.
(*Vienna Police*)

"Subculture of Sexuality" was the title of Jack's magazine story on the Hollywood Gay and Lesbian Parade, June 22, 1991. *(Vienna Police)*

Another shot of Jack enjoying himself at the Gay and Lesbian Parade. Los Angeles was a completely new world to him, and he appears to have been particularly fascinated by the city's black women, perhaps because he'd rarely if ever seen black women in Austria. *(Vienna Police)*

"They move to the city by the thousands, hoping for a better life, while thousands of others (some dead) leave." An L.A. prostitute in Jack's viewfinder
(*Vienna Police*)

(RIGHT) Marica Horvath, murdered in Salzburg in the early morning of April 1, 1973. In 1983, Inspector August Schenner made a strong case that Jack was the culprit, but strangely enough, Jack was never prosecuted for it. He was, in 1983, already serving a life sentence for a separate murder, but if he had been tried and convicted of murdering Marica Horvath, he would not have been released from prison in 1990.
(*Vienna Police*)

BIANCAS UNHEILBARE LIEBE

JACK UNTERWEGERS BRAUT ZIEHT BILANZ

FÜNF SEITEN BILDBERICHT

"Bianca's Incurable Love": her romantic adventures with Jack and her devotion to him were subjects of enormous popular curiosity.
(*Clarissa Gruber/Kronen Zeitung*)

from Mr. Unterweger . . . I have been informed by our Serology person-
nel that Jack Unterweger's blood has been submitted for DNA analysis.
They expect the results in 8 to 10 weeks.

Geiger imagined the uproar if Jack was sentenced to the gas chamber in the United States. The Austrian intelligentsia considered the
Americans barbarous to maintain the death penalty. He himself didn't
favor it, but he wouldn't lose sleep if Jack was sentenced to death.

He doubted it was going to happen. The DNA test result wouldn't
be available before the ninety-day period prescribed by Austria's extradition treaty with the United States expired on May 27, and without the
DNA result, Geiger knew it was unlikely the Los Angeles D.A. would
prosecute. If Jack was tried in L.A. without the DNA result and found
innocent, it would be a great victory for him, but Geiger knew he didn't
want to take his chances in L.A., where he had no supporters. The L.A.
press would regard him as a strange "Austrian guy," and his status as a
writer would mean little to the local literary establishment. It would be
a lonely trial, and if he were convicted, a lonely incarceration in a California state penitentiary. Most frightening was the prospect of death in a
California gas chamber.

What were Jack's chances in Austria? Geiger feared they were good.
Just as the investigators in Los Angeles hadn't found conclusive evidence, in Austria the Special Commission was still struggling to find it.

CHAPTER 51

VLAD THE IMPALER

"DON'T WORRY, ERNST," Wladkowski told Geiger over lunch. "This *will* go to
trial. If the *Amis* don't try him, we will." That the arrest warrant had
come from Graz instead of Vienna was, in Wladkowski's opinion, the

best thing that could have happened. Vienna was a court society; the dissolution of the monarchy in 1918 hadn't changed that, and like all court societies, it was governed by influence and patronage. Yet Wladkowski was the magistrate overseeing the investigation, and at his provincial court in Graz he was beyond the influence of Jack's friends in Vienna. No one in the capital could pressure him.

Forty-four-year-old Wolfgang Wladkowski. "Vlad the Impaler," as he was sometimes called. That he'd been assigned to the two prostitute murders in Graz had been a matter of chance. At the time the police started examining suspects for the first murder, Wladkowski had been next in the rotation. It was as though Fortuna had turned against Jack, because Wladkowski was the last magistrate in the country he would have chosen.

In his youth Wladkowski had studied music and voice, but he'd ultimately chosen a career in the army instead of the opera. After reaching the rank of captain, he decided that a legal career promised a brighter future, though he never lost his affection for the army. Impatient with bullshit, he liked the disciplined, no-excuses style of the military.

He was passionate about investigative work, especially its scientific and medical aspects. Though Graz has a low crime rate, it is home to the oldest Institute of Crimininalistics in the world, founded by the Graz examining magistrate Hans Gross (1847–1915). Gross's *Handbook for Examining Magistrates as System of Criminalistics* is considered throughout the world the pioneering work on the subject.

Despite Wladkowski's contempt for criminals, he wasn't a hard man. He loved wine and had a large collection. After work on Fridays he liked to hang out at the Zorba's Place Greek restaurant near the court, sip wine, and listen to the bouzouki player. He had a lot of sympathy for the defenseless in society, and he believed prostitutes were just as worthy of protection as everyone else.

Following his return from Cuba, Wladkowski studied the files on Jack and interviewed 160 men and women who'd had contact with the suspect. Everything he learned about Jack indicated that the suspect was monstrously selfish and dishonest. He had an uncanny ability to find troubled women and to exploit them with shocking ruthlessness.

Wladkowski marveled at how little Jack had changed between his twenty-fourth and fortieth years, especially given his status as the poster boy of the successfully rehabilitated offender. He'd gone to prison a killer and exploiter, and come out just the same. Like Geiger, Wladkowski resolved to end Jack's depredations forever. Unlike Geiger, he wasn't worried about journalists taking a pro-Jack posture. Nothing was going to stop the investigation from proceeding, and if the Los Angeles D.A. decided not to prosecute Jack at the end of the ninety-day period, he would be transferred to Graz, where Vlad the Impaler would be waiting for him.

On May 28, 1992, Jack arrived at the Vienna airport. As he descended the stairway of the Delta aircraft, wearing blue jeans and a white oxford shirt, a U.S. marshal on either side of him, he seemed relaxed, as though he'd just returned from a holiday in Florida. He smiled for the cameras as he was led to a bus waiting to take him to Graz.

His lawyer, Georg Zanger, recently returned from the Cannes Film Festival, made a statement to the assembled journalists: "Unterweger has won the first stage. The American district attorney has confirmed to me that there is no evidence against my client for the three murders in Los Angeles. In my opinion, the Austrian police are making presumptions. I will petition for his release."

CHAPTER 52

PRAGUE

GEIGER DIDN'T GREET JACK at the airport because he was in Prague, attending a conference of the Central European Police Association. He enjoyed being in the ancient and beautiful city. For forty-five years Prague had been stuck behind the Iron Curtain, and its people, with whom almost every Viennese has some relation from Czech immigration, had become foreign. Likewise the police in Prague had lost contact with the Vienna police. The mission of the Central European Police Association was to reestablish contact to prevent criminals from evading arrest in one country by crossing the border into the other.

Geiger looked forward to meeting his Czech colleagues—and not only to talk about future cooperation. He also had a current case to discuss. In the search of Jack's apartment they'd found an "auto book" in which he'd recorded his long road trips. Under the date September 14–16, 1990, he'd written: "Vienna—Prague—Vienna."

Geiger figured that Jack had heard about the burgeoning prostitution industry in Czechoslovakia. With no jobs available, a girl might sell her body to the Westerners that came flooding in after the fall of the Iron Curtain in November 1989. In September 1990, not only was there an abundance of full-time professionals in Prague, but also many women who occasionally bartered a sexual favor for basic goods and services. It was kind of like the American zone of occupation in Austria following the war, when the G.I.s were well provisioned and the local girls weren't.

In April, Vienna investigators had sent a query to the Interpol office in Prague about unsolved prostitute murders, modus ligature strangulation, from the weekend September 14–16. *Negative.* But then, just a few days before the Central European Police Association conference, Vienna headquarters received a brief report from Prague, stating that an unsolved murder had indeed been committed on September 15, 1990. The Prague police had not initially reported the case because it had been investigated by the Central Czech Police, which handled crimes committed outside of the city limits. At the conference, Geiger asked to speak with the head of Central Czech homicide, and he was put in touch with Major Jaroslav Hlavac.

CHAPTER 53

THE TRUTH ABOUT YOU

FROM THE VIENNA AIRPORT, Jack was transported by van to Graz, where he had his first meeting with Wladkowski in a police interrogation room. The examining magistrate explained to him that freedom was one confirmable alibi away. The Special Commission had stated its conviction that all seven Austrian women had been murdered by the same killer, and the L.A. cops had stated the same for the three women murdered in their city. If he had an alibi for one of the ten nights, it would gravely weaken the case against him.

From Miami, Jack had written another one of his girlfriends in Vienna—a lady named Mrs. Müller, the wife of a wealthy manufacturer—and begged her to say that he'd spent the night in her sauna (her hiding place for him when her husband came home) on one of the nights the Vienna hookers had disappeared. When she'd written back that she couldn't lie to the police, he'd called her and made a threat: "If it goes badly for me, it will go badly for everyone," insinuating that he would tell her husband of her betrayal if she didn't give him the alibi. Instead of yielding to the threat, she told her husband everything, and together they went to the police.

Two details from her statement had value for the investigation. First, she was with Jack on the evening of October 25, 1990; at about 10:00 p.m. he left her to get on the highway to St. Veit (which runs through Graz). Just over two hours later—the amount of time it takes to drive from Vienna to Graz—the Graz prostitute Brunhilde Masser was last seen. Second, in the summer of 1990 Jack visited Mrs. Müller's country house just north of Graz and went for a long walk in the woods in the area where Brunhilde Masser was murdered a couple of months later.

Mr. Müller had been under the impression that Jack was one of his wife's charity projects. Not only had Jack slept with her and sponged her husband's money from her, he'd also had the nerve to show up at Mr. Müller's office and ask for a large loan. To add insult to injury, Jack had stolen a pistol from his study. In the March 3, 1992, edition of a Viennese tabloid there was an image of Jack in a nightclub, pointing the weapon at a photographer (who sold the picture to the tabloid). The pistol had been a gift from Mr. Müller's father, and he didn't appreciate Jack stealing it and throwing it in a ditch in France.

Wladkowski told Jack that none of the alibis he'd thus far offered or tried to obtain had been confirmed. Had he, in the meantime, remembered anything pertinent to the ten nights in question? Jack told his recollections of the period, which included dozens of anecdotes, people, places, cultural events, and women. After a while his continuous talk *around* the critical hours had the effect of emphasizing the holes in his story rather than distracting attention away from them. Listening to him was like reading *Purgatory*, which related everything in the life of a prisoner except the reason for his imprisonment.

Wladkowski ran out of patience. "Mr. Unterweger, I admit I find your stories interesting, but it's time to come to the point. You remember everything about where you were before and after. Now I want you to tell me where you were when these women disappeared. Let's start with the first one: Brunhilde Masser, Graz, around 12:30 a.m., October 26, 1990. Where were you?"

"I estimate that I departed for Carinthia between 5:00 and 6:00 in the morning of October 26. Before that I was certainly in Vienna," Jack replied.

"Mrs. Müller stated that she was with you on the evening of October 25, helping you to write notices for your play, and that you departed for Carinthia at around 10:00 p.m.," said Wladkowski.

"I don't remember if she helped me that evening."

"Why, in your earlier statements, did you not address the question of where you were at around 12:30 in the morning of October 26?" Wladkowski asked.

"I don't know."

"Why not?"

"I just don't."

"Well, to me that can only mean one thing." Jack glared at him furiously, waiting for him to say it.

"You murdered that woman." Jack leaped out of his chair, fists balled, and Wladkowski leaped up to meet him.

"Go on, hit me, and then we'll see how this turns out for you."

A couple of days later Inspectors Windisch and Brandstätter took a crack at it, and a similar scene occurred. Windisch concluded, "Mr. Unterweger, I've probably interrogated a thousand suspects, and not one of them preferred to sit in jail rather than say where and with whom he was when the crimes were committed. You don't have an alibi for a single one of the ten nights, do you?" Jack turned to Windisch, a man of fifty and probably the most respected police officer in the country, and spat in his face.

Geiger had no desire to repeat the show, but he did have a couple of things he wanted to tell Jack. Together with Hoffmann he drove down to Graz. As they walked into the interrogation room, Jack warmly greeted Hoffmann, but refused to extend his hand to Geiger.

"I'm not going to ask about your alibis, because I know you don't have any."

"I know what all this is about," Jack interrupted.

"Yes, what then?"

"You're just trying to get rid of me because you want Bianca." Geiger was at first taken aback. Did Jack really feel that way, or was he just trying to throw his antagonist off balance?

"You really think that?"

"I know that's what this is about."

"Think what you want. I'm here to tell you that you've never told the truth about why you murdered Margret Schäfer. You've never told the truth about it because it's the truth about you. It was a sadistic, sexual murder. You are a sadist."

Again Jack leaped out of his chair, enraged.

"You're lying!"

"No, I'm telling the truth. That's why you hate me. You killed her because you enjoy killing."

"Wrong! That's not what happened. You're lying about me." Jack glared at him and then stared at the wall.

"And now we come to our current theme."

"What's that?"

"Prague."

"What are you talking about?"

"The weekend of September 14, 1990, you drove from Vienna to Prague. Just after midnight on the morning of the fifteenth you met a Czech girl named Blanka Bockova on Wenceslaus Square and you offered to give her a lift home. And then you murdered her."

CHAPTER 54

BLANKA

MAJOR HLAVAC of the Central Czech Police had arrived at the Central European Police Conference with a file about the murder of a woman on the morning of September 15, 1990. He remembered the case well. He'd spent a lot of time investigating it.

Blanka Bockova was thirty years old, married, and worked in a butcher's shop. She lived with her husband and two children in an apartment block southwest of the historical center, but in the evenings she often went into the old town and met other men. On the night of Friday, September 14, 1990, she met her friend Martin on Wenceslaus Square and had a drink. They got into an argument about something, and just before midnight, she got up and left. When Martin walked out of the café onto the square a few minutes later, he didn't see her.

The next day her body was found in the Brezany brook, a tributary of the Vltava River outside the city, a couple of miles south of her apartment. It appeared that her killer had started to give her a lift home, but had then continued on until he came to the little valley surrounded by

woods. Except for a pair of gray knee-high stockings and the gold wedding band on her finger, she was naked, lying in the shallow stream on
her back, her legs spread wide apart, covered by a couple of tree
branches. She had been strangled, both manually and with a ligature,
though the ligature was missing. In one of her buttocks was a stab
wound. Her clothing and purse were missing, though shortly thereafter
someone found her I.D. on the shoreline of the Vltava. It appeared that
her killer had taken it, and then, on his way back into town, tossed it in
the river.

Major Hlavac had examined dozens of possible suspects, but none
of them had been strong enough to warrant arrest. And so the case had
remained unsolved for almost two years.

Blanka's I.D., found on the shore of the Vltava, was an interesting
detail. In Salzburg in 1973, Marica Horvath's killer had also driven her
to a body of water surrounded by woods, and after he'd murdered her
and left her in the water, he'd taken her clothing and purse. From the
Salzach Lake he'd driven to the Salzach River and tossed her purse into
it. A fisherman downstream of the city snagged it a few days later.

An important question remained: Had Blanka known any German?
Before the war, German had been the language of Prague's ethnic Germans and Jews, but by the end of 1945, both groups were gone, and for
the most part, their language went with them. In 1990, if a man had approached a Czech girl and tried to chat her up in German, he might run
into a language barrier. Unfortunately for Blanka, she had known a little.

Among the women in Jack's electronic book were two university students who had accompanied him to Prague, where they'd stayed in the
same apartment, in separate rooms. The landlady was a fifty-year-old
woman named Ruzena Bacova, who spoke fluent German. She told a
strange story about Jack.

While his two companions spent the weekend sightseeing, touring
the castle, hanging out on the Charles Bridge, he was strictly interested
in the city's red-light district. It wasn't the only peculiar thing she'd noticed about him. Shortly after he arrived, as she was chatting with him
in the kitchen, he made a pass at her.

"I think I'm a little too old for you," she'd said. All right, but would she work as his interpreter? He was writing a story about the Prague red-light milieu and he wanted to talk with prostitutes and pimps, but he didn't know any Czech. She agreed to help him, and on the night of Friday, September 14, they drove his BMW across the river to the National Theater parking lot. As they were about to get out of the car, he opened his glove compartment and pulled out a pistol and switchblade, and sprang the blade to show her it was real.

"Just in case we have trouble with an aggressive pimp."

They talked with some women near the train station, and a couple of pimps did tell them to go away. Around 11:30 they finished interviewing and walked to Wenceslaus Square, where they parted company around 11:45. She remembered the time because she'd then gone to her sister's apartment, about fifteen minutes away, and as she'd entered, a television program that ended at midnight was concluding.

Mrs. Bacova's apartment was located on the opposite side of the river from Wenceslaus Square, not far from a bridge. Just downstream from the bridge, on the shoreline, Blanka Bockova's I.D. had been found. Not long after Jack returned to Austria, Mrs. Bacova received a letter from him, asking if she'd seen any interesting newspaper reports about the Prague milieu.

CHAPTER 55

MANEUVER AND COUNTER-MANEUVER

SINCE HIS TRANSFER from Miami, Jack's home was the jail at the back of the Graz criminal courthouse. Wladkowski's office was located on the second floor, and he occasionally met Jack in an interrogation room. One day in June, Jack had some news.

"The Interior Ministry is going to remove Counselor Geiger and appoint a new head of the Special Commission," he said.

"Really, why is that?"

"Because he talks too much. He's prejudicing the people against me."

"Is that so?"

"Yes."

"And you think he'll be removed from his post?"

"I know he will."

"We'll see about that."

It was true that Geiger had made some indiscreet comments to the press, like when he was in Los Angeles and a reporter for the ORF *Inland Report* asked him, "If you've found evidence, why hasn't the Los Angeles district attorney filed a complaint?"

"For opportunistic reasons, I suppose," he'd replied, meaning that the Los Angeles D.A., who knew Jack could be tried in Austria for the L.A. murders, preferred to let the Austrians deal with it. It was a dumb statement, an expression of Geiger's inexperience with being put on the spot. Many reporters seemed willing to believe Jack's protestations of innocence, and Geiger felt compelled to offer assurances that the police had good reason to suspect him. The trick was to think of the right words off the cuff.

Wladkowski drove to Vienna and met with the Interior Minister's secretary, who confirmed that the Ministry had indeed decided to remove Geiger. As always, Jack was well-informed.

"That's not going to work," said Wladkowski. He argued that Geiger knew the case better than anyone else, and that his removal would be a major setback for the investigation. Wladkowski prevailed and Geiger remained at his post.

It was a setback for Jack, but it paled in comparison with the bad news that broke at the end of June, when Bianca traveled to Graz for her third visit and learned upon her arrival that her mother had petitioned the court to forbid her from visiting Jack until her nineteenth birthday, the age of legal adulthood in Austria. She threw a fit and Wladkowski relented to a final visit.

It was a heavy half hour. Jack wept and raved about her mother's coldheartedness. How could she be so cruel? Now he would be left all alone. The guard knocked: their time together, at least until November, was up.

Separation from Bianca was a disaster. Not being able to see her at all meant a total loss of control. Jack had made Bianca a member of the *Schikeria* in Vienna (he'd heard she'd been running around in Munich as well), staying out all night at the *in* clubs. Her youth, which had been an advantage when he was free, worked against him while he sat in jail, because to an eighteen-year-old, just a few months seemed like a long time.

Jack was afraid that another four months was long enough for her to meet another man, perhaps a successful one who could show her a good time. He might not be as charming and funny as Jack, but he would have the advantage of being present. Even a pimp could catch a glimpse of the green-eyed monster.

Wladkowski was pleased with the decision of Bianca's mother. It was high time that an adult separated the girl from her murderous fiancé. He knew from her letters to Jack that she was still brainwashed. Perhaps not seeing him for four months would break the spell.

On Monday, June 29, Wladkowski received the results of the American DNA test and had Jack brought into the interrogation room.

"I don't need your confession," the magistrate said. "I've got a DNA test that proves you're the murderer."

"What are you talking about? Which case?"

"Think about it and you can probably figure it out on your own."

Wladkowski returned to his office and Jack was returned to his cell, where, later that night, he slashed his arm below the elbow with a razor.

"Unterweger slashed his wrist in his cell!" was the next day's front-page news. Margit was concerned at first, but then she read the statement of the surgeon at the Graz hospital: "Unterweger didn't cut his wrist artery, but the veins in his arm. He lost a lot of blood, but his wound is not life threatening."

Everyone who'd served a long sentence knew the trick. A phony suicide attempt could get a prisoner transferred to a hospital or, even better, into a psychiatric ward, where the security was much lighter and from which he could try to escape. Margit had once had a conversation with Jack about suicide in prison.

"Everyone in the pen knows that to end it all, you've got to slash up the artery, not across it," he'd told her. Suicide threats and attempts had often served him well. His transfer from the Salzburg jail to the Salzburg Nerve Clinic in 1974 after a drug overdose had been a key moment in his criminal career. In 1992, even if slashing his arm didn't win him a permanent transfer to a hospital, it would still win him sympathy.

CHAPTER 56

ASTRID

TWENTY-NINE-YEAR-OLD Astrid Wagner heard on the radio that Jack Unterweger, the celebrated writer sitting in the Graz jail awaiting a possible trial, had cut his wrist. She'd never met Jack, but she'd read *Purgatory*. She'd also read newspaper reports about the warrant for his arrest, his dramatic flight to Miami, and his transfer to the Graz jail, which happened to be a few blocks from her apartment.

Astrid knew something about the jail because she had, the year before, interned for a judge at the criminal court. In 1990 she'd completed her law degree and announced her Socialist Party candidacy for a seat in the Styrian state legislature. She was an attractive woman, with pretty brown hair, hazel eyes, and a shapely figure. In her childhood she'd attended school in Paris, where she'd learned to speak French. The judge she'd assisted, Dr. Bourcard, considered her a talented jurist with a promising career ahead of her.

And then she heard on the radio that Jack Unterweger had cut his wrist.

Thank God he survived, she thought, and sat down to write him a

letter. Jack received it in his cell and thought about it. What did it sig-
nify? On the one hand, the author appeared to have the makings of a
hopelessly devoted helper, just like the various women who'd served him
while he was in Stein. On the other hand, she mentioned that she was a
lawyer who had, the year before, been an intern at the court. Had Wladkowski decided to plant a woman to win his confidence? Wladkowski
was sly and bold. Jack imagined him attempting such a scheme.

After nine days of studying Astrid's letter, he took a gamble: her sympathy was real. He wrote her back, a regular correspondence ensued,
and then, around the first week of August, he suggested she come for a
visit. On August 14, Wladkowski was on vacation, and the intern on duty
didn't even ask her for an I.D. She received a pass and walked down the
corridor to the visitors' room. Jack was sitting on the other side of the
wire mesh, waiting for her.

Such a small, pitiable-looking man, she thought. His face was pale
from not having seen the sun. He noticed the Taurus figurine hanging
from her necklace.

"Taurus women are self-righteous," he said with an ironic smile. His
buoyant spirit and wit, despite his dreadful circumstances, moved her.
She perceived that he was determined to retain his humanity, in spite of
what awful things would come. She felt sorry for him, but was also filled
with admiration for his courage and strength. In only fifteen minutes she
felt a unique connection forming between them.

In the first of three books she would write about Jack Unterweger,
And the Hunt for the Murderer Must Go On!, she described her visits:

> I came two or three times per week, always between eight and nine
> in the morning, before I went to the office . . . In such a situation,
> you learn to speak quickly, to say as much as possible. The topics of
> conversation rapidly shift. Most of the time Jack had a little writing
> tablet with him on which he'd noted everything he wanted to say.
>
> These little quarter-hour visits in the morning could change my
> entire day. Already the night before was an expectation for the next
> morning.

Here we go again, thought Wladkowski as he read Jack's letters (to make sure he didn't try to acquire false alibis or manipulate witnesses) to the latest woman in his life. Astrid Wagner wasn't a schoolgirl from a desolate home or a desperate housewife. According to Wladkowski's colleague Judge Bourcard, she was a smart young woman. Why didn't she meet some nice law-abiding fellow who lived in an apartment instead of a jail cell, earned a living instead of exploiting others, and who didn't have an incurable urge to torture and strangle women?

Over the weeks and months that followed, Wladkowski often wondered why Astrid had become so consumed by Jack Unterweger. He sensed that she was enthralled by what she perceived to be the masculine power of a violent outlaw, and some of her statements to the press had a leftist ring. Though Wladkowski didn't know it, Astrid had once read a biography of the German terrorist Andreas Baader and found him fascinating.

A high-school dropout and petty criminal, Baader had a natural charisma that he used to become an early leader of the German Red Army Faction (RAF), a radical leftist organization that was active in the seventies and eighties, committing robberies, arson, bombings, kidnapping, and murders to protest the "capitalist and imperialist state." In 1970, the renowned journalist Ulrike Meinhof helped him to escape from prison and then spent two years committing crimes with him— heady stuff for a woman who'd earlier led a quiet life with her husband and two children.

Jack was aware of how Baader and his fellow gang member had romanticized violent crime by proclaiming it to be a form of protest. In January 1975, when he and his girlfriends Maria and Barbara robbed a jewelry store in Germany, they announced to the owner that they were members of the Baader-Meinhof gang. In his 1989 interview with the ORF journalist Peter Huemer, Jack said that, had he been at university in 1968, he would have "certainly been a terrorist."

Astrid was no RAFer, but she found the idea of struggle between the underprivileged and their bourgeois oppressors compelling. As her relationship with Jack developed, his letters to her and to Bianca became ever more duplicitous. Bianca became aware of Astrid's devotion through her passionate statements to the press, and a rivalry developed between the two women. Jack pretended to be equally devoted to both. In a letter to Bianca, he said that he needed to maintain his friendship with Astrid because she was an invaluable helper in Graz. In a letter to Astrid, which he wrote on the same day, he said that he needed to maintain his relationship with Bianca so that she would testify favorably if it came to a trial. Wladkowski read the letters, and then accidentally placed the one to Astrid in the envelope addressed to Bianca and vice versa. So many briefs crossed his desk—he couldn't keep perfect track of them.

Margit laughed as Bianca recited Jack's letter to Astrid. How witty of Wladkowski, she thought. She also thought it was possible that the examining magistrate wanted to help Bianca break free of Jack for her own well-being. Bianca's nineteenth birthday was approaching, at which point she would have the right to visit him again.

Margit couldn't help admiring Wladkowski for the letter swap, even though she knew that he was doing his best to send Jack back to prison. She still believed in his innocence, and under a pseudonym she gave an interview to *Viennese* magazine in which she said the cops had the wrong guy.

She knew that Jack was a neurotic man with a lot of resentment, as well as a persecution complex, but she just didn't see how her friend could be a serial killer. Jack was weird, but he wasn't a monster. He'd also often expressed affection for hookers. He'd once told her he thought they were the most honest women in society, and in an interview with *Viennese* in October 1991, he'd said the same thing. Margit figured the cops had fixated on him because of his past. He'd then aggravated their suspicion by fleeing.

Such was her conviction, though she had to admit that a couple of times she was haunted by the question: My God, what if he is the killer? After the warrant was issued for his arrest, she read a newspaper report that listed the women he was alleged to have murdered, and she saw that one of the Viennese victims had been found in the Scots Woods. Instantly she remembered her outing with Jack on Easter Sunday, 1991, when he had taken such a roundabout way back to Vienna and had slowed down to a walking pace as they passed the Scots Court restaurant in the Scots Woods. She wondered what he had been looking for when he peered around into the trees.

Then she saw in the papers that one of the women had been murdered in Vorarlberg on December 5, 1990, which reminded her of the time that Jack had called her from Vorarlberg twice in one night—stressed out during the first call, relaxed and humorous during the second. Was his dramatic mood swing connected with the woman's murder?

And yet, for some reason that she couldn't entirely articulate, she still had a hard time believing that he was a serial killer. She also thought it possible that her memories themselves had been colored by all the sensational media reports.

CHAPTER 57

FRUSTRATION

THE AMERICAN DNA TEST was inconclusive. The DNA, isolated from semen found on the Los Angeles victim Shannon Exley using the PCR (polymer chain reaction) method, contained the genetic marker HLA-DQ alpha type 3.4. DNA isolated from Jack's blood contained the same marker.

The trouble with the HLA-DQ alpha marker was that it was useful chiefly as a means of excluding a suspect, but not of *proving* that a suspect was the origin of a biological trace, because the marker was evident in the DNA of 10.9–11 percent of the Caucasian population and 9 percent of the black population in the United States. In other words, roughly one out of every ten men in Los Angeles could have been the origin of the semen.

Additionally, the hair fibers found stuck to the trailer at the Rodriguez crime scene in Los Angeles didn't match Jack's hair. That spoke in his favor, though not enough to exclude him, because someone else—a driver or mechanic or a homeless person—might have bumped his head on the trailer.

Wladkowski's assurances that the case would go to trial were consoling, but Geiger knew they could hold Jack only for so long before the Graz D.A. would have to submit his indictment and get on with the proceedings. Their case had to be stronger by December, when a hearing would be held to review the grounds for Jack's detention, or he would be released and the investigation suspended.

The search for material evidence had become an exercise in frustration. Many times the Special Commission found something that seemed promising, and everyone got their hopes up, only to have them dashed. Four dark hairs had been found in Jack's VW that were morphologically identical to the hairs of the Vienna victim Sabine Moitzi, but they didn't have good roots (in 1992, the method of extracting mitochondrial DNA from the hair shaft hadn't yet been developed). DNA could be extracted only from skin cells adhering to the roots.

Also frustrating was their experience with Jack's Mustang Mach I. In November 1990 he paid $17,000 for the car, which had a brand-new engine, and by all accounts he was wild about it. At the end of March 1991 he took it on a long road trip in Italy and returned to Vienna without it.

The car finally turned up in a garage north of Padua in excellent condition. No mechanical problem could account for why he'd abandoned it, and given that he'd ditched it at a time when he was strapped for money, his decision made no sense—unless he had reason to believe that keeping the car posed a risk.

A lot of hookers walked the streets of northern Italy, especially in the towns along the Adriatic coast between Venice and Trieste. Many of the girls were illegals from the Balkans and Africa, and if they disappeared, their pimps might not file a missing-person report. The Italians didn't share the Austrian love of walking in the woods; a corpse might sit in a patch of forest for years before it was discovered. If a farmer stumbled across a skeleton, he might call the local police, but with no missing-person report, not much could be done about it. The regional mentality of the Italians also didn't help. Geiger wondered if Interpol Rome had any contact with police precincts in the north.

In the end, the Mustang turned out to be another letdown. The red leather interior was immaculately clean—no traces whatsoever—and the Italians never turned up any murders similar to those in Vienna, Graz, Bregenz, Los Angeles, and Prague.

Despite the negative results, Geiger never lost his conviction that Jack had a compelling reason for abandoning his beloved Mustang in Italy. Maybe he was afraid that someone had seen a girl getting into the conspicuous car.

The Los Angeles D.A. declined to prosecute at the end of May for lack of material evidence, and by the end of August 1992, Geiger became haunted by the specter of a similar outcome in Austria. For months they'd been looking for a smoking gun and they still hadn't found it. They would continue the search, but in the meantime, Geiger returned to the starting point of their case. A few months after Jack Unterweger was released from prison, a series of women were murdered in a similar way in three Austrian cities, as well as in Prague and Los Angeles, on nights when he was in each city, in some cases within a couple of blocks from where the victims were last seen. What were the odds it was just a coincidence?

CHAPTER 58

FORENSIC PATHOLOGIST

IN THE LONG and distinguished history of the Vienna Institute of Forensic Medicine, thirty-one-year-old Dr. Andrea Berzlanovich was the second woman to hold a staff position. Her institute had played a key role in the development of forensic pathology and the germ theory of disease, but in 1991 it had become a relic. It was part of a complex of medical buildings called the Josephinum, after the "Enlightened Emperor" Joseph II, best known for commissioning operas from Mozart. Next to the institute was the dreadful Narrenturm (Fools' Tower)—a giant, mausoleum-like building that had been an insane asylum in the eighteenth century (Salieri's final home in the film *Amadeus*).

In the spring of 1991, Andrea read in the papers about the prostitute murders and wondered if they were indicative of a growing trend of brutality against women. And so she decided to do a study on prostitute murder in postwar Austria. She began with the year 1960 and ended with 1991. From various institutes of forensic medicine and police precincts she compiled data on every recorded case.

In January 1992 she was surprised to get a call from Ernst Geiger, who had just been promoted to deputy director of the Security Office. In the institutions of Vienna, chiefs spoke with chiefs, they didn't call underlings, and yet Dr. Geiger wanted to speak directly with her.

In a meeting at his office, he asked her hundreds of questions about her study. While she had initially focused on the forensic medical aspects of the murders, he was interested in whether the victims had worked on the street or in an apartment. At what time of the day and what day of the week were they murdered? Were they murdered near where they worked or taken somewhere else? Were their bodies found naked or clothed?

In May 1992, Andrea completed her study, and Geiger was stunned by its implications for the Unterweger investigation. If the case went to trial, he knew that Dr. Berzlanovich would be a powerful witness for the prosecution.

Not included in Dr. Berzlanovich's study was Jack's aunt Anna Unterweger. The forty-six-year-old woman had been sexually murdered in a wooded area near Salzburg in 1967. Her killer, a man named Franz Kracher, had already served time in Stein prison for sexual assault, and had been released two years before he murdered Anna. She wasn't included in Dr. Berzlanovich's study because she wasn't a prostitute. Nor was she Jack Unterweger's aunt.

Geiger obtained a copy of the newspaper report to which Jack referred in *Purgatory*, with its images of Anna and her murderer "blinking at the camera." It was the May 6, 1967, edition of the *Salzburger Nachrichten*. As a sixteen-year-old boy, Jack had read it and seen that the victim shared his last name. That, and perhaps the fact that she'd been sexually murdered in the woods, had appealed to his imagination. The story made such a strong impression on him that he incorporated it in the autobiographical novel he began writing ten years later. Only instead of the actual headline: VIOLENT VAGABOND INCRIMINATED, he invented the headline: HER LAST CUSTOMER WAS HER MURDERER! In a January 1989 radio interview in Stein prison, Jack told the ORF journalist Peter Huemer: "She was murdered by a man who had, almost symbolically, served four years in Stein prison, and who then, the day after his release, looked for a prostitute in Salzburg and stabbed her."

CHAPTER 59

SPECIAL AGENT

IN AUGUST 1992, Special Agent Gregg McCrary of the FBI Behavioral Science Unit got a call from Robert Farmer, the FBI legal attaché at the American Embassy in Vienna, who explained that the Austrians appeared to have their first serial murderer.

"They've made an arrest and are sure they've got the right guy, but because of his celebrity status and some other issues, they're afraid they might lose him at trial. They want you to profile him." McCrary replied that if they had the right guy, they didn't need a profile but a signature crime analysis. Before he learned anything about the suspect, even his name, McCrary wanted to see descriptions of the crimes. He would examine each one to determine if they were linked.

After receiving the files on the eleven murders, McCrary perused the crime scene descriptions and was struck by how far and wide the anonymous suspect had traveled. It was rare for a killer to strike outside his familiar realm. That this one had traveled from Austria into neighboring Czechoslovakia didn't seem so remarkable, but to have ventured all the way to Los Angeles and continued his crimes—McCrary had never heard of such a killer.

Geiger figured that any contribution from the FBI would bolster the case against Jack, not only in its substance, but also in how it was perceived by the public. From the success of *The Silence of the Lambs* the year before, the special agents at Quantico had become celebrities. Expert testimony from one of them would carry weight with a jury.

It was an unseasonably warm October when Geiger and the fledgling criminal psychologist Thomas Müller arrived in Arlington, Virginia, and checked into the Ritz Carlton near the Pentagon. The next morning they rose early and drove to Quantico, and were surprised by the spartan quality of the FBI Academy campus, a former Marine Corps base. They met Gregg McCrary, who showed them their rooms in the Jefferson dorm and then invited them to his office—yet another surprise. The world's top research institution for studying violent criminal behavior was located in tiny basement offices, about the size of a walk-in closet. Everywhere, on every surface, were stacks of files.

In their introductory conversation, McCrary could see that the case was weighing on Geiger. He sensed the Austrians didn't know exactly what they wanted from the FBI, just some kind of expertise to help them bolster their case.

"Let's start with looking at each case to see if there is some kind of pattern that connects them," McCrary suggested. They moved to a conference room, and for the next few days they went over every detail of every case, noting all of the similarities and differences.

A signature crime-scene analysis begins with the idea that a serial killer has developed a personal routine for carrying out his crimes, just as a chef might develop a personal routine for organizing and preparing his ingredients and executing a dish. If the same killer is responsible for multiple murders over time, each crime scene will bear the signs of the same routine. The best indicators that the same hand is responsible for different murders are the things the murderer didn't have to do. Whoever killed the eleven women didn't have to do the following:

1. Drive them so far out of town.

2. Use an article of their own clothing to strangle them (he could have used his own tool).

3. Leave their jewelry on their bodies (he took other personal effects, why not their jewelry?).

4. Take their I.D.s (why not just take their cash?).

5. Partly cover their bodies, though not enough to hinder their discovery.

6. Place the bodies near trees or water.

Because the victims and circumstances of each crime were not identical, it followed that the crime scenes weren't identical. The killer may have felt more comfortable at one site than another and thus taken more time and care. One woman might have been docile, another might have fought. All such variables, things over which he didn't have complete control, might have caused variations in his routine. Finally, with each successive crime, he might have become more confident and efficient. As with all skills, he probably improved with practice. The technique of signature crime-scene analysis involves weighing the similarities against the variations.

For the three murders in Los Angeles, McCrary entered six variables into the VICAP data base, and the computer generated a list of matches. The results would definitely impress a jury.

CHAPTER 60

JACK, GEORG, AND THE SUPREME COURT

ON NOVEMBER 25, 1992, a hearing was held in the Graz court to review Jack's pretrial detention. The judges ruled that the grounds for suspecting Jack of murdering eleven women were substantial enough to detain him further while the investigation continued.

Jack appealed to the Graz High Court, and a few weeks later it rejected his complaint that he was being detained without sufficient grounds. The court extended his pretrial detention for twelve months, which relieved the pressure on the Special Commission. Now they would have another year to search for evidence. For the first time in so long, Geiger felt as if he could relax a little and enjoy the holidays.

On Christmas Eve, at home with his wife and daughter, he found himself momentarily not worrying about the killer in the Graz jail. So many good people all over the world were working on the case. Surely, he thought, they would have enough to go to trial and win the following year. After a few glasses of hot spiced wine, his wife began to sing the carol that was first performed near Salzburg in 1818 and since then exported all over the world. The Austrians have a tradition of singing it just one time, strictly on Christmas Eve. Geiger wasn't a religious man, but joining his wife and child in the song, for a moment he felt its peace.

Stille Nacht, Heilige Nacht . . .

It wouldn't last long.

In January, Jack became the first pretrial detainee in Austrian history to petition the Supreme Court for his release. He claimed the Graz criminal court was infringing his fundamental right to freedom by detaining him without legitimate grounds for suspicion. His lawyer, Georg Zanger, stated to the press that the investigators had nothing.

During the same month that Zanger filed Jack's complaint with the Supreme Court, a report appeared in the monthly magazine *Basta* about his film project. He'd persuaded the Austrian director Max Vrecer to participate, and Vrecer was working with the Hollywood screenwriter Patricia Louisianna Knop (co-writer of *9½ Weeks*) on the script. Vrecer imagined Jack and Zanger as a double role to be played by the same actor. The opening scene would be purely visual, Vrecer explained. "We see the lawyer in his blue Jaguar convertible, speeding the wrong way down the one-way streets of Vienna's central district, waving at cops along the way. Cut to the same actor being released from prison . . ."

The double role made sense. Jack and Zanger were both men who compensated for their short physical stature with a superabundance of self-assertiveness. Just as Jack had, in his youth, a taste for formal clothing that was unique among small-time pimps, Zanger's taste for well-tailored suits during his student days contrasted with the threadbare style of his fellow '68ers. Just as Jack had claimed in *Purgatory* to have been a competitive boxer, Zanger adorned his desk with a pair of red boxing gloves, a memento from his days in the ring.

By February, the impending Supreme Court decision was the center of media attention. Had the investigators indeed failed to find enough evidence to warrant detaining Jack any longer? On March 11, 1993, the court issued its ruling: Jack Unterweger remained under suspicion for eleven counts of murder, and would remain in pretrial detention.

CHAPTER 61

"ISN'T THAT UNTERWEGER'S TRAMP?"

THE SUPREME COURT decision made it clear that Jack wasn't getting out of jail anytime soon, and his landlord wanted a new tenant. Bianca was obliged to find a new place. A broker showed her several that she liked, but there was always another prospective tenant ahead of her. It seemed odd, given there was no housing shortage in Vienna. Then one day she realized what was going on.

"They won't rent to me because they're afraid my boyfriend will get off and move in with me," she said to her broker. He admitted that that was the case.

It wasn't the first time that Bianca had been confronted with the harsh reality that, though her fiancé was a darling of the radically chic, he wasn't popular in other quarters of society. One day as she was walking out of the subway on St. Stephen's Square, she overheard a well-dressed girl say to her friends, "Hey, isn't that Unterweger's tramp?"

The attention she got from men wasn't deliberately hurtful, but it, too, was demeaning. When the Beverly Hills go-go dance club opened for business in 1993 in Vienna's First District (on the back side of the Coburg Palace, which once belonged to relatives of Queen Victoria), one of its owners offered Bianca a large sum to perform the opening dance (everyone loved the story of her dancing at Miami Gold to finance her fiancé's flight from justice). Other men apparently fantasized about her being a uniquely kinky nineteen-year-old, the embodiment of the mysterious association of desire and death. On a few occasions she was approached by prominent men who never would have noticed her before. She even claimed that Prince Albert of Monaco hit on her one night in Take Five.

Finally she found a landlord willing to take the risk, and began clearing out Jack's apartment. The biggest job was packing up his library and manuscripts. Margit came over to help. While Bianca boxed books, she cleared out Jack's file cabinets. One of them contained letters, and Margit couldn't resist the temptation to read them. The first that grabbed her attention was from the actress Senta Berger. Like Marisa Mell and Erika Pluhar—fellow graduates from the Max Reinhardt Seminar—she had gone on to have a major stage and film career. While Jack was sitting in Stein, he had written her, asking her to join the campaign for his release. As Margit would later recall the letter, its pertinent sentence was so reasonable: "I cannot fulfill your request, as I know nothing about your character or the offense for which you are serving a life sentence."

After Senta's letter, Margit found one by Barbara Scholz, Jack's German girlfriend in 1974. Jack had visited her while attending the Frankfurt Book Fair in 1990.

"She was a bit surprised when she opened the door to find me standing there, but we ended up having a nice reunion," he'd told Margit about the occasion. As Margit would later recall, Barbara's letter, which she'd written shortly after his visit, told a different story:

> I let you stay over because I thought it might help me to understand what, in my youth, I saw in you—you who sent my life in a direction in which it should have never gone.
>
> You haven't changed. You will do something criminal again.
>
> Barbara
>
> P.S.—Please return the radio you stole from my apartment.

Margit wondered why the police hadn't seized the letter. Moving on to the next binder, she saw it contained police and court files from the years 1975–1976.

"This is interesting," she said to Bianca. "It's copies of Jack's old police files. He must have gotten them from his lawyer back then. Do you mind if I take them home and read them?"

"Go ahead," said Bianca.

That night, Margit stretched out on her couch with the files on her jailbird friend. One of the first documents she came across was the transcript of Barbara Scholz's police interrogation, shortly after she was arrested with Jack in Basel.

Barbara was the link between the murder victim, Margret Schäfer, and the suspect Jack Unterweger. A few months prior to Margret's murder, Barbara had run off to Switzerland with a German boy dodging military service. In Zurich they'd broken up, and shortly thereafter she'd met Jack. When, in January 1975, Barbara was arrested in Basel with an Austrian boy with a record of violence against girls, the police drew the connection between the young couple and the murder victim Margret Schäfer, as the two girls had lived in the same street in the town of Ewersbach.

The interrogator asked her what she and her boyfriend had done on the night of December 11, 1974, and she freely confessed. A couple of pages into her statement, Margit began to feel nauseated.

CHAPTER 62

REVELATION

THE HESSIAN TOWN OF EWERSBACH lies twenty-five miles west of Marburg—home of the oldest Protestant university in the world, where Jakob and Wilhelm Grimm began collecting folk stories. The wooded hills along the upper Lahn River, which flows through Marburg and just north of Ewersbach, are thought to be the origin of "Little Red Riding Hood." The traditional peasant costume of the region's young girls featured a red cap.

Eighteen-year-old Margret Schäfer probably knew the story of the archetypal predatory male as well as any girl, but no knowledge or caution could have saved her from the wolf she encountered on December 11, 1974. On that night, Jack and Barbara drove from Frankfurt up to Ewersbach to get some money and other things from her parents' house.

Upon finding the house locked, with Barbara's parents asleep inside, Jack suggested they rob someone. Right then Barbara spotted her neighbor Margret, who happened to be walking home from an evening of bowling with friends.

At the moment she saw Barbara getting out of the Mercedes and walking toward her, Margret had no way of knowing the danger she was in. As Jack understood when he told Barbara to lure her into the car, why would Margret fear her old friend and neighbor?

Barbara recounted the story to the police interrogator:

We chatted for a minute, and I asked her if she had to be home. She said no, and I asked her if she wanted to hang out with me and my boyfriend. We got in the back seat and chatted while Jack drove. She told me about her evening at the bowling alley and some of our friends who were there. Jack asked if we wanted to go somewhere for a drink, and we parked across the street from a bar.

"Do you have anything else you want to tell her?" he asked me.

"No."

"Then now we'll get to the point." He grabbed Margret by the front of her shirt and jerked her into the front seat. Naturally she was surprised and afraid and asked him what he was doing. He told her that nothing would happen to her if she stayed calm and didn't resist him, and using the belt from my coat, he tied her hands behind her back. He then stuffed her on the floor between the front and back seats, with her head down and her legs up. With her hands tied behind her back she couldn't move.

"Why are you doing this to me?" she asked him.

"Shut your mouth unless you want something to happen to you," he said. He went through her purse and found 30 Marks [$12] and her key, and he asked her if she had any more money at home. She said she kept 100 Marks [$40] in her dresser, and so we drove to her house. I let myself in, snuck back to her room, and took the money and some clothes.

I put the clothes in the trunk and got in the front seat. Jack asked me if I'd found the money. I said yes, and he got on the main

road out of town, headed south. We stopped for gas and he told me,
"It's time to make your friend disappear."

The way Margret was lying on the floor with her hands tied behind her back, she couldn't sit up. She kept crying, and every time
she asked Jack what he was doing, he told her to shut her mouth.
No, I did nothing to persuade him to let her at least sit on the back
seat. We drove for about an hour, and in Herborn, he asked me if I
knew of a place in the woods. I directed him to a country restaurant. We drove past the parking lot and onto a forest road. We had
to drive slowly, and after about five minutes, he pulled over.

He ordered her to take her clothes off. She begged him to leave
her alone, said he could take whatever he wanted and that she
would do whatever he told her.

"Barbara, what is he going to do with me?" she asked. I told her
I didn't know. She refused to undress, and he hit her in the face. He
untied her hands so that she could undress, and we pulled her
clothes off. He then got out of the car to go around to the other side,
and we were alone for a few seconds.

"Barbara, can't you help me? What does he want from me?" I
couldn't say anything. All I could do was shrug. At that moment,
I instinctively knew what he was going to do to her. He opened the
door and pulled Margret, who was completely naked, out of the
car. It was very dark and cold, and there was snow on the ground.

"Do you want to come with me?" he asked.

"No," I said. I was terribly afraid for her, but also for myself. I
couldn't form any clear thoughts of what to do. He tied her hands
behind her back again and grabbed his steel truncheon from the
center console; I didn't see him grab her bra. He then grabbed one
of her arms and pushed her into the woods.

About fifteen minutes later he came back to the car, and after he
sat in the driver's seat, he handed me the steel rod, which was covered with blood and hair.

"What did you do with her?" I asked him.

"There's no way she can betray us now," he said. I knew then
that he'd murdered her. On the drive back to Frankfurt he told me

to throw the steel rod out. Because he'd somehow broken the heel off one of his boots while he was in the woods with Margret, he said he needed to get rid of them as well. We kept her fur coat but threw the rest of her clothing away.

Three weeks later, hunters found the naked corpse of Margret Schäfer at the foot of a larch tree, lightly sprinkled with leaves and soil, a bra tightly knotted around her neck. Her jewelry was left on her body, but the rest of her clothing was missing. Her autopsy revealed that she'd been repeatedly struck on the head, neck, and upper body with a blunt instrument, manually strangled, and then finally strangled with her own bra.

PART III

CHAPTER 63

THE TRIAL OF THE CENTURY

THE PRESS BILLED IT the "Trial of the Century," and in fact, never in Austrian history had a single man been accused of so many counts of murder. In a way it was three trials rolled into one, because the accused was alleged to have murdered not only seven Austrians but also three Americans and one Czech. Witnesses from Los Angeles and Prague were scheduled to give testimony, as were top forensic scientists from Switzerland, Germany, and the United States. It was to be the first trial in Austrian history in which the prosecution would present DNA, microscopic fibers, and a signature crime-scene analysis as evidence. The proceedings were to last thirty days, with testimony from 160 witnesses. In preparation, the main courtroom was renovated and a new room was built to accommodate the flood of reporters.

Originally the presiding judge was to have been Helmut Bourcard, but in November 1993 the press reported about his friendship with his former intern Astrid Wagner. Astrid's devotion to Jack was public knowledge from her interviews; she'd described him to the ORF as having "stumbled" in his youth. And so the court ruled that Bourcard's impartiality was in question.

The decision made Astrid furious, and it deepened her suspicion that the court and the D.A.'s office were conspiring to stack the deck against Jack. Most distressing was his replacement: Judge Kurt Haas.

Bourcard was an unassertive man who played the role of moderator rather than leader and was extremely attentive to the formal, procedural aspects of a trial. Haas was the opposite. With his imperious personality and his handsome looks, he struck awe in the jury and forcefully led the proceedings. His approach to the procedural aspects of a trial was instinctive, with no hand-wringing.

For two years, Jack had pitted his fans against his critics, cops against journalists, journalists against journalists, intellectuals against ordinary people, and political party against political party. Every adult citizen had more or less followed the story of his arrest and detention, and the question of his guilt or innocence had been the subject of millions of heated conversations in cafés, bars, and living rooms all over the country. Two years after his arrest in Miami, a jury would finally decide.

The trial opened on April 20, 1994. The Austrian monster Adolf Hitler was born on April 20, and when a journalist asked Jack if he thought it was a bad omen, he replied, "Hitler was an innocent baby on the day he was born."

At 4:30 a.m. a crowd gathered in front of the courthouse, everyone hoping to get a seat card when it opened for business. A reporter asked what exactly was motivating them to stand in the dark for three hours on the slim chance they would get one of the few seats left in the courtroom.

"My wife stayed at home to feed the animals while I drove into the city," said an old farmer.

"What are you hoping to see?" asked the reporter.

"I don't know. I just don't want to miss it."

"I want to see Jacky," said a thirty-six-year-old woman. "Just to see him once."

Across the street, the Café Paragraph, which had fallen on hard times and closed before the trial, had reopened and was doing a spanking business selling coffee and sandwiches, as well as order forms for Jack's latest book, 99 Hours, an account of his high life after his parole, his unjust arrest and detention, and his suicide attempt. As an example of the book's lyrical content, the magazine NEWS reproduced "Love Poem to Death," which Jack had "written" just before he tried to kill himself. NEWS didn't know it was the same poem that had so impressed Jack's first patroness, Sonja Eisenstein, eighteen years earlier.

The porter opened the doors at 7:30, distributed thirty-two seat cards, and made way for the television crews who herded into a specially erected corral at the front of the courtroom, a gigantic jumble of microphones and cameras. At 8:30, a bomb threat obliged everyone to file back out of the courtroom while it was searched.

The first leading player to show up was Dr. Zanger, who walked toward the front of the courtroom, shaking hands like a campaigning politician. On his desk he laid a copy of Scott Turow's *Presumed Innocent*, facing the photographers. And then Jack's second attorney, Hans Lehofer, entered.

Unlike the arts and entertainment lawyer Zanger, Hans Lehofer was a criminal defense attorney—the best in Graz. Probably realizing that Zanger's media campaign wasn't going to get him off, Jack had hired Lehofer eight weeks before the trial. A national judo champion in his youth who'd competed in the 1964 Olympics, the bearded fifty-year-old still projected a lot of masculine strength and was a charismatic speaker. With his charm and infallible sense of timing, he had a way with juries, especially the female members.

If anyone could get Jack off the hook with a Graz jury, it was Lehofer. The problem was that he'd entered the game with little time to prepare himself for the gigantic trial. He would also play second fiddle to the Viennese Zanger, who had no experience before a Graz jury (which would have a certain amount of prejudice against all things Viennese). Lehofer wanted to help Jack, and he agreed to defend him for free, but he knew going into the trial that he was going to be cast in Zanger's shadow.

The prosecutors Martin Wenzl and Karl Gasser entered. Originally Wenzl was to have prosecuted the case on his own, but a few months before the trial opened, the D.A.'s office appointed Karl Gasser as co-prosecutor. The official reason was that Wenzl needed assistance because of the size and complexity of the case. Another reason, not mentioned in the press, was Wenzl's friendship with Zanger. Wenzl was a passionate violin player who loved going to concerts, and Zanger was well connected with Vienna's cliquish music scene.

Wladkowski had first noticed their budding friendship in Los Angeles, when the three men visited in October 1992 to examine the L.A.

murders. One night, instead of going to a big party at the Austrian Consulate, Zanger and Wenzl attended a concert of the L.A. Philharmonic, with Itzhak Perlman as soloist. At a meeting a few days later in the U.S. Attorney's office, the Americans noticed the peculiar chumminess between the prosecutor and the defender.

"They're not very adversarial, are they?" the U.S. Attorney remarked to Wladkowski.

And so the fiery young Karl Gasser was appointed to put some bite into the prosecution.

At 9:00 a.m. Judge Haas took his place on the bench, and at 9:07 the show began. Jack entered wearing an ensemble that Astrid had bought for him—dark gray double-breasted suit, light blue shirt, and navy tie with a red-and-gold paisley print. His two years of "Canadian vacation," as some call a jail term, with its lack of direct sunlight, had left his face deathly pale and noticeably aged. Nevertheless, he appeared in good spirits, ready to fight. He stopped before the horde of photographers in their corral and smiled for a thousand shutter clicks and flashes.

That night he noted the morning's events in his diary:

> Alexander, a conscientious warden, bent me over and looked up my butt. I imagine the scene: In the courtroom, trousers dropped, I pull a weapon out of my ass and open fire.
>
> The animal was led through a passage, prepared for the media. Cruel. Roman arena, cordoned off with iron bars for my protection. Reporters with cameras, their calls make me nauseated: "Jack, look over here. Jack could you turn this way!" I smile, feel empty, not nervous. What is it with me? Have they degraded me into a machine? I grin. I am now an animal: lion, wolf, cat, or snake. I myself don't know.

A veteran reporter named Doris Piringer also observed the gladiatorial atmosphere of the courtroom. "There was so much tension in the room, and immediately after the proceedings opened, I sensed the enormous enmity between Jack and Zanger on one side and the prosecutor Gasser on the other. Both sides attacked with such ferocity. It was as though neither was going to be satisfied until the other's blood flowed. I had never seen anything like it, and I was appalled that such a trial could take place in a lawful state."

Judge Haas gave the photographers five minutes to shoot the animal or superstar, depending on one's perspective, and then started to swear in the jury. Dr. Zanger rose and said he wished to present some motions.

"No, you don't really want to do that," said Haas.

"Yes," said Zanger.

"Not now. First I must swear in the jury."

Zanger began to recite the motions—the expulsion of Wladkowski (who was in the Canary Islands) and certain journalists (who were also absent) from the courtroom because he intended to call them later as witnesses, the suspension of the trial because of the media witch hunt against his client, and the postponement of the trial.

"That's enough," said Haas.

"Pardon me, but I'm not doing this for fun."

"Of course you're doing it for fun."

Zanger's most original motion was for Judge Haas to be replaced by the originally appointed Judge Bourcard.

"I'm not going to listen to a motion about something that was adjudicated long ago," said Haas.

Zanger defiantly carried on, and as he began to enumerate his successful lawsuits against newspapers, Karl Gasser said, "Dr. Zanger is just seeking publicity for his success as a media attorney and trying to still his vanity."

After Zanger had spoken for an hour and a half, a jury member interrupted: "I motion the court to excuse the jury until the proceedings begin."

Judge Haas appeared to be in a bind. If he ordered Zanger to be silent and Zanger kept talking, the judge could hold him in contempt. However, Lehofer reckoned that Haas didn't want to do anything that would further delay the already long overdue trial. Lehofer also figured that Haas was happy for Zanger (Jack's lead defender) to get on the jury's nerves. The result was a bizarre trial that sometimes seemed to verge on being completely out of control.

CHAPTER 64

OPENING STATEMENTS

AFTER ALL OF ZANGER'S MOTIONS were rejected, the proceedings finally began. Martin Wenzl made his opening statement. Echoing the prosecutor's statement at Jack's murder trial in 1976, Wenzl warned about the winning charm of the accused.

"Who is this man who was arrested in Miami with a couple of dollars in his pocket but about whom men in the highest circles of government wanted to be kept informed? That is one of Unterweger's facets: a winning, friendly presentation, not at all a caricature from a horror film. He was a darling and a benefactor; women chased him in flocks. He fooled a Justice Ministry section head, media people, a court president, and artists. He has an unbelievable effect on women, but also unbridled aggression against women."

Prosecutor Gasser took over and began his statement by berating Jack and Zanger: "Your defense strategy has exceeded the bounds of good taste, because you disseminated untruths and half truths in a massive attempt to manipulate public opinion and the opinion of the jury." Turning to the jury, Gasser continued: "He is a master of manipulation, a master showman. Do not allow yourselves to be taken in by him."

Gasser then pointed out that, even before Jack murdered an eighteen-year-old girl in 1974, he had already raped a girl with a steel rod and committed fifteen other offenses. "I can think of nothing good to say about him . . . His parole four years ago was a curse for his victims."

The following day (April 21) began with Zanger's opening statement:

"From the very beginning, this has been a media case. The media has branded Unterweger a monster. You, the jury, must realize that you have been prejudiced against him, because the media has flouted the principle of presumed innocent until proven guilty." Opening his well-worn copy of Scott Turow's *Presumed Innocent,* he quoted the elegant defense attorney Sandy Stern: "You must begin your work with the presumption that the accused is innocent." As Zanger went into a lengthy digression about the media's power and "greed for sensation," Judge Haas reached for his letter opener and a stack of mail and began reading.

Zanger then asserted that the prosecutors had no evidence, that their entire case amounted to an arbitrary exercise of power designed to hang the murders on Jack because of his past.

> *A green light was given for a happy hunt, and after the investigators became convinced of Unterweger's guilt, all objectivity and impartiality were thrown aside. The lead investigator, Ernst Geiger, is so personally engaged in the matter that he refuses to consider other suspects. He aspires to solve seven, nay eleven, murders in one swoop! Every indication was bent toward Unterweger, and the investigation against every other suspect was suspended.*

Zanger claimed he would demonstrate that the alleged times at which particular women disappeared—times during which Jack was in the area—were not accurate. He would also show how blood traces found under the fingernails of the Prague victim, Blanka Bockova, excluded Jack. It was, he asserted, highly significant that none of the victims had been found with dog hair adhering to their clothing, given that Jack's German shepherd often rode in his car and had certainly shed hair on the seats.

> *And you must also consider the psychology of the accused. Jack Unterweger is a narcissist who is compelled to be at the center of attention. It would have been impossible for him to have committed such high-profile murders and to have remained anonymous.*

He would have left a sign of himself at the crime scenes—a red rose, for example . . .

The district attorney wants to put Unterweger behind bars, but instead of evidence, he has only arbitrary presumptions. There are no indications of his guilt, only indications of his contact with a single victim.

Zanger's assertion that the blood trace found under the Prague victim's fingernails (from scratching her assailant) excluded Jack was bold and dramatic, and the jury wondered when he would present evidence to support his contention. The part about the dog hair adhering to the victims' clothing was less impressive because almost all the victims were found naked. Zanger's foray into his client's narcissistic psyche was even weaker, because Jack didn't remain anonymous in the case of the high-profile murders but produced a radio documentary and co-wrote a newspaper report on them.

Jack's second attorney, Hans Lehofer, made his statement:

This is my most difficult trial. None of us know if we have here before us a murderer of eleven women or if this is all just a fatal error of justice. You will hear and see many things in the course of this trial—for example, a video of a corpse. Shocking. The ladies will faint. But you may not identify such images with Unterweger. You will hear a lot about the unbelievable collection of coincidences in this case—a Viennese is in Vienna when murders are committed. What a coincidence! A condom is found at one of the crime scenes and is put in storage until it is analyzed, at which point its contents are no longer usable. How coincidental! The finger of a rubber surgical glove with blood and hair stuck to it is found at another crime scene, put in storage in Vienna, and then sent to Graz, but the traces are destroyed. And so you will see that a single hair [found on the seat of Jack's BMW] will decide the outcome of this trial, because the true indications—those that could have led to the culprit—have disappeared, were destroyed. Ladies and gentlemen of the jury, be just and give Jack Unterweger a chance.

Jack's turn. In an Austrian trial, the accused is allowed, at certain moments, to address the jury and to question witnesses for the prosecution. Sitting before him on the jury bench were eight men and four women. All twelve would attend the entire trial, but only eight would render a verdict. The other four were substitute jurors in case one or more of the main jury members suffered an illness or emergency. As Jack addressed the twelve men and women, he didn't know which eight would decide his fate, and as he'd done his entire life, he paid more attention to the women. Two of the three women who were substitute jurors had already made up their minds he was innocent, though he didn't yet know it.

His overall strategy was to present himself as charming, witty, friendly, and engaging, to make the jurors think he was too human to be the monster. He made direct eye contact with them, frequently smiled, and animated his speech with a cheerful tone.

Ladies and gentlemen of the jury, we will be together for the next two months, and I'm not going to be a sterile actor. No, I want to talk with you as though we were sitting in a coffeehouse. If you have questions, then simply ask them, and I will answer them spontaneously and tell you everything—really everything. You see, I have a great advantage in that I have nothing to hide, because I'm not the murderer. If you catch me lying to you just once, then go ahead and judge me.

The prosecutors have spoken about my adventures with women and underage girls, and yet, after my long imprisonment, only five of my partners were under twenty. The average age was thirty. I'm not going to tell you I came, I saw, and the women swooned. As to whether I'm a ladies' man, I'll leave that judgment to women. The prosecutors have reproached me for my inability to form a steady relationship, but how was I supposed to form a steady relationship with married women? Nevertheless, there was one woman who I was about to marry—a woman from Guatemala. She came to Vienna, but when I learned from a newspaper report that I was under suspicion, I wanted to clear everything up first, so I put her on a plane back to Los Angeles. I told her that after a month every-thing would be okay . . .

The prosecutors will talk a lot about my past. What should I say about it? At the end of my trial in 1976 I admitted that I had lived like a rat and had been justly convicted—indeed for sixteen of-fenses. I don't deny it, but in this matter, shouldn't you set the past aside?

He then spoke about the negative things the prosecutors had said about him in their opening statements, all of which, he claimed, were an attempt to create a prejudicial atmosphere against him. Sometimes he insinuated that their statements weren't true; at other times he tried to refute them.

"The prosecutors said that I dumped all of my advocates from liter-ary circles when I was released from prison. Why? Because the pseudo-humanists and pseudo-romantics from the left tried to lead me like a poodle to five o'clock tea. I broke with them because I wanted to have my own life . . .

"Prosecutor Karl Gasser said he knew of nothing good to say about me. Now, I don't want to boast, and I've never said anything about it to the public, but I did transfer the income for my children's stories to the SOS–Children's Village. Anonymously."

"How much?" Judge Haas interrupted.

"Is that relevant?"

"Well, someone might say you only gave thirty Schillings [$3]."

"I don't want to boast, but between 10,000 and 20,000 Schillings."

"Please don't interrupt the accused," said Zanger.

Judge Haas let it slide.

"I'm not going to wait for my innocence to be demonstrated on its own—now I will go on the offensive and prove my innocence. On Mon-day I will present my diaries, in which every day of my freedom between my release in May 1990 and my arrest in Miami in February 1992 is re-constructed. I will also present to you the names of my alibis. They have clear memories of experiences they shared with me at the critical times, and they will prove that I cannot be the killer. I have never named them before because I wanted to protect them from the police. Speaking of the police, soon you will see the material with which they have sent the prosecutor into battle, and you will learn what's really behind it." With that he pulled a rubber surgical glove out of his briefcase, and with a quick motion he tore one of the fingers off.

"Look—blood and hair were stuck here," he said, reminding the jury of the torn-off fingertip of the surgical glove found under the body of Karin Eroglu.

"Ladies and gentleman of the jury, be strict with me, but be just as strict with all the others who will come before you. Thank you for your attention."

Though Jack's presentation was excellent, the substance of his statement was a bit sloppy. Proclaiming that he'd had *only* five sex partners under the age of twenty during his year and a half of freedom suggested that a man getting laid so much with nubile girls had no motive for committing sexual murders. And yet, at the time he murdered Margret Schäfer in December 1974, he was living with two young and pretty girls who were infatuated with him.

His statement that before he married the woman from Guatemala (Carolina) he wanted to "clear up" the suspicion he read about in the newspaper was also clumsy, because he hadn't gone to Edelbacher's office to discuss the matter but to talk about his adventures with the cops in L.A. Most awkward was his claim that he would present his diaries and alibis the following Monday, because when Edelbacher had asked him to present his alibis in October 1991, he'd claimed he couldn't remember and that he hadn't kept any records of the period during which the women disappeared. At his trial almost three years later, his assertion that he hadn't mentioned his alibis before because he "wanted to protect them from the police" made no sense. Edelbacher had been open and friendly with Jack; nothing about his manner had suggested he would have checked his alibis in an indiscreet or bullying way.

The substantive problems of Jack's opening statement were not obvious to the jury members because they didn't have a comprehensive familiarity with the background of the case. Most people can digest only so much information at a time, and as everyone who has studied public speaking knows, most members of any audience are more sensitive to the appearance, style, and gestures of a speaker than to the substance of his statements. The job of the prosecutors was to point out the substantive weaknesses of Jack's assertions in order to neutralize his rhetorical and theatrical gifts.

CHAPTER 65

INQUISITION

IN AN AUSTRIAN TRIAL, the judge plays an inquisitorial role, and Judge Haas began his examination by going to the heart of the Jack Unterweger story.

"You have always presented your life differently from how it really was. Often you've told the story that you received your first prison sentence because you stole twenty Schillings out of hunger. How much did you really steal?"

"Twenty-seven Schillings," Jack replied.

Haas lifted one of Jack's books off the pile in front of him. "In the bio on the back cover here it says twenty Schillings."

"I didn't write that."

"In the file it says that you stole 457 Schillings."

"That's not true," said Jack, shaking his head.

"The part about you doing it out of hunger also isn't true, and you were only jailed for three days."

"It must be a lot of fun for you to begin this trial by talking about my past. Or is it merely a substitute for evidence?"

"In your statement you acted insulted by the prosecutor's statement that you had often assumed aliases. And yet you often *did* assume aliases, didn't you?"

"Yes, but—"

"How many women have you promised to marry—just one?"

"Yes."

"Well, what about . . ." The judge named two other women whom Jack had promised to wed while he was in prison (thus turning them into errand girls).

"Is it true that you sent young girls onto the street and lived from their earnings?"

"Not only from them. I was also a waiter." The judge then quoted a recording of Jack's conversation with a prison psychologist about his past.

"You said that your mother was a prostitute and that your aunt was a prostitute. You called yourself a protector of prostitutes. The fact is, your mother never had anything to do with prostitution, and your—"

"I see through your tricks," Jack interrupted. "You'll have me judged by depicting me as a liar."

Haas opened his copy of *Dungeon* and quoted the passage in which the narrator poses as a male prostitute in Rome, holds his client at knife-point, ties him up, and drives him to an isolated spot outside the city and abuses him.

"*I worked on him without seeing him. He was only an object.* What do you have to say about this?"

"Must everything I write be a description of an actual experience, or does a writer have some poetic license?"

Haas opened a file and quoted another passage: "*There is nothing more poetic than the death of a beautiful woman.* Did you write that?"

"No, Friedrich Nietzsche did," Jack replied.

The laughter in the courtroom gave him a boost of confidence, and when Zanger tried to object that the judge was creating a prejudicial atmosphere, Jack said, "Leave him be. He promised a fair trial."

Judge Haas was renowned for his ability to memorize files, and he'd become acquainted with the 17,000-page file on Jack. Though the law requires a judge to keep his opinion about the accused to himself, it cannot prevent him from forming one. From Haas's initial questions it was clear he regarded Jack as a fraud who'd used his position as an author to propagate myths about his life. The judge was going to cooperate with the prosecutors in showing the jury that the accused was a liar who'd deceived an entire country.

Step one was destroying Jack's credibility. Step two was demonstrating that he was present in each of the five cities on the nights the women were last seen, and that he didn't have an alibi for a single one of the eleven nights. Step three was to use character witnesses to demonstrate that he was the same sociopath when he got out of prison in 1990 that he was when he committed the murder in 1974. Step four, the weakest, was the presentation of evidence linking him to the murders.

Prosecutor Gasser began his examination.

"This morning you claimed that you have always acknowledged your guilt for the murder of Margret Schäfer—that you admitted it shortly after your arrest in 1975. In fact, you continually denied it, even during your trial."

"Am I here for the murder of Margret Schäfer, for which I have already been convicted, or am I here for the eleven murders?"

"For the eleven murders," said Judge Haas.

"Thank you," Jack said.

Gasser then asked Jack where he was on the night of September 14–15, 1990, when Blanka Bockova was last seen shortly before midnight on Wenceslaus Square in Prague. Jack began with a detailed account of what he'd done before the evening of September 14, and then skipped over the critical time and offered an equally meticulous account of what he'd done afterward.

"Yesterday Mr. Unterweger said he'd lived like a rat," said Gasser to the jury. "Right now I get the impression he's a rabbit who runs a zigzag course every time a question makes him uncomfortable."

"What did you do on the night of September 14–15, 1990?" Judge Haas demanded, and Jack admitted he did research on Prague's red-light milieu with a Czech translator, from whom he parted at around midnight, continued his research alone for a while, and then drove to his quarters.

"Were the women in the apartment when you got home?" Haas asked.

"I didn't look."

"Witnesses have said that you were unusually calm and quiet the next day. Why was that?"

"We were in a beer hall with horn music and people gabbing in Czech. Please, your honor, concede that I have the right not to be chummy with foreigners."

Regarding the early morning of October 26, 1990, when the Graz prostitute Brunhilde Masser disappeared, Jack again began by talking about the days before the critical nights.

"On October 22 I was in Augsburg."

"No, no. Where were you on the night of October 25?" Haas asked.

"It's not so simple," Jack replied, and began recounting his activities during the days leading up to the night of the twenty-fifth. Finally he came to the point.

"On the evening of October 25 I still hadn't finished making the notices for my theater piece, and so I didn't depart for St. Veit until between 3:00 and 5:00 on the morning of October 26."

"That isn't what you wrote in your initial statement," said Haas.

"When I wrote my defense in Miami, I had no records with me. Now I can reconstruct much more."

"Why then, on the twenty-fifth, did you tell your girlfriend in Vienna that you were departing for Carinthia that evening?" asked Gasser.

"When we stepped out that evening to walk my dog, I saw another girl, Martina, who worked at the Café Florianihof. I'd already had an eye on her for a while, and I wanted to chat with her, so I told my girlfriend that I was leaving for Carinthia to get free of her. I couldn't just tell her to get lost."

"You say you have alibis that you will name on Monday," said Prosecutor Wenzl. "Why have you chosen to sit in jail for two years instead of naming them?"

"I have always said that I would present everything at the moment someone explained to me why I am accused of murdering these women, for only then would I be able to refute your grounds for suspicion. If I had named my alibis during the investigation, the police would have gone straight to them with horrifying crime scene photos and shocked them. I wanted to spare them that, and so I decided to keep them to myself until the trial. They are my jokers, and I will play them only at the right time."

On Monday morning (April 25) Jack was asked his whereabouts on the nights of the other nine murders. On the evening of December 5, 1990, when the Bregenz prostitute Heidemarie Hammerer was last seen, a filling-station receipt indicated he'd bought gas in the nearby town of Dornbirn between 7:00 and 9:00 p.m.

"I arrived at the hotel [in Dornbirn] in the early evening, reviewed the script of my radio piece in my room, and then went to bed."

"And you never left your hotel room that night?" asked Judge Haas.

"No."

"Had you ever gone for a walk in the Lustenauer marsh?"

"No, nor had I ever visited it by car," Jack replied (falsely).

"What were you wearing during your two days in Dornbirn?"

"A white sweater and a red scarf," Jack replied.

"Let's talk about the night of March 7, 1991" (when Elfriede Schrempf was murdered), said Haas. "What did you do?"

"I would like to read from my daily notes," Jack said, referring to his typed "reconstruction" of his 673 days of freedom.

"Just answer the question."

"I was at a reading in Köflach."

"How long did the reading last?"

"Two hours, more or less."

"When did the reading end?"

"I didn't look at my watch."

"What did you do after the reading?"

"I got on the South Autobahn and drove straight to Vienna."

"You didn't make a stop in Graz?"

"No."

"Did anyone see you when you arrived in Vienna that night?"

"No. I took my dog for a walk alone and didn't see anyone before I went to bed."

"Why did you initially tell the police you were with your girlfriend in Vienna?" asked Gasser.

"Because at the time I was asked [January 1992] I didn't remember the reading in Köflach, but I did remember picking up my girlfriend from school almost every day during that period."

"And in the defense you wrote in Miami, you still didn't remember the reading in Köflach?"

"No."

Jumping ahead to the Los Angeles murders, Jack admitted he'd stayed in the Hotel Cecil on the nights the two downtown women were murdered, though he insisted he'd spent both nights alone in his room.

"And we're supposed to believe that?" said Prosecutor Gasser.

"No, you're supposed to prove the opposite," Jack shot back.

"On the morning of June 20," said Hass, "a few hours after Shannon Exley was murdered, you returned your car to the rental agency with a broken windshield, and in the American autopsy report it is written that the victim had a head injury. According to the forensic pathologist, the injury could have been caused by her head striking the windshield in a struggle with her assailant."

"The damage to the windshield was caused by a stone that fell off a truck in front of me," Jack replied.

Regarding the night the third prostitute was last seen in Hollywood, he admitted he'd stayed at a motel on Sunset Boulevard (a few blocks from her corner).

"But for the third murder I have a firm alibi," he asserted.

"Who?" Judge Haas asked.

"I will state it with the rest of my alibis, after the public has left the room."

Judge Haas ordered the public and press to leave the courtroom while the accused named his alibis: Carolina in Los Angeles, with whom he claimed to have had a long cell phone conversation on the night of July 3, 1991, when Sherri Long disappeared in Hollywood; a woman named Karin, with whom he claimed to have had a long telephone conversation on the night of April 8, 1991, when Silvia Zagler disappeared in Vienna; a woman named Sylvia, with whom he claimed to have spent the night of April 16, 1991, when Sabine Moitzi disappeared in Vienna, and finally his mother in Munich, whom he claimed to have visited on May 7, 1991, the night Karin Eroglu disappeared in Vienna.

"Why did you insist on naming your mother in secret?" Gasser asked. "Your attorney has already told the press that you visited her on the night of May 7."

"And I scolded him for it."

"And the woman with whom you say you spent the night of April 16—why didn't you mention her when Counselor Edelbacher asked for your alibis in October 1991?"

"Because I couldn't take seriously that I was a suspect for these murders."

"Don't tell us fairy tales. You became aware you were a suspect in September 1991, and you had two months to think about your alibis. And why did you lie to the police when they asked you if you'd ever had contact with prostitutes?"

"I ask you not to say that I lied," Jack said.

"You will *not* tell me how to pose my questions!" Gasser roared. "Not you!"

"The police asked me if I'd had contact with the milieu," Jack said.

"Don't lie. The question was if you'd had contact with prostitutes."

Jack's last-minute alibis were subpoenaed and scheduled to give testimony.

CHAPTER 66

CALLED TO ACCOUNT

ON APRIL 27, former Justice Ministry official Wolfgang Doleisch was called to the stand. A lot had gone wrong during his lifetime, which began the year the *Titanic* sank, but it hadn't diminished his belief in the ability of human beings to change for the better. As director of the Department of Penal Executions, he'd taken an interest in the prisoner Jack Unterweger, for whom he'd been a devoted and powerful advocate.

"I'm sorry it has come to this," Jack said to the old man as he took the stand.

"The truth will be found," he replied.

"I was inspired by the prisoner's hunger for education," Doleisch explained. Unlike the Stein prison director Karl Schreiner, Doleisch had never gotten any publicity for Jack's transformation from murderer to celebrated writer, even though he was a supporter at a time when Schreiner was still skeptical. Doleisch had helped Jack to get around the prohibition against prisoners publishing their writings, and yet Jack had dedicated *Purgatory* to Schreiner, probably as a way of pushing the ambivalent prison director onto the bandwagon.

After his release, Jack never phoned or visited his old patron Dr. Doleisch.

"The only time I heard from him was when he sent me a postcard from Los Angeles," he explained. So in the end he received nothing for his help but the ignominy of having to explain it at Jack's eleven-count murder trial.

———

Next was Dr. Michaela Happala, a young psychologist at Stein prison who had written a favorable evaluation of Jack's psyche in the autumn of 1989. Almost five years later, she still looked like a teenager with her blond bangs and Hawaiian print shirt. At the time she evaluated Jack she had just completed her training and arrived at her post.

"How long did you talk with Unterweger?" Judge Haas asked.

"We had two conversations, about half an hour each. A test was also conducted, which showed no abnormalities, but that wasn't especially meaningful. I got the impression that Mr. Unterweger had a mental block. He didn't go into the motive for his crime. He evaded me, and he was not ready to talk about it."

Judge Haas read aloud from her report: "Jack Unterweger grew up with his grandfather, an alcoholic. His aunt was a prostitute." All her statements about his background were from *Purgatory*. Had she done any independent research into his past?

"It wasn't a formal evaluation but a mere statement," she said.

"Yet in this statement you wrote of a positive development in Jack Unterweger. You wrote of his fitness for society, that he had worked on his mental problem with intellectual rigor."

"Yes, I wrote that," she said softly. "But it was so difficult to form an opinion. I had six hundred prisoners to tend to. It was impossible to delve deeply into all of them."

"Yes, well, why didn't you say that at the time?"

"The prison director [Dr. Karl Schreiner] asked me to, as much as possible, write nothing negative."

Dr. Schreiner was lucky to be in his grave and not in the courtroom (he died in 1990, the year his favorite prisoner was paroled).

"Was that not an abuse of office?" Prosecutor Gasser interjected.

"One could see it that way," she said.

"You speak always of one case [the murder of Margret Schäfer]. I must tell you, there are numerous cases. That Mr. Unterweger went to work on a woman with a steel rod was also a case."

"I didn't read his entire file," she replied.

"I don't think you understood the responsibility of your office," said Gasser.

A juror interjected (in an Austrian trial, jurors are free to ask questions at will): "Is it not the case that the decision had already been made and that your statement was a mere formality?"

"Yes" was her soft, almost inaudible reply.

The probation officer Helmut Haselbacher took the stand. His responsibility had been to monitor Jack following his release from prison, and Judge Haas wanted to know about his experiences with the accused.

"Shortly after Unterweger's release I sensed he wouldn't remain free for long," he explained.

"Why?" asked Judge Haas.

"He consciously led the life of an outsider. Guys like him view the world differently." Haselbacher described his two-year struggle with the accused, who had deeply resented his probation.

"Why doesn't the President just pardon me?" Jack asked irritably in the autumn of 1991. He couldn't be bothered to meet his probation officer, because he had more important things to do, like entering his Mustang Mach I in a private race near Monaco and making film deals in Hollywood.

"It was a constant fight to reach him, a power struggle in which it quickly became clear that Mr. Unterweger would win." Haselbacher paraphrased Jack's children's story *The Dachshund Without a Leash* to illustrate the personality of the author.

"A dog without an owner looks after himself. Unterweger saw in his probation assistant an instrument for binding him on a leash—a sort of master. But there was no sense in trying to leash a dog against his will. And so eventually the dog ends up in the pound."

"People aren't put into pounds," Lehofer replied.

CHAPTER 67

JOKER

THE FIRST OF JACK'S "JOKERS" (as he called his alibis) arrived. Karin, a thirty-nine-year-old graphic designer, had told the police and Wladkowski that she'd "possibly" had a phone conversation with Jack on the evening of April 8, though she'd been unable to say when exactly. Silvia Zagler had last been seen on her corner, ten minutes from Jack's apartment, around 10:30 p.m., so the time of Karin's conversation with him was critical.

"Certainly the conversation lasted until 12:00," she told Judge Haas.

"Why, now, are you so sure?"

She tried to make eye contact with Jack.

"Don't look at the accused, just look at me," the judge said.

"Initially I didn't realize how precarious it would become. Later I meditated on the occasion and was able to recover a clear memory of it."

Prosecutor Gasser then asked her about a letter she'd written to Jack in jail—a letter that Gasser interpreted as asking the question: "What do you need?" Reacting to the pressure; she said, "I feel that he couldn't have done these things. He is an exceptionally tender man."

"Do you believe he was capable of committing the murder in 1974?"

"Yes, but that was when he was young."

"Do you believe he was capable of raping a girl with a steel rod?"

"No."

"No further questions."

On her way out, Karin tried to give a parcel to Zanger.

"What is that?" Judge Haas asked.

"Just some things for Jack."

———

That evening, an ORF television news program reported Karin's testimony as "the first successful Unterweger alibi." Alibis would have been more helpful on the nights the women disappeared from cities other than Vienna. The Vienna victims had last been seen on Sunday, Monday, and Tuesday nights, between 10:30 p.m. and 1:00 a.m., and because Jack lived in the city, it would have been plausible for him to say that he was at home. "A Viennese happens to be in Vienna—what a coincidence!" as Lehofer exclaimed. If Jack hadn't mentioned all his girlfriends, he could have said, "So *what* that I was home alone on those nights. I'm a single man." Asserting that he was with women or talking with them on the phone *around* the time the prostitutes disappeared might convey the idea that he *could* be excluded, but it also prompted the thought: He had regular contact with so many women, and yet not *one* of them was with him on a *single one* of the eleven nights the prostitutes were last seen.

His second "joker"—a woman named Sylvia with whom he claimed to have spent the night when Sabine Moitzi disappeared in Vienna—also couldn't confirm the alibi. The court attempted to contact Carolina (his "joker" for the night Sherri Long disappeared in Hollywood) in the States, but didn't succeed (she was apparently in Central America visiting family).

CHAPTER 68

MOTHER

THREE OF JACK'S "JOKERS" failed to make a winning hand. The final one—his mother in Munich—would have to be checked. If Jack really had been in Munich on the night of May 7, 1991, it would exclude him as a suspect in the murder of Karin Eroglu in Vienna and create doubt that he was responsible for the other murders. The prosecution was confident he hadn't been in Munich on the night of May 7, 1991, but there was still the possibility that his mother would try to protect him.

For two years, Theresia Strasser had been besieged by the media. One day she looked out the window of her apartment in Munich to see a television cameraman on a crane filming her in her living room.

"Look at my boy," she said to a journalist as she held a framed picture of Jack. "He's a pretty boy; or does he look like a murderer? My boy hasn't traveled halfway round the world murdering a football team of hookers." On the other hand, she was offended by what he'd written about her in *Purgatory*.

"I was never a whore and I don't have a sister. I don't know why Hansi wrote that." Regarding Jack's famous claim that he'd envisioned his mother before him at the moment he murdered his victim in 1974: "It's not true that he saw his mother in every female—such foolishness. He could have just murdered me. And if I'm the one to blame for everything, then they ought to lock me up."

CHAPTER 69

NEMESIS

ON MONDAY, MAY 2, retired Salzburg inspector August Schenner took the stand. For twenty-one years he'd sought justice for the murder of Marica Horvath, the Yugoslavian girl found in the lake near Salzburg. Once again Schenner confronted the man he was convinced had murdered her.

"To me there was nothing that exculpated Unterweger, and I investigated a long time," he said. He described the one-of-a-kind necktie used to bind the girl's hands behind her back, purchased at a shop in Wels when Jack was in the city. The m.o. of the murder was identical to the m.o. Jack had used when he raped Daphne in Salzburg a year later, with the same kind of knot used to tie her hands behind her back. Then there was his initial false alibi that he'd been in Switzerland, when in fact he'd been in Salzburg on the night in question, and gone out alone. The following day he'd dropped off his girlfriend in Wels and unaccountably driven to Switzerland. In his hotel room he'd collected newspaper reports on the murder.

Schenner then described Jack's uncooperative behavior during the 1983 interrogation in Stein, and the bizarre fact that he appeared to be running the prison.

"When Dr. Schreiner tried to attend the interrogation, Unterweger bluntly told him to leave the cell. Afterward, I asked Dr. Schreiner why he tolerated it, and he said, 'Unterweger has many powerful advocates, and I have no desire to be called to the Justice Ministry to explain myself.'"

"Why was Unterweger never tried for the murder of Marica Horvath?" Judge Haas asked.

"The district attorney told me it was senseless, because he could receive only one life sentence," Schenner replied.

Judge Haas probably knew that "Unterweger's powerful advocates" were the real reason for the Salzburg D.A.'s decision, but they weren't on trial.

CHAPTER 70

EX-GIRLFRIEND

ON THE AFTERNOON of Wednesday, May 4, the excitement mounted in anticipation of Bianca's arrival. From her press interviews during the lead-up to the trial, it was public knowledge that she didn't love Jack anymore.

"He got on my nerves, always whining and complaining," she said to a Viennese tabloid. "And then his suicide attempt—cut himself with a dull razor blade. Oh really! If I wanted to do that, I'd do it properly, not just to get sympathy." What had caused her to see him in a different light?

"I read the file on his murder of Margret Schäfer. She was also eighteen. As I read it, I thought, My God, he must have been a brutal pig."

So Jack's spell over Bianca had finally been broken. Did that mean she would offer new, incriminating testimony against him?

A crowd greeted her as she got out of the taxi in front of the courthouse wearing a cream-colored suit and sunglasses, her hair in a ponytail. With a police escort, she entered the courtroom, took the stand, and once again recounted her three months with the accused.

"Was it your great love?" Judge Haas asked.

"For me back then, yes. When we returned from Miami, I didn't want to hurt him, and so I didn't tell the police about a couple of sacks of women's clothing I saw in his basement, as well as some panty hose in his glove compartment." In the course of her testimony she didn't turn her head to make eye contact with Jack, who was sitting to her left and slightly behind her, but she felt his gaze.

"In the meantime, I have emotionally distanced myself from him," she explained. "I don't hate him; he means nothing to me. As a person he was okay," she said. For the second part of her testimony—the most intimate part—Judge Haas dismissed the public and press. As Bianca answered the judge's questions about her intimate experiences with the accused, she could feel Jack staring at her. Yes, he had hit her, though never with a closed fist. Yes, he had shown a preference for certain sexual practices that one might describe as sadomasochistic, and yes, he had tried to put her to work as a prostitute. That a forty-one-year-old man had so exploited a troubled eighteen-year-old girl wasn't evidence that he'd murdered the eleven women, but it once again showed the jury that the accused was selfish and ruthless.

CHAPTER 71

DAUGHTER

OVER THE NEXT FEW DAYS a parade of character witnesses took the stand, some for, most of them against, the accused. Many female witnesses felt bitter that Jack had used them for sex and money and then discarded them.

"Anyone who is emotionally unstable will trust Jack entirely," as one woman put it. "I was going through a very difficult time when I met him, and I was even foolish enough to allow my daughter to be alone with him. Thank God, nothing happened."

She then offered an example of Jack's dishonesty. "When I called him and Bianca answered the phone, he later told me she was his cleaning lady."

Jack shook his head, and she turned to face him.

"It's true, Jack."

The jury's sympathy for her and others like her was probably limited, because most had known in advance that he was a convicted murderer and a womanizer. There was, however, one character witness whose testimony was undeniably sad: Jack's daughter, Claudia.

The public was excluded during her testimony, and to disguise her appearance, the twenty-three-year-old girl wore a wig and sunglasses.

For the first fourteen years of her life, Claudia hadn't known her father. In the summer of 1970, her mother, a sixteen-year-old chambermaid at the White Horse Hotel in the town of St. Gilgen, had met the twenty-year-old disc jockey and fallen in love. A passionate affair ensued, her mother got pregnant, and shortly thereafter Jack moved on. Fifteen years later, as an inmate in Stein, he was allowed to travel to Vienna for the premiere of his play *End Station Prison* at the People's Theater. Claudia attended the play with her mother, who walked up to the author.

"This is your daughter," she said.

"Who are you?" he asked.

"I'm Margret."

A photographer captured Jack embracing them.

For the remainder of his incarceration, Jack corresponded with Claudia, who in the meantime had two children of her own, and after his release he occasionally visited them. When one of her children called him Grandpa, he acted mortified, as though the child had deliberately shattered his youthful self-image. Afterward the kids called him "the man with the big dog."

"He stopped visiting us in the autumn of 1991," Claudia explained. "He called once in February 1992, and the next day I heard on the radio that he was under suspicion for murder and had fled."

Claudia's testimony wasn't really relevant to the prosecutor's case, though it did demonstrate Jack's lack of family feeling. He'd written in *Purgatory* and spoken in interviews about his feelings of despair from being unwanted and abandoned by his parents. It was sad enough that he'd done the same to his own child, but what was most upsetting was the shame and humiliation the girl obviously felt as she testified against her own father, an alleged murderer of eleven women.

On her way out of the courtroom, she handed a folded slip of paper to Lehofer. "Please give this to my father." Lehofer unfolded it and saw the words: *Why have you done this to us?*

"What's that?" snapped Judge Haas.

"It's nothing, your honor, I promise," he said, and stuck the note in his pocket.

CHAPTER 72

A STORM IN THE COURTROOM

ON MAY 19, fifty-year-old Rudolf Prem, the husband of the murdered Regina Prem, took the stand wearing a white sand suit and moccasins, his hair permed and his mustache neatly trimmed. In an interview with *NEWS* the week before, he'd already warned of a possible showdown.

"If Unterweger provokes me, there will be a storm in the courtroom."

"You say you received anonymous telephone calls after your wife went missing," said Prosecutor Gasser.

"Yes. In July and in October."

"What did the caller say?"

"A bunch of miserable nonsense," Rudolf said in thick Viennese dialect. "Phrases like: *When the figure eight at the zenith stands* and *They lie in the place of atonement, facing downward, toward Hades* and *To eleven I have carried out the just punishment.* I said, 'Listen, fool, what was she wearing?' And he said, 'White, eh, and white high heels.'"

"And you say you later recognized the voice?"

"Yeah, later I heard it on the radio when Unterweger was talking."

Judge Haas wanted to know about Regina's typewritten diary, which Rudolf claimed to have found tucked behind a wardrobe as he was cleaning the apartment in May 1992, after Jack's arrest. The eight-page manuscript contained colorful descriptions of her clients, and on the final page was the entry:

Yesterday the comedian came by, says he's a writer. I drove with him to a side street where we take care of quick customers. He chatted about his readings and books, and after 20 minutes he gave me 1,500 Schillings . . . Today the writer came by again. I went with

him to his apartment in the Florianigasse. The guy has a kink for
handcuffs and satisfies himself perversely on top of me . . . After-
ward he told me about his film projects and readings. Most of all,
he jabbers about his shepherd . . . He is very proud of the tattoos on
his upper arms and chest, something I don't understand.

"Had you already seen your wife typing this diary?" asked Haas.

"Yeah, but I figured it was none of my business. I mean, nowadays every public restroom cleaner writes her memoirs."

Some of the diary's phrasing and content, sprinkled with social and political commentary, didn't look like the work of a woman with only an elementary education. The possibility that Regina's diary had been written by someone else was reminiscent of *The Memoirs of Josefine Mutzenbacher*, a classic of Viennese erotic literature that was actually written by Felix Salten, best known for his children's story *Bambi*.

"We know exactly what to think of the diary," Judge Haas said reproachfully. Geiger lamented Rudolf's loss of credibility from the diary, as it undermined his testimony about the anonymous phone calls, which were probably made by Jack. After Jack was arrested, Rudolf became convinced he was the killer and got frustrated that the investigators had such a hard time proving it. He had wanted Regina's diary to contribute to the case against Jack, but in the end it hurt more than it helped.

Zanger and Lehofer took a few shots at Rudolf regarding his statements in a civil court (he'd filed a suit against Jack for the cost of his son's psychological counseling).

"You said in a civil court that you'd seen your wife getting into Unterweger's car, which is obviously false," said Lehofer.

"I've never heard such stupidity! I don't have to take this bullshit from you!" Rudolf yelled.

"That's enough of that," said Judge Haas. "We're not in Hütteldorf [a rough part of Vienna]."

Though Rudolf came off as more of a comedy act than a witness, Jack couldn't resist confronting him.

"This anonymous caller—sometimes you talk about him speaking in a Styrian-Carinthian [Jack's native] dialect, and sometimes you talk about a Viennese [Jack's adopted] dialect."

"Yeah, well, as you would know, you can imitate an accent, but your voice tone remains the same."

CHAPTER 73

PSYCHIATRIST

ON MAY 25, a few days after Rudolf's testimony, Dr. Reinhard Haller observed Jack and jotted an occasional note. The court had contracted him to evaluate the accused, but Jack refused to speak with him, claiming that he was "biased." And so instead of talking with Jack, the psychiatrist watched him.

Jack knew he was being observed by the most renowned court psychiatrist in Austria. He knew the doctor had read the bleak psychiatric evaluations from his trials in 1975 and 1976. It would be difficult to manipulate him, and he regarded anyone immune to his manipulative charm as biased against him.

During the midday recess, Haller approached him and introduced himself. Jack greeted him warmly, and then, about an hour into the afternoon session, he announced, "Of course I'll talk with Dr. Haller. Anytime and anywhere he wishes to speak with me, I'll gladly make myself available."

During the next break, he approached the psychiatrist. "I mistook you for a different doctor, and then I realized that you are the famous Dr. Haller from Vorarlberg. I've heard of you."

Haller figured Jack had sized him up and sensed a weakness, most likely from his youthful appearance. Many people thought he was much younger than his actual age. In fact, Jack was well informed about all the expert witnesses, including Haller.

CHAPTER 74

WITNESSES FOR THE DEFENSE

AND THE PROSECUTION

ON THE AFTERNOON OF MAY 25, the defense enjoyed one of its strongest moments when Dr. Elisabeth Friedrich of the Vienna Institute of Forensic Medicine was examined about what had happened to a five-centimeter hair found adhering to the torn-off fingertip of a surgical glove discovered near the body of the Viennese victim Karin Eroglu. On July 25, 1991, the institute examined the hair and concluded that it was morphologically dissimilar from Eroglu's hair, indicating that it probably came from her assailant. However, in a subsequent attempt to extract DNA from the hair, a molecular biologist at the institute committed the entire sample to the test, thereby dissolving it, while at the same time failing to extract any DNA.

"The entire hair—all five centimeters—was fully dissolved without yielding any result!" said Lehofer.

"Yes, the entire five centimeters." In other words, the hair was destroyed before it could even be morphologically compared (viewed under a microscope) to Unterweger's.

Dr. Friedrich's testimony didn't make sense. Even though the molecular biologist at the Vienna institute was a novice at DNA testing, it seemed very strange that he would use the entire hair for the extraction, as he had to have known that only the root could yield DNA. Dr. Friedrich's testimony was highly compromising for her institute and for the prosecution.

Probably in an effort to negate the bad impression she made, the prosecution called a witness immediately after her testimony—an actor who'd toured with *Scream of Fear*—who recounted how Jack had once remarked to a young actress, "Your nipples should be cut off and preserved in vinegar."

"Oh, come on, that was just guy talk," said Lehofer in a rare occasion of missing the mark with the jury.

"Guy talk, Mr. Defender!" snapped Prosecutor Gasser. "Don't count me among the guys who talk that way."

CHAPTER 75

HEIDI

THE MURDER OF Heidemarie Hammerer on the night of December 5–6, 1990, was the topic of the day on May 27.

"We investigated fifty-four suspects, and at the end only Jack Unterweger was left," explained the Vorarlberg gendarmerie inspector Kurt Obergschwandtner. Among other things, hairs found on the victim's body were morphologically indistinguishable from Jack's, though none of them had sufficient roots for extracting DNA.

Jack testified that he'd checked into his hotel in the neighboring town of Dornbirn that evening around 9:00 and didn't leave his room until the next morning. Two eyewitnesses contradicted him.

Johann F. testified that on the night Heidemarie disappeared, he saw her in her apartment building garage between 11:00 and 12:00 p.m. with a shorter man wearing a red scarf and leather jacket. The witness had contacted the police in February 1992 after reading about Jack's flight from arrest and thinking that his image in the newspaper resembled the man he'd seen with Heidi Hammerer. Given that the eyewitness was the victim's neighbor, it seemed odd that he hadn't contacted the police when her body was found on December 31, 1990, in the Lustenauer marsh.

"I figured they would find her killer without my help" was his lame explanation. Jack had indeed worn his favorite red scarf to Dornbirn—the same red scarf he was wearing in the newspaper photo. He'd also worn a beige leather jacket that *wasn't* in the photo—the same jacket he'd discussed with Bianca on the phone during his detention in Miami (he asked her to tell the police it was hers, and became enraged when she told him they'd confiscated it).

The second witness claimed he'd seen a white Mustang Mach I with the Vienna plate w JACK 1 near the Bregenz train station (and Heidi Hammerer's corner) at around 9:30 that evening. He'd contacted the police in July 1992, after seeing a photo of Jack's Mustang in the paper.

Zanger asked the witness why, over a year and a half later, he remembered seeing that particular car at that particular time and date.

"When I saw the car, I was driving to the station to pick up my wife, who was returning from a meeting in Vienna, and I thought to myself, Look at that, a Viennese pimp in Bregenz." Checking the documentation of his wife's business trip, he saw that she had returned on the evening of December 5.

The eyewitness accounts suggested Jack's guilt, but didn't prove it. The testimony seemed questionable, given that both witnesses had come forward so long after the events had happened. Their statements gave the jury a glimpse of the gray zone in which the investigators had worked for two years. So many things about the accused were suspicious, and so little amounted to proof.

Jack insisted he'd never visited the Bregenz red-light district, but a while later he referred to a specific location in the neighborhood.

"I thought you said you'd never visited the Bregenz red-light district," said Judge Haas. Jack paused for a second, and then said, "In my conversation with Dr. Haller [who lives near Bregenz] yesterday, he mentioned the location." Dr. Haller wasn't present to confirm the statement (he later denied it).

Further muddying the water was the testimony of a Bregenz pimp named Manfred. Two weeks after Heidi Hammerer's body was found, he told a waitress about her violent death, and mentioned that her killer had crammed her slip down her throat—a detail that hadn't yet been

mentioned in the press. The Bregenz police investigated him and ultimately excluded him. In the initial questioning of prostitutes and pimps,
it was likely that an officer had carelessly mentioned that the victim had
been choked with her slip and strangled.

Zanger tried to play the former suspect for all he was worth, and began his examination by handing him a handkerchief.

"Why are you sweating so much?"

"Spare us the theater, Mr. Defender," said Judge Haas.

Manfred denied he was the killer, and though he admitted to talking
about her murder, he denied the rumors that he'd boasted about committing it himself.

"I wouldn't brag about murder!" He'd never been suspected of murder before the Hammerer case, but he did have a rape conviction. Had
he committed murder on the same night Jack Unterweger happened to
be in town?

CHAPTER 76

BLANKA

LEHOFER GREETED JACK as he entered the courtroom on the morning of May 31.

"My wife is here today to watch her old man in action and to see the
great Unterweger for herself."

"Excellent. Where is she?"

"Guess," said Lehofer, knowing that Jack had never seen a photograph of her.

"She's the blonde sitting on the left side toward the back," he said. It
wasn't a brilliant guess, because Lehofer had told Jack of his taste for full-
bodied blondes. Jack shared Lehofer's preference for women with round
hips and large breasts. "The kind of girls you see working at country restaurants," as he'd put it. Lehofer called the type "Valkyrie-like," an expression

of his love of Wagner's operas ("The Ride of the Valkyries" played on his law-office answering machine), and Mrs. Lehofer looked like one of Odin's priestesses. What was impressive was the speed with which Jack had scanned the thirty middle-aged women in the room and identified her.

After the session opened, Lehofer realized he'd made a mistake by inviting his wife to attend on that particular day—the day the prosecution showed the video of the Prague crime scene. A screen was pulled down, the lights were dimmed, and an image appeared of a naked woman lying on her back in a shallow brook, her legs spread wide apart. The background sound of the gurgling water added to the stark realism of the scene. A close-up of the woman's throat revealed deep red marks from a strangulation instrument; red marks on her wrists looked like chafing from handcuffs. She was a young, healthy blonde (sort of "Valkyrie-like") with a shapely figure and breasts. As the camera zoomed in on her pubic region, a hand entered the frame and pulled a tampon from her vagina, indicating that she hadn't had sexual intercourse with her assailant.

Lehofer imagined his wife fifty feet away, having an emotional meltdown. He glanced at Jack and saw him watching intently, without the slightest expression on his face. The instant the lights came back on, he felt Jack nudging him with his elbow.

"Go on, say something," he said, probably thinking it would interrupt the jury's train of emotion. He really is ice cold, Lehofer thought.

"No, Mr. Unterweger," he whispered, "now is not the time to say something."

CHAPTER 77

AN EXPERIMENT

LEHOFER'S JOB WASN'T TO FIGURE OUT THE TRUTH but to defend his client. Determining the truth was the jury's responsibility. And yet there was something about the Unterweger case that made him want to know the truth. Maybe it was all the social and political dimensions. Where did wishful thinking end and reality begin? Did the accused really make such an ass of the influential people who'd pressured for his release with such sanctimonious rhetoric?

Jack had a remarkable ability to make people question the reality that all the indications denoted. Lehofer had represented many men who were guilty of murder, and few if any had been good at concealing it. Most of them just weren't very good liars; within a couple of conversations they revealed knowledge of something that only the murderer could know.

Jack was different. He could discuss the murders for hours without mentioning a single detail that wasn't in the police files. It must have been strange for him to read reconstructions of crimes they claimed he'd committed. If he was innocent, he must have thought, I can't believe they're saying I did this. If he was guilty, he would recognize what the police had noticed and what they had missed. He could use the gaps in their reconstructions and their erroneous deductions to his advantage, but he had to be careful not to reveal too much understanding of the crimes.

One day he gave Lehofer a thirty-eight-page handwritten critique of the investigation, laying out all the mistakes the police had made. It included his own signature crime-scene analysis, in which he pointed out many differences from one scene to the next. His critique was presumptuous, but it was also clear that he had a solid grasp of the techniques of gathering and evaluating evidence—techniques he had learned from his own mistakes in the past, and from studying literature on forensic science. He'd also written a screenplay titled *Naked Life* for the ORF television series *Crime Scene*. Soon the first expert witness would take the stand, and as the pressure mounted, Jack became ever more industrious in coming up with ideas for challenging the prosecution. One day as they were reviewing crime scenes, he had an idea. One of the Graz crime scenes suggested that the woman's assailant had killed her, perhaps in his car, and then moved her body into the woods.

"You say she was a big woman?" he asked.

"Yes. Somewhere I've got a note of her height and weight."

"Well, I'm a little guy. How could I have carried her body up the hill between the road and the woods?" he said as he stood up and mimicked bending forward, using his hips and back to leverage the weight. "Up that steep slope, all slippery with dead leaves," he said, making gestures of pulling on the body, struggling to move forward. "It would have been impossible."

Lehofer said nothing, but pretended to be lost in thought.

"Something strange happened today," he said to Anna, a young medical student he'd hired to help him understand DNA. As Anna would later recall, Lehofer was visibly perturbed by the day's events, and what he said left a strong impression on her. "We were talking about one of the crime scenes, and as Jack described what it must have been like for the killer to move the body into the woods, I got the feeling that he was using words and gestures that only the killer would use," Anna recalled Lehofer saying. "He says he's never been to that crime scene, and in none of the files have I seen such a precise description of it."

"That's creepy," said Anna. "So you think it's him."

Lehofer didn't answer. "How would you like to meet him?" he asked.

Lehofer invited Anna to meet Jack because he wanted to see for himself how a woman reacted to him. The attorney had heard so much about Jack's legendary powers as a seducer—the way he could sit in a coffeehouse and draw girls like moths to a light. What was it about the strange little man that women found so fascinating? Anna was the perfect subject upon which to conduct the experiment because, though she was young and feminine, she was also highly intelligent and would be able to articulate her perceptions.

The following evening she dressed up like a secretary, with a long skirt and blouse, and they went to the jailhouse.

"She's my support staff," Lehofer said as they signed in. A security guard led them down a corridor to the interrogation room, where they sat down at the table. Anna had never been in a jail before, and it made her extremely nervous.

"Just relax and try to set aside everything you've heard about him," said Lehofer. "I'll do most of the talking; you just watch him." The door opened and Jack entered, wearing jogging pants and a T-shirt.

"May I introduce my assistant Anna Schmidt," Lehofer said, presenting her like a sumptuous dish. Jack was surprised. For two years a wire partition had separated him from all his female visitors, with the exception of Dr. Zanger's assistant, and Anna was no ordinary woman. A star medical student, she also looked like a supermodel.

"It's very nice to meet you," he said. His demeanor was formal, as though he really were addressing a legal assistant (as he noted in his diary, he knew she wasn't one). For her part, Anna was astonished by the little man who stood before her. He in no way corresponded to her notions of a woman killer. He had a strangely childlike face, and when he smiled, he looked like an impish but sweet little boy. If she had known nothing about him and met him on a dark street, she wouldn't have felt the slightest fear of him.

She watched him and noticed that he avoided eye contact with her. Lehofer watched her and noticed her hand quivering as she touched her face. Jack talked about the fix he was in and asked what more could be done to win the trial. As he spoke, Anna watched his facial expressions and evaluated his phrasing and tone, trying to detect a sign that he was dissembling. She saw and heard none. His conviction and his despair sounded authentic, as if he were a helpless little man pulverized by the crushing power of the state.

"So what do you think?" Lehofer asked as they walked out of the courthouse.

"I can't believe how small and childlike he is."

"Maybe he's short and slender, but did you see the size of his forearms?"

"I didn't notice them."

"How did he affect you?"

"Like seeing a wounded animal."

"Really?" Lehofer asked.

"Yes, definitely. I understand why he makes women feel motherly and protective, and any woman with a helper syndrome would be devastated."

"How did you feel about him?"

"Mostly I was just amazed by his sweet-little-boy appearance. I can't imagine a more harmless-looking man. No wonder he's so dangerous."

CHAPTER 78

CHIEF OF POLICE

ON JUNE 2, MAX EDELBACHER, chief of the Vienna police, took the stand.

"It kind of bothered me that Mr. Unterweger interviewed me first, for the ORF, and only later did I learn from my wife that I had spoken on the radio with a convicted murderer. After he returned from Los Angeles, he visited me a second time to tell me about his trip. At that point I began to have a funny feeling in my gut, and I asked myself, Why is he seeking contact with us?"

"If you had a funny feeling about him, why didn't you confront him with it during his second visit?" asked Judge Haas.

"Because we didn't have anything on him. The tip to look at him was only one of 130. At that point it didn't make sense to tell him of our suspicion."

Haas wanted to know how Jack had managed to slip surveillance and flee to America in February 1992.

"He simply ditched us."

"When Unterweger first interviewed you about the murders, did you tell him any details about the crime scenes?" Prosecutor Gasser asked.

"Certainly not."

"How then did he know that no jewelry was missing from the victims?" Gasser said, referring to Jack's statement in his Miami Defense.

"Ah ha," said Edelbacher. "That's a very good question!"

Lehofer took a turn.

"Didn't you think it was remarkable that a man released from a life sentence on probation didn't flee straightaway when he learned he was under suspicion?"

"I consider Unterweger a very cold and calculating man. Fleeing was what one would expect, and so he did the opposite and came to us. He played with us."

"You knew he didn't have a driver's license, but you nevertheless had your men follow him in his car round the clock. Why?" asked Judge Haas.

"When one is under suspicion for several murders, then frankly I don't care if he drives without a license."

Jack was angry that Edelbacher had turned on him.

"A lot of what you are saying about our first meeting isn't correct," he told the police chief.

"Yeah, just like the reason you offered for why you were doing a story on the prostitute murders—because your aunt had been murdered while working as a prostitute. That also wasn't correct."

CHAPTER 79

THE AMERICANS

SERGEANT STEVE STAPLES OF THE LAPD had been amazed to receive a summons to a trial in Graz, Austria, and a plane ticket, courtesy of the Austrian Consulate. They wanted him to testify at the trial of the journalist who'd gone on a ride-along three years before. Staples had heard of Homicide inspectors traveling to Chicago or Boston for a murder trial, but a patrol sergeant sent to Europe was unheard of.

It was frustrating how no one would tell him any specifics. In theory it was to avoid prejudicing him, but Staples wondered if it was necessary to be kept so completely in the dark. All he knew was that the Austrian journalist was being tried for murder.

"And if he's convicted, we're gonna try you as an accessory," Ronnie Lancaster at the Sheriff's Department had joked.

In the waiting lounge at the airport, he saw Detective Harper.

"What exactly did this guy do?" Staples asked.

"You'll soon find out," Harper replied.

It was a long way to Graz. The little city was so far east of L.A., and so different. Staples had never seen anything like it. The ancient buildings with steep pitched roofs, the narrow cobblestone streets, the churches with Gothic spires and onion domes, the castle perched on the hill above—it was like something out of a fairy tale. And God was it orderly. Walking around the pedestrian zones in the old town, Staples heard only his footsteps and the soft chime of a church bell every quarter hour. At one point as he was strolling along, the smell of fresh-baked bread stopped him in his tracks. He looked around and saw a bakery, its door propped open. He went inside as a woman was pulling a tray of brown rolls out of the oven.

"May I have one of those?" It was a heavenly piece of bread, all crunchy on the outside and dense on the inside, and as he bit into it, his mind flashed back to a lunch at the Captain's Table seafood joint on Sixth and Main exactly three years earlier.

"You don't have very good bread in this country, do you?" said the Austrian journalist as he eyed the crappy little white roll.

Lynne "the Boa" Herold of the L.A. County Crime Lab arrived the following evening and was told the Graz police were hosting a party for the Americans at a wine garden in the countryside. She was met in the lobby by an officer of the court who spoke pretty good English. The first stop of the evening was the home of a ranking Graz officer who was keen for the Americans to try his home-distilled schnapps. She thought it tasted pretty good, but she didn't care for it as much as the Austrian cops did. Following them on the windy road out to the countryside, she noticed their car was weaving. It was hard to get too indignant, because they were such a cheerful bunch and they treated her like a queen.

On June 6, 1994, the fiftieth anniversary of D-Day, the L.A. cops testified. Just before the session began, Ronnie Lancaster bumped into Jack walking down the courthouse stairs, escorted by security guards. Unlike Miller and Harper, he'd never met the accused. A Vienna cop with whom Lancaster had just been talking made the introduction.

"Nice to meet you," Jack said, smiling warmly and shaking his hand. "Are you having a nice time in Graz?"

"Yeah, a great time," said Lancaster. "It's a beautiful city."

"I'm glad. But you know, Lancaster, you guys aren't going to convict me, because you don't have any evidence."

"You don't think so?"

"No. But I do hope you enjoy your visit. See you later."

Because of his back injury, Fred Miller couldn't make it to the trial, and so James Harper took the stand and told the story of the two downtown L.A. prostitutes who were found strangled with their own bras in the summer of 1991. Lancaster then took over and explained how the third victim had been picked up in Hollywood and driven to Malibu. He opened his map of L.A. County to show the jury where Hollywood was located.

"So you see, the girl was picked up here." He started to point at the map, but didn't see Hollywood. *Where's Hollywood?* He frantically scanned the streets, still holding up his index finger. *Holy shit, this is embarrassing. Where's Hollywood?*

"Well, anyway, I can't find it on this map, but it's in this area somewhere. He picked her up here and drove her out to Malibu on the Pacific Coast Highway," he said, pointing to the coast.

The thrust of the Los Angeles testimony was that, long before they'd heard of Jack Unterweger, they knew that all three women had been murdered by the same killer—a killer who'd started in downtown L.A. and then gone to Hollywood. They had expected him to continue, and when he didn't, they assumed the he'd moved on, gotten locked up for a separate offense, or died. And then, eight months later, they learned that Jack Unterweger had stayed at the Hotel Cecil in downtown when the

first two girls disappeared, and had then moved to a motel on Sunset
Boulevard in Hollywood the day before the third girl disappeared from
her corner a few blocks away.

What emerged from Staples's testimony was Jack's voracious curiosity about police work in L.A. His interest wasn't in particular crime stories but in the methods of controlling and investigating crime in general,
as though he were acquiring an education. After Staples's testimony, a
journalist asked him his official position.

"Back then I was a patrol sergeant. Now I work in vice."

The next day, out for a stroll, he passed a newsstand and saw his face
on the front page of a tabloid. SERGEANT STEVE STAPLES, MIAMI VICE,
read the caption.

Special Agent Gregg McCrary's testimony on June 8 was billed by the
press as one of the biggest moments in the trial. A month before he arrived, the papers began reporting on the "FBI Man, the director of the
special unit in *The Silence of the Lambs*," who was coming to Graz, as
though McCrary were an international celebrity about to bless the
provincial city with his presence. For his part, McCrary found the experience one of the most memorable of his career. What impressed him
most was the accused. "Despite his small stature, this guy was larger
than life. He was a *presence* . . . a malevolent thoroughbred. His smile
was gracious and disarming, his gaze penetrating. He clearly loved the
limelight, and his abundant charm filled the room."

"Would you please tell the court and the jury exactly what you did in
this case and what conclusions, if any, you drew," asked Prosecutor
Wenzl. McCrary explained his analysis of the cases and how computer
database searches had linked the eleven homicides while simultane-
ously eliminating thousands of others. He then described how the common features of the crime scenes were revealing of the personality of the
offender. "If we were to know who committed one of these crimes, and
if that individual was in the same area at the same time the other murders were committed, it's highly probable that this one perpetrator committed all eleven homicides."

What were the odds that the opposite was the case—that is, that various killers were at work in each of the five cities? Though McCrary did not mention it to the jury, it was a remarkable fact that Jack was in five different cities on nights when women were not only murdered in the same way he'd murdered his victim in 1974 but murdered by a stealthy killer who evaded the intense investigations that were conducted in each city.

A break was announced, and as McCrary was organizing his notes, he glanced up and was amazed to see Jack walking toward him. A security officer ordered him to stop, but he didn't listen. He walked right up to the FBI agent, smiling.

"The first murder was not a sexual homicide," he said, referring to his murder of Margret Schäfer in 1974. McCrary could see that Jack was trying to engage him, to form a personal connection.

"Is that right?" he replied. "But the others were?"

Jack paused for a moment, and then his eyes flashed with understanding.

"A clever question!" he said, just as the guards grabbed him and pulled him back.

Zanger cross-examined McCrary after the break.

"Have you ever heard of a man who has frequent consensual sex murdering a prostitute?" he asked. McCrary replied with an account of the Arthur Shawcross case. Like Jack, Shawcross had been imprisoned for murder and was released after serving fifteen years. Despite having regular consensual sex with his wife and mistress, he frequently went to prostitutes, and murdered eleven of them.

It was a classic example of why a defense attorney shouldn't ask questions whose answers he doesn't already know.

Of all the expert witnesses who testified at the Unterweger trial, Lynne "the Boa" Herold from the L.A. County Crime Lab made the strongest impression. As Lehofer watched her approach the stand, wearing a light blue dress and what appeared to be bedroom slippers (orthopedic shoes for a bad disc in her lower back), she reminded him of the Westerns by the German author Karl May he'd so loved as a boy, because Dr. Herold looked like a Navajo squaw.

Judge Haas asked her about the bra ligatures from Los Angeles.

"I have analyzed several hundred cases of ligature strangulation, and I have never seen ligatures like these. They are extremely unusual and have seven conspicuous similarities. When I saw them, I immediately said, 'Look for the same killer for all three.'" She pulled two bras out of a bag (the bra found on the third victim was wrapped in plastic because of the decomposition fluid), and as she held one up, Lehofer heard gasps.

Dr. Herold pointed out the tiny circumference of the nooses. "These ligatures were, with very high probability, made by the same killer," she explained.

"Could you demonstrate how they were tied?" asked Judge Haas.

"To see the exact combination of loops and turns, they would have to be untied, which I'm not prepared to do."

"Perhaps Mr. Unterweger can show you how the knot was tied," Prosecutor Gasser said.

Lynne didn't understand the German words, but from the stir in the courtroom, she knew they were provocative. As the interpreter translated them, she raised her eyebrows, glanced at Gasser, and said nothing.

Judge Haas spoke: "You said at the time that one should look for the same killer of Rodriguez, Long, and Exley. What would you have said if you had, at the time, also seen the panty hose of Mrs. Moitzi?"

"The same," she replied.

"And the tights of Mrs. Eroglu?"

"The same. All five ligatures were, with a very high probability, tied by the same killer."

"We thank you," said Judge Haas.

She felt around under the witness stand with her toes, looking for her slippers, slid her feet into them, and shuffled out of the courtroom.

———

Lehofer figured that if any jury member had been sitting on the fence, Dr. Herold had just pushed him onto the "guilty" side. All around him he sensed people looking at Jack in a new, darker light. Tools are one of the things that distinguish humans from animals, and the bra ligatures— relics of murder—had a devilish ingenuity about them. They were a particularly disturbing expression of the culprit's warped intelligence. Prosecutors relished such presentations because they overwhelmed jury members with the enormity of the crime, causing them to forget about the trying situation of the accused.

Prosecutor Gasser's suggestion that Jack demonstrate how the knot was tied was an example of his sharp-tongued style. From his harsh words and his way of shouting at the accused and his lawyer when they tried to distract or confuse the jury, it was obvious that he despised Jack Unterweger. Throughout the trial, Zanger suggested that the prosecutor was too personal, his attacks too annihilating, and that it was all just posturing for the media. "Now that the press is back in the courtroom, the prosecutor may start yelling again," he remarked on one occasion.

Lehofer, who knew Gasser, believed his sentiment was genuine. Gasser felt a passionate desire for justice for the murdered women, and he was incensed by the prospect of Jack manipulating his way out of it. In the thirty-two days of the trial, he and Jack had only one friendly exchange. Judge Haas was trying to untie a piece of twine binding some files together.

"Who tied these files together?"

Suspicion fell on Gasser.

"I can show you how to tie a knot," Jack said to the prosecutor. "You asked me to show Dr. Herold. I can show you, too."

Gasser looked at him and couldn't help smiling.

CHAPTER 80

A HISTORY LESSON

ON JUNE 13, Dr. Andrea Berzlanovich from the Vienna Institute of Forensic Medicine was feeling nervous. It was her first time giving testimony at a murder trial, and it was hard to imagine a bigger one. Geiger was supportive.

"Your work is solid; your facts speak for themselves. All you have to do is present them." He warned that Jack's defenders would try to rattle her. They would try to undermine her credibility in the eyes of the jury by emphasizing that she was young and female. An emotional response was what they wanted from her.

Zanger began his cross-examination by addressing her as "Mrs." instead of "Dr." Berzlanovich. Andrea knew that if his "What does this girl know?" strategy was going to work, he was going to have to be more subtle about it, because the jury knew she was a doctor. The day before her testimony, the country's largest circulation newspaper printed a two-page report on her work that included her education, experience, and achievements.

On the stand, Andrea stated that she'd begun her study of prostitute murder long before she'd heard about Jack.

"The study was not directed at Unterweger," she said. She then explained how, during the thirty-five-year period between 1959 and 1994, fifty-four prostitutes were murdered in Austria, or 1.5 per year on average, and of those, there were only eight cases of street prostitutes picked up in the city, strangled or apparently strangled, and dumped in the woods naked or partly naked. One of the cases had been solved in the 1970s. The other seven were those the accused was alleged to have committed. Seven prostitutes murdered in six months was a dramatic spike from the 1.5 per year average.

While Zanger tried to call into question her credentials, Jack tried a more effective strategy. Politely addressing her as Dr. Berzlanovich, he focused his questions strictly on the substance of her testimony.

Afterward she found a place on the second-floor gallery from which to watch Geiger's testimony. Under questioning from Judge Haas, he recounted how the investigation had started to take shape in January 1992.

"For months he was just one tip among many, but as we began to focus on him, our most striking realization was that he was always in the vicinity when each of the women disappeared from the three cities. It was then that we thought, This can't just be a coincidence. Later we discovered that the same was true of his trips to Los Angeles and Prague."

As she was listening to Geiger, Andrea noticed a group of about twenty women in the rows below her, sobbing. At first she figured they were friends and relatives of the victims, but after watching them for a while, she realized the true cause of their distress: their beloved Jack was getting fried.

Andrea had always resented the cliché that women are too governed by their emotions to make rational judgments. As she watched the chorus of weeping women, it bothered her to think how much they were reinforcing the cliché. Were they incapable of listening to Geiger and thinking about his statements? She found the women incomprehensible.

A few female journalists covering the story felt the same way. They believed that Jack hated women, and they were flabbergasted that so many women were willing to man the barricades for him. Three journalists, Eva Deissen, Marga Swoboda, and Doris Piringer, were relentlessly critical of Jack and the women who supported him. Toward the end of the trial, Swoboda wrote an editorial titled "The Serpent and the Bunny" about how the young lawyer Astrid Wagner had lost possession of herself and was going to get burned if she didn't snap out of it.

In his diary Jack wrote: "Deissen, Swoboda, Piringer, have you looked at your mugs in the mirror? Does it lift your wrinkles to slime me? No more orgasms for you. Sad. No hatred, just feel sorry for you."

In cross-examining Geiger, Zanger focused on the minutiae of the crimes that the investigators hadn't been able to reconstruct. He knew there were many things about how the murders were committed, the precise sequence of events, that Geiger didn't know, and it was at these gaps that he aimed his questions in an attempt to make the jury think, There are many things the lead investigator doesn't know. By asking an enormous volume of questions, Zanger tried to make Geiger lose his bearings and contradict himself.

"In a single one of these cases do you know exactly when the woman was picked up?"

"No."

"Do you know for certain that all the victims were murdered on the same night they were picked up?"

"No." Geiger answered most of the rhetorical questions with a simple no or yes. To the questions that required a statement of facts, he replied immediately, without contradicting himself. Zanger pursued the theme that the investigators hadn't reconstructed the precise timing of the murders relative to Jack's movements, and then he tried to spring a little trap.

"Do you know what time it is right now?"

Geiger glanced at his watch. "Seventeen thirty-six."

After Zanger and Lehofer asked about 500 questions, Jack confronted the witness.

"You focused your investigation exclusively on me, without considering other suspects or evidence that exculpated me, didn't you?" he said.

"We spent months reconstructing your activities, looking for anything that could exculpate you, and we found nothing," Geiger replied. While watching Jack pretend to be outraged, as though he'd suffered a great injustice, Geiger imagined the scene that he'd replayed in his mind so many times over the previous two years.

A car parked on a forest road at night. Inside, Jack has a woman in handcuffs, abusing her, savoring her screams of fear and pain. He makes the noose out of her underwear, puts it around her neck, and jerks her "out of the car, into the cool night air." He then marches her into the woods, walking behind her, compelling her forward by choking her with the noose and by pushing her arms, locked behind her back, up toward her head. She tries to resist, and he stabs her in the buttock with his stiletto.

"You say you looked for things that exculpated me?" Jack asked.

"Yes," Geiger replied.

"I don't know whether to laugh or cry," Jack sneered.

"It wouldn't have been necessary to look if you'd cooperated with us, but instead you offered a false alibi and fled the country."

CHAPTER 81

TEXTILE FIBERS

ON JUNE 15, Walter Brüschweiler from the scientific bureau of the Zürich police gave a presentation on textile fibers. The technique of collecting microscopic fibers at crime scenes using sticky tape had been developed by his retired colleague Dr. Max Frei-Sulzer, best known for his controversial analysis of the Shroud of Turin and the "Hitler Diaries."

With his heavy accent, his slow, deliberate manner of speaking, and his talk of precision instruments, Brüschweiler gave a thoroughly Swiss presentation. He began by explaining the enormous variation of textile fibers. The smallest units of textile material, fibers are produced in various shapes and of various lengths. They may be natural or man-made, spun with other fibers into yarn, or woven into a fabric. The chemical composition of dyes also varies tremendously, as does the way the dye is applied and absorbed along the length of the fibers.

"Red is not exactly red, and green is not exactly green," explained Dr. Brüschweiler. "There are thousands of variations of each color."

Using a microscope and an infrared spectroscope, he had analyzed 142 red fibers and 153 black fibers found on the clothing of the Bregenz murder victim Heidemarie Hammerer. The red fibers were compared with fibers from a red scarf found in Jack's closet. The black fibers were compared with fibers from a pair of black wool trousers also found in his closet. Both comparisons yielded a perfect match.

Brüschweiler's conclusion: it was highly probable that Jack's red scarf and black wool trousers had come into contact with Heidemarie Hammerer's clothing. Fibers from the lapel of a leather jacket found in his closet also matched six fibers found on the victim's clothing, but their spectrograph was far less unique.

Jack admitted to having worn his favorite red scarf on his trip to Bregenz on December 5, 1990. How many other men in Bregenz on the same night wore textiles made out of identical material was impossible to establish. Brüschweiler explained that police officers in Switzerland and Austria had looked in various markets and found twelve different red scarves, two of which were indistinguishable from Jack's.

Jack was engrossed in Brüschweiler's presentation. In a friendly tone he asked intelligent questions about fiber analysis, and he seemed deeply impressed by the scientist's testimony. But when he was confronted with the red scarf upon which the tests had been conducted, he said, "That can't be mine. It's ragged. I don't have such a scarf."

That night, Jack lamented the performance of his lawyers in his diary:

> It seems to me that Lehofer's entire role has been to block Zanger's attacks on the authorities, because Lehofer has never really studied the files, and has never used the material and the questions with which I have provided him.
>
> And Dr. Zanger: all of the (since Feb. 92) "sensations" in this case that he has announced to the media have shown themselves to be sacks of hot air. For example his "100 red textiles" (scarves, etc.) and his "Bockova's missing skin"—fundamentally nothing! 80 percent showman with me as his advertisement.

The part about the "100 red textiles" referred to Zanger's claim that the fibers in Jack's scarf were commonplace. The part about "Bockova's missing skin" referred to the skin and type B blood traces found under the left-hand fingernails of the Prague victim Blanka Bockova (Jack was type B, as was she). Zanger claimed that Blanka had bits of missing skin from her own body, indicating that she had accidentally scratched herself in struggling with her assailant. That meant, he claimed, that the blood traces under her right-hand fingernails—which included types AB, A, and B—were those of her assailant. However, the Prague forensic pathologist stated that the traces under her right-hand fingernails included animal blood from her work at a butcher's shop. The type B traces under her left-hand fingernails were definitely human, and there were no defects on her skin from fingernail scratching and gouging (though she did have a stab wound in her buttock).

CHAPTER 82

DNA

MANFRED HOCHMEISTER, the DNA specialist from the Bern Institute of Forensic Medicine, wasn't going to testify about the hair found on the seat of Jack's BMW 728, because he wasn't a professor, and also because he was too young-looking. Thirty-seven years old, he appeared to be in his early twenties. The jury would definitely think, What could this little boy know about this cutting-edge science? And so Professor Dirnhofer, the head of the institute, was going to present the results of Manfred's work.

Just before Dirnhofer took the stand, Manfred reviewed a few things with him in the men's room, and was surprised to see that the professor was nervous. Taking a seat, Manfred glanced over at Jack's attorneys and was astonished to see them reading textbooks on molecular biology. Surely they didn't think they were going to challenge his work on scientific grounds.

Jack knew that Manfred was the only true expert on the subject.

"Zanger + Dirnhofer / DNA = hot air. Lehofer also zero. Only talk of studying DNA with his 'student' for weeks . . ." he wrote in his diary.

DNA evidence was something the jury had to accept on the authority of the scientist who presented it. With visual aids, Dirnhofer gave a thorough presentation on deoxyribonucleic acid, the double-helix bond, and the genetic code, but in the end, all the jury could really do was have faith that he was telling the truth when he stated that DNA was a scientifically established fact of life, and that DNA extracted from the root of a blond hair found on the seat of Jack's BMW was identical to the DNA of the Prague murder victim Blanka Bockova.

If, as Jack maintained, Blanka Bockova had never ridden in his car, then why was her hair found on his car's passenger seat?

Because the police put it there was Astrid Wagner's answer. Manfred considered it very unlikely but not impossible, though it occurred to him that if the lead investigator had decided to break the law to achieve his desired result, thereby risking total disaster and a prison sentence, he might have planted hairs with decent roots.

In May 1993, Manfred received three blond head hairs from the scientific bureau of the Zurich police, which claimed they were morphologically indistinguishable from hairs taken from Blanka Bockova. According to the Zurich police, the three hairs submitted for testing had been found on the passenger seat of Jack Unterweger's BMW by the Vienna police trace evidence team. Two of the three hairs had negligible roots; one had a small, damaged root that yielded the absolute smallest amount of DNA on which the tests could be conducted. Because tests for revealing an ever-greater number of genetic markers were coming onto the market almost monthly, Manfred conducted the final test during the trial, in May 1994, and it revealed a constellation of ten genetic markers found in the DNA of less than a thousandth of a percent of the female population. It was 99.99 percent certain that the hair found on the passenger seat of Jack's BMW was Blanka Bockova's.

Dirnhofer did a good job of presenting the evidence, and during the break, Lehofer walked up to Manfred. "Thank you, Dr. Hochmeister, for your excellent presentation of DNA."

CHAPTER 83

MALIGNANT NARCISSIST

ON JUNE 20, 1994, the psychiatrist Dr. Haller presented his findings.

"Jack Unterweger is legally sane, but mentally abnormal. He is suffering from a deep-reaching narcissistic personality disorder with sadistic tendencies." From where Dr. Haller was sitting, facing Judge Haas, he couldn't see the reaction of the accused. Jack had tried hard to win over the psychiatrist—to deceive him about the reality of his character. But Haller was invulnerable to his manipulative charm, and no one told the doctor to "write nothing negative."

It was remarkable how precisely Jack's character conformed to Otto Kernberg's theory of the "malignant narcissist." Kernberg, a Viennese Jew who'd fled the Nazis and ultimately settled in New York, had occasionally returned to the land of his birth to give talks, and Haller found his work on narcissism compelling. At the time Kernberg formulated his theory on the "malignant narcissist," he might as well have been writing a case study of Jack Unterweger.

"Is there anything you wish to say about the doctor's findings?" Judge Haas asked the accused.

"What should I say? He's the expert," Jack replied.

CHAPTER 84

A LIFE OF LIES AND GAMES

AS JACK ENTERED THE COURTROOM the next morning (June 21), he walked over to the press bank.

"I'm mentally abnormal. That sounds good, doesn't it?"

"You're right," shouted a female journalist. It was a bad start to another bad day. Another judge from the Graz court, Prosecutor Gasser, and Zanger had just returned from Munich, where Jack's mother had been sworn in at a local court and asked if she could confirm her son's statement that he'd visited her in Munich May 6–8, 1991 (Karin Eroglu had disappeared on the night of May 7–8).

A video of her statement was played for the jury.

"My son often visited me, but I don't remember any concrete dates. Around Mother's Day in 1991, he gave me his dog as a gift, but I can't remember exactly when."

"Mother?" he wrote in his diary after she failed to confirm the alibi. "No. A life of lies and games. When I was prostrate in the filth, she never gave me a cloth to clean myself, though later she was happy to bask with me in the sun. Never once was she prepared for the truth."

CHAPTER 85

THE LORD'S PRAYER

IT WAS FRIDAY, JUNE 24, and the trial was almost over; the summations were scheduled for the following Monday and Tuesday, and then the verdict.

"Is there anything left for me to do?" Jack asked Lehofer.

"You could pray," said the attorney.

"I don't know how to pray. I've never done it before."

"Then just say the Lord's Prayer."

"I don't know it."

"Come on, man, everyone knows the Lord's Prayer." Lehofer wasn't very religious, but it struck him as odd that Jack didn't know the Lord's Prayer. He had an excellent memory, and as a boy he'd gone to church occasionally. Every Austrian child was taught the prayer.

On Sunday evening, Astrid went up on the roof of the high-rise student dorm behind the courthouse jail. During the two years of Jack's incarceration, she had often gone up on the roof. Though it commands a panoramic view of Graz, it wasn't the sight of the pretty old city and surrounding countryside but the prisoner in the second floor cell 150 yards away that engrossed her.

It was a mild summer evening, and some students were setting up for a roof party. Jack waved his handkerchief at her through the bars, and she could see that he was shirtless. The students were excited about the fun that lay ahead. Their carefree happiness contrasted with the morbid obsession that had taken hold of Astrid.

In her mind, the man in the cell had assumed the mystical significance of a divine victim. Jack suffered not as a result of his behavior but as a result of the bloody-mindedness and stupidity of every man, woman, and institution with which he'd come into contact. Everyone was guilty except him.

Astrid wasn't crazy, but she had focused all her critical intellect on the faults of society and none on the faults of her beloved. She mistook the weaknesses and errors of Jack's opponents for his own innocence. Yes, the police had made mistakes, Geiger and Wladkowski were ambitious, Haas was probably biased, Gasser was zealous, and the press didn't care if its sensational reporting prejudiced the people against Jack. And yet, rationally speaking, the most important question for Astrid was not whether Jack was *proven* guilty, but whether he was *probably* guilty. Lawyers and epistemologists could spend a lifetime debating about proven fact vs. probability, but on what psychological terms was Astrid planning to spend the rest of her life with a man who had, in all probability, tortured and murdered eleven women? Though she hadn't mentioned it to her friends or to the press, Jack had proposed marriage to her, and she had accepted.

CHAPTER 86

SUMMATIONS

PROSECUTOR KARL GASSER gave a powerful summation:

Ladies and gentlemen of the jury, I was afraid you would be overwhelmed by this monster trial, but I see that you have understood. I am absolutely convinced the accused is the killer, and I won't lose a second of sleep if he is convicted . . .

For thirty-five years, the average number of prostitute murders in Austria was 1.5 per year. But then, in the six months between Oc-

tober 1990 and March 1991, seven murders were committed. Unterweger was released in May 1990. He needed a bit of time to get used to freedom, and then, after four months, the series of murders began. Conspicuously, he was always in the area at the time each murder was committed in the same way—once in Prague, twice in Graz, once in Bregenz, four times in Vienna, three times in Los Angeles. No reasonable person will attribute that to mere coincidence.

Gasser then reviewed the indications of Jack's guilt—the highly unusual and matching ligatures found on the victims in L.A. and Vienna, the red fibers found on the victim in Bregenz, the hair of the Prague victim found on the seat of Jack's car, his inability to produce a single alibi and his attempt to obtain false alibis.

And so you see how all of this finally tightens the net around Unterweger . . .

The accused has often tried to confuse you. He has charm and a powerful capacity to convince and to manipulate. In an instant he can think of a plausible-sounding lie. Every time he was caught in a lie, he claimed he'd simply been mistaken. Naturally one makes errors, but in every case? . . .

At various times in his life he has shown his true face. Twenty-one years ago he showed it to a hitchhiker in Tyrol when he picked her up and drove her to a wooded road. "Suddenly he jumped on me and said I would never get out," Gasser quoted the girl's statement. "He strangled me, ripped my stockings off, and tried to tie my hands behind my back, but I was able to get out of the car and run."

The accused has not changed since then. In prison he occupied himself with the question of how he could commit his crimes without being caught, and after his release he almost succeeded . . . His motive wasn't love or jealousy, money or revenge, but the desire for power. Unterweger takes a sinister pleasure in power, and its summit is the mastery over life and death. Such power gives this deeply disturbed personality a special satisfaction . . .

The expert witness Professor Dirnhofer told you that the total is greater than the sum of its parts. You must regard each individual indication not separately but as links in a chain. At the beginning of the chain stands the question: Who is the killer? At the end stands the name: Jack Unterweger. Do not allow this man who has so often lied to you to make suckers of you. Consider that the parole of Jack Unterweger was the irresponsible product of a few people. Now you have a responsibility to the citizens of this republic. Earlier Jack Unterweger told you: If you catch me lying just once, then judge me. Do not fail to fulfill his request.

In Zanger's reply, he insisted to the jury that "there is not a single indication, not a single piece of evidence," and that the entire trial was in reality an effort to undermine the project of criminal rehabilitation. Lehofer took over, and instead of proclaiming that the prosecutors had nothing against Jack, he emphasized that none of it was beyond a reasonable doubt.

In doubt, ladies and gentlemen of the jury, you must rule in favor of the accused. I said earlier that this entire trial hangs on a hair— the hair found on the seat of Unterweger's car. You must decide if the DNA analysis of the hair is proper evidence. Consider that it is a very young science and that Professor Dirnhofer's evaluation has not been confirmed by any other institution . . .

Over the last two months we've heard about how many women Unterweger has been with, his favorite sexual positions, and how long it took him to have an orgasm, but we've heard nothing about evidence. Instead of evidence the prosecutors have talked about probability and coincidence, and in a lawful state, these are not sufficient for a judgment. Coincidence is the cultivated brother of chaos . . .

In every murder there was at least one other suspect. In the case of Brunhilde Masser there was the prominent member of Graz society. In the case of Elfriede Schrempf there was the driver of a white Golf with red stripes. In the case of Regina Prem there was the loving husband and pimp . . .

Ladies and gentlemen of the jury, if you are free of doubt, then throw the stone.

CHAPTER 87

EXPLOSIVE

THE EVE OF THE LAST DAY of the trial—in the morning, Jack would give his summation and the jury would begin deliberating. At 11:45 p.m., Lehofer was at his judo club working out, when he heard an explosion in the distance. Someone had detonated 300 grams of the military high explosive Nitropenta on the outside window of Wladkowski's chamber (he'd since become a trial judge) at the courthouse. The blast, which was heard as far as five miles away, shattered the room and blew a radiator off its mounts beneath the window, rupturing the water pipe and flooding the floor.

Because the main courtroom wasn't damaged, the proceedings began as scheduled the following morning. An investigation was launched and a couple of Yugoslavian boys, active in the Graz underworld, fell under suspicion, but were never arrested for lack of evidence. Wladkowski had a hypothesis about who had commissioned the job, but with no evidence, he was obliged to keep it to himself.

Astrid yearned to see Jack one last time before the verdict. At 8:00 a.m. on June 28, she met him in the jailhouse visitors' room and told him about the glass shards scattered on the ground next to the courthouse.

"Shards bring luck," he said, and forced a smile. He then told her about the stir the bomb had made in the jailhouse.

"They even got Haas out of bed. I saw him peek into my cell. He looked tired, and I overheard him say something about how hard it was for him to wake up with his low blood pressure." Jack had often spoken about Haas, and Astrid sensed that he couldn't help admiring the powerful and handsome man.

"I hope you've filled your tank, because when I walk out of here, the last thing I want to do is spend another night in Graz."

Soon the fifteen minutes were up.

"It's funny," he said, "I don't have a bad feeling."

Astrid stood to leave, but as always, the partition stood in the way of a farewell embrace. Sometimes they'd pressed their palms together, and the previous Friday they'd even managed to steal a kiss through the small aperture in the middle. This time not, because a kiss on the lips signified a true goodbye. Instead, she raised her arm for a kiss on the hand. As she exited the room, she looked back for a final glance. Standing there in his gray, double-breasted suit, he looked so small, the expression on his face so infinitely sad.

Jack wrote in his diary:

> *Today I will hardly listen to the proceedings, but think about friends, and deep within me I will feel happy because I sense that I am loved, and am still capable of loving, not at all devoured by hate. I am a guest at a feast of beautiful feelings because YOU ARE THERE. And I wish to leave the party at its high point, because I cannot bear the stale taste of early morning, and because I have the fear of losing—not the trial—but you, dear one. You are greater than the worries of this life. Your smile. Your presence. That is life, also when it's past.*

Jack gave the final summation—an advantage, given that his words were the last the jury would hear before it went into deliberation. Under Austrian law, a simple majority was sufficient for a conviction, which meant he needed to succeed with at least four of the eight main jury members—to introduce enough doubt to make them reluctant to send him to prison for the rest of his life. If he could speak well enough—passionately enough, with the right gestures—he would appear as a man with too many human qualities to be a sadistic, serial killer of women.

I've been sitting here not knowing what to do. For the last thirty-one trial days, I've been spun through the washing machine of my past, and sometimes I've asked myself, Are you not the idiot who has maneuvered yourself into this position?

It's true what Prosecutor Gasser said about my past. I've often been forced to lie about it because I didn't want to be forever chained by it. What else should I have done? I worked in the public eye; I wanted to write and to direct theater.

. . . Regarding my credibility: I argued with Dr. Zanger. He said, "For God's sake, admit that you had a hooker in your car in Prague. That doesn't mean you killed her." I told him no, lies don't interest me. I go my own way. I want to tell the truth.

. . . Ladies and gentleman of the jury, I don't believe I've made a show here. Earlier I made a giant error: that was my jackass behavior, my boastful manner. Such a lifestyle would have been permissible for a Klaus Kinski or a Helmut Berger, but not for Jack Unterweger.

It's true what the prosecutor says about me consuming women instead of living with and enjoying them, instead of loving them. But fifteen years in Stein: How should one learn to have feelings? It's not possible . . .

After my release from Stein, I was a greedy, devouring individual full of hunger for life. It gave me a feeling of happiness and triumph to have prominent people sit at my table. It gave me the impression of rising above from below.

It made me ill yesterday to hear Dr. Lehofer describe me as a beetle who tries to crawl up a glass wall but never reaches his goal because he always falls onto his back while everyone laughs. I never felt that way. I have always felt that I would eventually arrive at the top . . .

Even if you disapprove of Jack Unterweger's morals and lifestyle,
I ask you to consider if it's enough to say: "Such a man has no busi-
ness being free." I should have been more humble, more prudent,
but I ask you to consider only the arguments and indications that
pertain to the crimes for which I am accused.

I am counting on a verdict of not guilty, because I'm not the
killer. Your decision doesn't only affect me but also the murderer
out there, who is laughing up his sleeve. I will not fall into a hole
if you find me innocent. I have an apartment and a job. There are
so many people who stand behind me, who know me from my two
years of freedom. For that I am humbled, but also proud that they
have not made a mistake.

I am innocent. Thank you.

CHAPTER 88

TENSION

GEIGER WENT FOR A WALK. With eleven counts to consider, he knew the jury would deliberate for a while, and he figured he'd go crazy waiting in the courtroom. It was a fine early-summer day, perfect for a stroll in the historic city center. He walked along, looking at the old buildings, occasionally checking the reception on his cell phone (Dr. Lambauer, the head D.A., was going to call him with the verdict). He popped into a pub for lunch, and then continued his stroll, all the while feeling his anxiety grow.

It's a rule of thumb that the longer a jury deliberates, the greater the likelihood it will find the accused innocent. Deliberation means uncertainty; uncertainty means doubt. Over the previous two years, Geiger had had recurring nightmares of Jack beating the rap. Sometimes they had awakened him in the middle of the night, sometimes after he'd gotten just enough sleep to keep him from drifting back off.

It was hard to explain exactly why he'd taken it so personally. Unlike his wife, he didn't worry that Jack would murder again in Austria if he was released.

"What if he gets off and decides to stalk Katja when she's old enough to go out?" she'd asked during one of their discussions about when Jack would be tried.

"He would never do that. He knows that if anything happens to my daughter he'll be the first guy we go to."

"What if he hates you so much that he decides to take that chance?"

"No, he's too cowardly to do that."

If Jack beat the rap, would it be his fault or the jury's? God knew, he'd done his best. He and Wladkowski and the rest of the guys—Hoffmann, Kucera, Windisch, Etz, Steger, Brandstätter; Miller, Harper, and Lancaster in L.A. and Hlavac in Prague—they had all worked so hard together, and that by itself had been a glorious thing. For all the apprehension and frustration of the previous two years, Geiger had never before felt such camaraderie. Jack had given him and his colleagues a challenge, a compelling reason to get to the office early and to stay late. He'd given them a sense of purpose.

Geiger knew that many considered him a careerist, which he was. Since his adolescence in his little village, he'd wanted to have a career. He'd wanted to make something of himself and to be recognized for it. He didn't want to live out his days in rustic obscurity, nor did he want to be just another bureaucrat who expected no reward for his work other than a pension at the end of it. He knew the Unterweger investigation was the defining moment of his career. Jack's crimes had given him a reason to travel to Los Angeles to work with the most experienced homicide inspectors in the world, and to Quantico to learn from the most experienced criminal psychologists. For all of the above, he knew he could only be grateful to Jack Unterweger. As strange, even disturbing as it sounded, Geiger was the beneficiary of Jack's murders.

And yet, if Jack was found innocent, there would be no triumph. For the rest of his life Geiger would have to live with the fact that he and his colleagues hadn't made a strong enough case. They hadn't looked hard enough, hadn't asked witnesses the right questions, simply hadn't been smart enough. The triumph would be Jack's, which was precisely the thought Jack had relished from the moment he'd started murdering again. He had always considered himself smarter than the police, and in some ways he had been. Geiger knew that if it hadn't been for old Schenner in Salzburg, Jack might have never even become a suspect. Even after he'd learned he was under suspicion, he'd still been confident the investigators wouldn't be able to prove it.

"There can be no evidence," he'd proclaimed again and again. If the jury found him innocent, he would publish another book about the "injustice" he'd suffered, and get a new, if temporary, lease on life as a literary celebrity. The press would clamor for interviews and women would jockey for a place in his bed. And then, when he felt the urge to kill again, he would move to South America.

Geiger wandered over to the head D.A.'s office and found Dr. Lambauer sitting at his desk.

"Still no word?" Geiger asked.

"Still in deliberation." They talked about the trial, reviewing the testimony, going over the strongest and the weakest moments for the prosecution, trying to form a picture of what the eight jury members were thinking. They were ordinary citizens with no experience in evaluating what they were called upon to evaluate. Everything that was presented—DNA, microfibers, ligature analysis, signature crime-scene analysis, the theory of the "malignant narcissist"—was new to them. Had they found it compelling or incomprehensible?

As the afternoon wore on into early evening, other players drifted into Lambauer's office—Wladkowski, cops from Vienna and Graz. Everyone had their own observations, and each player's best and worst moments were reviewed. At dinnertime, no one dared leave Lambauer's office, because everyone knew he would be the first to receive the call. At around 8:00, a thunderstorm approached the city. The wind came

first, shaking the beech trees outside and rattling the windows of the
Justice Palace.

CHAPTER 89

VERDICT

A FEW BLOCKS AWAY, a crowd had gathered outside the courthouse, and in its
midst stood the Viennese ex-pimp Cadillac Freddie, holding up a sign
that read, DEATH TO THE HOOKER MURDERER! Inside, the jury was still
deliberating. Lehofer sat at his desk, reading a magazine.

Judge Haas approached him. "Congratulations," he said, referring to
the probable outcome of the long deliberation.

"Thank you, your honor," Lehofer replied, even though he could see
that Haas was furious.

Forty minutes later, the jury foreman announced that they had
reached a verdict. At 8:50 p.m., just as everyone had reassembled and
the last reporter had scrambled back into the courtroom, the electrical
storm broke. Lightning so bright that it flashed in the courtroom and
thunder like cannon shots created a horror-film atmosphere for the reading of the verdict.

"Is the accused, Jack Unterweger, guilty of the murder of Blanka
Bockova in Prague?" Judge Haas asked.

"Six yes, two no," replied the foreman. That alone was enough to
send him back to prison for the rest of his life, but there were ten more.

"Guilty of the murder of Brunhilde Masser in Graz?"

"Six yes, two no." Down the list they went: "six yes, two no," for all
the murders except Elfriede Schrempf in Graz and Regina Prem in Vienna. Because their bodies had been too decomposed to establish a definite cause of death, five jury members decided to give him a pass. The
"six to two" vote didn't come as a big surprise to Jack. He'd once told Dr.

Haller: "Two of the main jury members are definitely with me, four are definitely against me, and two aren't sure."

"Do you have anything to say?" asked Judge Haas.

"I will appeal," Jack said, teary-eyed but defiant. The court watch-men led him toward the entrance.

"Look after him," Lehofer said, and saw one of them kick him in the ass as he passed through the door.

At the head D.A.'s office a wild celebration got under way. After much cheering and embracing and backslapping, the whole gang moved to a beer cellar a few blocks away, the taps were opened, and all the tension of the previous two months was relieved. Among the Vienna crew, everyone got drunk except poor Hoffmann, the designated driver. With early-morning appointments the next day, they couldn't spend the night in Graz, and at about 3:00 a.m. they stumbled to the car.

Shortly after they got on the Autobahn, all the drunks fell asleep, leaving Hoffmann alone, thinking about the two hours of driving ahead. It had been a long and tense day, and then the gigantic release when the guilty verdict was read. The thunderstorm subsided, with fewer and fewer lightning flashes on the horizon.

CHAPTER 90

"IS THAT THE ANSWER?"

LEHOFER'S SON BERNHARD would always remember the night of Jack's verdict. With the thunderstorm raging like a battle outside, he had a hard time falling asleep, and a couple of hours after he finally nodded off, he was awakened by the phone ringing in his father's study across the hall. Glancing at the clock and seeing that it was 4:00 a.m., he figured it must be something serious, and so he got up to ask what it was about.

Stepping out into the hall, he saw his father talking on the phone. "Yes, it's clear. I'll be there in a couple of hours."

Geiger was awakened by a jolt, and his mind emerged from the fog of beer and sleep to discern what was going on. Hoffmann had fallen asleep behind the wheel and drifted into the concrete median. The smashing and scraping had also awakened him, and he regained control of the car. They were lucky they'd drifted into the median instead of off the right side of the road, where they might have slammed into a tree at seventy miles per hour. UNTERWEGER GUILTY AND VIENNA INSPECTORS KILLED RETURNING FROM GRAZ! What a pretty headline that would have been.

The next morning, as Lehofer approached the entrance to the courthouse, he saw a young woman sitting on the steps, holding her face in her hands, weeping.

"I'm sorry, Miss Wagner," he said. For a moment she looked up at him, tears streaming down her face, but she said nothing.

My God, she must have really loved him, he thought.

At 6:00 that morning, Bianca was awakened by her clock radio. After blowing all the money she'd earned from interviews, she'd been obliged to get a nine-to-five job, and that meant getting up early.

> *Austrian Radio sends the news. Jack Unterweger has committed suicide. At 3:40 this morning he was found hanging in his cell in the Graz court. A few hours earlier the jury found him guilty of nine of eleven counts of murder and sentenced him to life in prison.*

It was strange for Bianca to think that, just two and a half years earlier, she'd loved him so much that she would have done anything for him. As she listened to the news of his death, she felt nothing, neither bitterness nor sadness nor regret—just nothing. She got up to brew her coffee.

———

Using a thin metal wire as the lead and the drawstring of his jogging pants as the noose, Jack had fashioned an ingenious instrument for strangling himself. Because the wire was so thin, he had double-looped it around a coat hook and tied it off with a braid in just the right place so that the load would be distributed equally over the two loops. The noose he'd made out of the drawstring displayed equally fine craftsmanship. The entire instrument hung down just low enough for him to get it snug around his neck, standing on the tips of his toes. With his back to the wall, he'd lowered himself to a flat-footed position, thereby putting most of his weight on the noose.

It was the worst day of Astrid's life. The most unbearable moment was when his body was taken to the Institute of Forensic Medicine for autopsy. She went to see him in the basement one last time before he was cut up, but then changed her mind at the last minute. No, she would remember him as he'd been in life, not in death. She walked out of the institute, and in front of an ORF television crew, she broke into tears.

In the autopsy theater, Professor Peter Leinzinger examined the corpse. What a strange, self-assertive man he had been. A couple of years earlier, the doctor had responded to Jack's complaint that he'd been roughed up by the jailhouse guards. Arriving at the prisoner's cell, Leinzinger found him completely unscathed.

"It was nothing really, I just wanted to talk," he'd said, and engaged the doctor in an interesting and entertaining conversation. Leinzinger looked at his swollen face and then sawed off the top of his skull to remove his brain.

Many pundits expressed outrage that he'd been left alone in his cell with at least two pieces of cord and a sloppy suicide watch. Lehofer believed his client had resolved to kill himself the moment he heard the guilty verdict, and that far greater precautions should have been taken to prevent it. When Margit Haas heard the news that morning, she figured Jack had made yet another phony suicide attempt to get more press and sympathy, but had accidentally succeeded. Her theory: he knew the watchman looked into his cell every half hour, and so his plan was to stand on his tiptoes, his head in the noose, just before he was observed. At the moment the watchman looked in, he went flatfooted. What he didn't calculate, Margit reckoned, was that the watchman wouldn't intervene.

Since the night she'd read about Jack's murder of Margret Schäfer in 1974, Margit had often wondered why he'd been set free, and why he hadn't received intense psychotherapy. After hearing about his suicide, she spent the day thinking about his life, so full of sorrow and destruction. She still didn't think of him as evil, but as disturbed. In the afternoon she called Astrid.

"No one knew him. Even you didn't know him, Margit!" Astrid cried. "I knew he would do it." That evening Margit saw her on the evening news as she walked out of the Institute for Forensic Medicine, beside herself with grief.

"I loved him so much," she said.

She's his last victim, Margit thought.

Despite everything Margit had learned about Jack, it was still hard for her to believe that he'd murdered women during the period of their friendship. She hadn't forgotten the good times they'd had together, talking on the phone, sitting in cafés, analyzing people. She remembered his mischievous little-boy smile and the twinkle in his eye as he told her a story. Most of all she remembered the times he'd made her laugh. It was bizarre to think of him picking up hookers, taking them out into the woods, and killing them.

That evening she went to bed early while her boyfriend sat in the living room listening to music, sipping a glass of wine. She drifted off, and then awoke with a start and sensed someone was in the room. In the dim light of her clock radio, she saw Jack standing at the foot of her bed, grinning at her.

"Get out of here!" she yelled.

A few seconds later, her boyfriend Peter opened the door. "Did you just yell something?"

"I just saw Jack Unterweger standing at the foot of my bed," she said, still shaken.

Peter told her she was just dreaming, which was only natural, given she'd been thinking about Jack all day. She could have sworn she'd been awake.

"His best murder" was how Michael Graff, the newly elected Conservative Party Justice Minister's spokesman, described Jack's suicide on national television. Zanger was outraged and demanded Graff's resignation. The lawyer pointed out that, because the judgment had not yet been reviewed and confirmed by the court, one could not, legally speaking, refer to Jack as guilty.

"On behalf of Unterweger's daughter, I am petitioning for a confirmation that he died innocent. In the name of his daughter I am also seeking a final ruling, and will take it to Strasbourg if necessary."

The following week, Zanger announced that he was about to start filming his movie *Jack*, which would include graphic re-creations of the eleven murders. *NEWS* excerpted the scene in which Blanka Bockova is murdered in Prague:

> *Unterweger drives slowly through the night. Cut to a young woman walking out of a disco, caught in the headlights . . . The young woman begins to run . . . As she looks back in panic, she is struck on the forehead with a dark object . . . Lightning fast, the gloved hands wrap an elastic band around her throat . . . The woman's eyes bulge as she thrashes with all her strength. Her fingernails dig into the underarm of her assailant, tearing out bloody skin. Slowly her desperate struggle ebbs and she becomes still.*

Zanger hoped to cast Anthony Hopkins in the lead role.

CHAPTER 91

PEACE

A WEEK AFTER THE TRIAL, Geiger took his family on an American vacation. He hoped that two weeks in the States, so far away from Vienna, would start to mend the rift in his family. Two weeks with no pagers or cell phones, no talk of murder or trace evidence or decomposition. Most important, not a word about Jack Unterweger. In America, the mythic land of "fresh starts," he and Eva would begin the process of reconciliation.

After a few days of strolling and shopping in New York, they flew to San Francisco. The highlight was renting an apartment in Sausalito, waking up with the sun shining through the patches of fog on the bay. They then headed south on the Pacific Coast Highway, passing through Monterey, Carmel, and Big Sur. Truly it was "the greatest meeting of land and sea in the world," as Robert Louis Stevenson had once remarked. In Santa Barbara they spent a day sightseeing with the chief of police, and then pressed on to L.A. Driving through Malibu on the Pacific Coast Highway, Geiger glanced at the entrance to Corral Canyon Road but said nothing.

Eva had a suggestion: "I know you want to meet your L.A. friends and relive the glory. Katja and I can spend a couple of days at Disneyland." The arrangement worked well. The ten-year-old and her mother played at the fun park while Geiger met Harper, Miller, Lancaster, and Lynne Herold. By the time he picked his wife and daughter up at Disneyland, he was ready to do some normal sightseeing in L.A.

One day he suggested they have lunch at Gladstone's.

"It's a terrific seafood restaurant, right on the beach in Malibu," he said. They drove down Sunset, through Brentwood, and down to the Pacific Coast Highway. Eva and Katja liked Gladstone's; they sat on the deck extending over the beach.

"Look!" Katja said. "Those people are eating peanuts and throwing the shells on the floor. Isn't that forbidden?"

"No, everyone throws shells on the floor," said Eva. "Later they'll be swept up."

"May I do it?"

"Of course." Katja grabbed a handful out of the basket on the table and began breaking them open, giggling each time she tossed the shells on the floor. A seagull swooped down from the roof and landed on a rail post next to her.

"Kind of forward, isn't he?" said Geiger.

"He's big!"

"He wants a peanut. Go ahead and give him one."

"How?"

"Just toss it up in the air and he'll get it."

"The whole thing?"

"Yeah, his beak is for cracking open sea creatures." She tossed one at him and he dove after it as it fell onto the beach below. A moment later, he was back on the post, begging for another.

After they ordered drinks, Eva noticed a distant expression appear on her husband's face—the expression she'd seen so many times over the past two years. Though he'd been chatty all afternoon, suddenly he was quiet, apparently distracted by the surroundings.

"Right now I get the feeling you'd rather be sitting with him than with me."

"What are you talking about?"

"I know this was his favorite restaurant in L.A. I just remembered you talking about the menu you found in his apartment."

"All right, you got me, but I didn't suggest we come here just because he came here. I figured you would enjoy it. Katja seems to be having a good time." She was standing at the rail, throwing peanuts at the hovering seagulls, enthralled.

"Isn't it strange to think that, exactly three years ago, he sat right here where we are sitting?"

"I think it's strange that you are so fascinated by him. You and your colleagues have spent *hundreds* of hours talking about Jack Unterweger. Can you explain why you are so fascinated by a killer?"

"Because he wasn't only a killer. He was an extremely clever killer, an actor, a manipulator."

"He certainly manipulated you."

"You think so?"

"Of course! Have you thought about how much that little man has affected you? And don't say it was just a professional thing. For two years you've been obsessed with him."

"You think I'm crazy?"

"No, just obsessed, though maybe that is a kind of insanity."

"I see. And what do you think now?"

"I think I want to enjoy our vacation and not talk about Jack Unterweger."

"Fair enough."

She looked out at the Pacific. "I'm just so glad he's dead. I don't know what I'd have done if he'd appealed. Thank God, he's dead."

LIST OF SOURCES

INTERVIEWS

POLICE: Ernst Geiger, Max Edelbacher, Ernst Hoffmann, Leopold Etz, Franz Brandstätter, Helmut Golds, Fred Miller, James Harper, Ronnie Lancaster, Steve Staples, Shawn Conboy.

FORENSIC SCIENTISTS: Andrea Berzlanovich, Lynne Herold, Peter Leinzinger, Manfred Hochmeister, Walter Brüschweiler.

PSYCHIATRISTS AND CRIMINAL PSYCHOLOGISTS: Reinhard Haller, Gerhard Kaiser, Gregg McCrary.

JUDICIAL OFFICIALS: Wolfgang Wladkowski, Karl Gasser, Franz Perschl.

JACK'S ATTORNEYS: Hans Lehofer, Anna Schmidt (Lehofer's assistant), Peter Cardona (at his trial in 1976), Joseph Slama.

JOURNALISTS AND PHOTOGRAPHERS: Peter Grolig, Hans Breitegger, Bernd Melichar, Frances Schoenberger, Paul Yvon, Doris Piringer, Ulrike Jantschner, Günther Nenning, Sonja Eisenstein, Thomas Raab, Andreas Hermann, Martin Vukovitz.

FILMMAKERS AND EDITORS: Willi Hengstler, Robert Dornhelm, Alfred Kolleritsch.

JACK'S FRIENDS AND FAMILY: Margit Haas, Astrid Wagner, Bianca Mrak, Carolina, Charlotte Auer, Odelia Vizthum.

VICTIM'S RELATIVE: Rudolf Prem.

POLICE AND COURT FILES

The Special Commission (SOKO) for investigating Jack Unterweger assembled:
1. Police and court files on his entire criminal career going back to the early 1970s.
2. Police files on all of the cases under investigation in Vienna, Graz, Vorarlberg, Los Angeles, and Prague. Included in the files are investigative reports on each of the crimes before Jack was identified as a suspect. Altogether, the files amount to thousands of pages of crime scene descriptions and photographs, autopsy reports, witness statements, interrogation transcripts, wiretap transcripts, forensic scientific evaluations of evidence, Interpol correspondence, correspondence between courts in different jurisdictions, and previous indictments, as well as letters, photographs, and other documents seized from Jack's apartment. The files document not only Jack's crimes but also

his education. In every confrontation with the police and courts, he learned something about the way they work. Quotations from the files are cited in the chapter notes.

DIARIES

As Jack noted in one of his diary entries, he had "a mania" for keeping records of his daily activities. The diaries document five distinct periods.

1. THE PRISON DIARIES: Starting in 1982, his breakthrough year as a writer, Jack made notes of his publishing triumphs, his correspondence and phone conversations with influential persons, his increasing numbers of visitors and admirers, and his extraordinary privileges as a prison inmate. His entries during the months between April and July 1983 pertaining to Inspector Schenner's renewed investigation of the Marica Horvath murder (see chapter 43) are especially noteworthy. As far as I know, no other journalist or writer has seen the prison diaries.

2. THE MISSING DIARY (APRIL 27, 1990–SEPTEMBER 4, 1991): When the police searched Jack's apartment, they found his prison diaries as well as a diary of his life between September 1991 and February 1992. Conspicuously missing was the diary of his life from May 1990 through August 1991 (roughly the time frame in which the eleven women were murdered). Geiger believed that Jack had kept a diary of the period but had hidden it because it was incriminating.

After his arrest in February 1992, Jack told the police that he had quit keeping a diary when he was paroled in May 1990, but had started again in September 1991 when he learned that he was a suspect for the murders. He claimed that he had resumed his old habit in order to document his whereabouts in case additional murders were committed.

Later, at his trial, he said that he wanted to read from his "reconstruction" of his days in freedom. The court denied his request, as it was interested only in what he was doing when the murdered women were last seen. Neither the court nor the police nor any journalist ever saw the document.

About a year after I began researching Jack's life, I obtained a copy of it, and I saw that it was not Jack's "reconstruction" (implying that he'd assembled it from memory and from other records) of his days in freedom, but a typed version of his diary of his days in freedom. In other words, it was the so-called "missing diary."

It contains no incriminating entries from the days the eleven women disappeared, but the entries for the rest of the days appear unedited. It is hard to imagine a more thorough documentation of a man's life—each day's appointments, accounts of conversations, arguments, and sexual encounters, movies he saw, cafés he visited, repairs to his car, work assignments, road trips, etc.

Though the typed version of the diary doesn't contain smoking guns, some entries would have bolstered the case against Jack if the investigators had seen them. But what makes the diary interesting is not so much its contribution to the case against him as what it reveals about his character and habits—his obsessions and his extreme restlessness.

3. THE UNDER SUSPICION DIARY (SEPTEMBER 5, 1991–FEBRUARY 7, 1992): Reveals Jack's initial fear when he realized that the police might be taking Schenner's tip seriously, followed by his increasing lack of concern about it in the autumn of 1991.

4. THE FUGITIVE DIARY (FEBRUARY 8–26, 1991): Jack recorded his maneuvers in the days just prior to fleeing the country, as well as his adventures in Miami with Bianca. The diary was seized by the U.S. marshals and handed over to the Austrian police.

5. THE TRIAL DIARY (APRIL 20–JUNE 26, 1994): Jack's account of the proceedings and his thoughts and feelings about them. He arranged for Astrid Wagner to receive the diary, and she gave parts of it to the weekly magazine *NEWS* for publication.

PSYCHIATRIC EVALUATIONS OF JACK UNTERWEGER

Haller, Dr. Reinhard. *Nervenfachärztliches Gutachten.* June 13, 1994.

———. "Forensisch-psychiatrische Aspekte des Falls Jack Unterweger." *Forensische Psychiatrie und Psychotherapie*, February 1995.

———. "Maligner Narzissmus und Sexualmord—dargestellt am Beispiel Jack Unterweger." *Archiv für Kriminologie*, July/August 1999.

Jayrosch, Dr. Klaus. *Befund und Gutachen.* July 15, 1975.

Laublicher, Dr. Werner. *Befund und Gutachten.* April 28, 1975.

Zigeuner, Dr. Richard. *Befund und Gutachen.* May 25, 1993.

BOOKS AND ARTICLES BY JACK UNTERWEGER

Fegefeuer oder die Reise ins Zuchthaus (Purgatory or the Journey to Prison). Augsburg: Maro, 1983.

Kerker (Dungeon). Vienna: J&V Edition Wien, 1990. Jack submitted this sequel to *Purgatory* after he was paroled, which was no coincidence, given that it contains softened depictions of crimes he had committed in his past—the kind of crimes he had started committing again at the time the book was published.

Tobendes Ich (Raving I). St. Michael, Austria: J. G. Bläschke, 1982. A collection of lyrical poetry.

Endstation Zuchthaus (Last Station Prison). Frankfurt: Haag & Herchen, 1984. A play that was repeatedly produced on stages in Austria and Germany.

Wenn Kinder Liebe leben (When Children Live Love). Krems: Edition Wortbrücke. A collection of children's stories, many of which were broadcast on an ORF radio program for children.

Mare Adriatico. Vienna: *free life* Edition, 1990. A short novel about Jack's adventures in Italy.

Schrei der Angst (Scream of Fear). Krems, Austria: Edition Wortbrücke, 1991. Jack started working on the play, for which he received the Austrian drama stipend (a state subsidy for playwrights) in 1986. He rewrote it after his parole and published it in 1991.

"Rote Laterne in Graz" ("Red Lantern in Graz"). *Basta*, October 1990.

"Die Angst im Rotlicht Milieu" ("The Fear in the Red-Light District"). ORF *Journal Panorama*, June 5, 1991.

"Sex, Blut und Tränen" ("Sex, Blood, and Tears"). With Thomas Rottenberg. *Falter*, June 20, 1991.

"Die Schattenseiten von Los Angeles" ("The Dark Sides of Los Angeles"). ORF *Zick Zack*, September 17, 1991.

"Hollywood: Luxus, Laster, Leidenschaften" ("Hollywood: Luxury, Vice, Passions"). *Tirolerin*, Autumn 1991.

"Subkultur der Sexualität" ("Subculture of Sexuality"). *Tirolerin*, Autumn 1991.
"Los Angeles: Traumfabrik Hollywood" ("Los Angeles: Dream Factory Hollywood").
ERFOLG, December 1991/January 1992.

BOOKS BY OTHER AUTHORS

Bargon, Michael. *Prostitution und Zuhälterei*. Lübeck: Max-Schmidt-Römhild, 1982.
Berg, Karl. *Der Sadist*. Munich: Belleville, 2004.
Berner, Wolfgang and Edda Karlick-Bolten. *Verlaufsformen der Sexualkriminalität*. Stuttgart: Ferdinand Enke, 1986.
Breitegger, Hans. *Die Grossen Kriminalfälle der Steirmark*. Graz, Austria: Styria, 2000. Contains a chapter on the Unterweger case.
Cleckley, Hervey. *The Mask of Sanity*. Augusta, Georgia: Emily S. Cleckley, 1988.
Depue, Roger L. *Between Good and Evil*. New York: Warner Books, 2005.
Douglas, John and Mark Olshaker. *Journey into Darkness*. New York: Scribner, 1997.
Edelbacher, Max and Harald Seyrl. *Wiener Kriminalchronik*. Vienna: Edition S, 1993.
Eggerer, Wilhelm and Ernst Theo Rohnert. *Sagen des Altertums*. Munich: Martin Lurz, 1972.
Geher, Robert. *Wiener Blut oder Die Ehre der Strizzis*. Vienna: Edition S, 1993.
Geiger, Ernst and Paul Yvon. *Es gibt durchaus noch schöne Morde*. Vienna: Kremayr & Scheriau/Orac, 2005. Contains a chapter on the Unterweger case.
Girtler, Roland. *Der Strich: Sexualität als Geschäft*. Munich: Wilhelm Heyne, 1990.
———. *Rotwelsch*. Vienna: Böhlau, 1988.
Haller, Dr. Reinhard. *Die Seele des Verbrechers*. Sankt Pölten, Austria: Residenz Verlag, 2006.
Hare, Robert D. *Without Conscience: The Disturbing World of the Psychopaths Among Us*. New York: The Guilford Press, 1999.
Krafft-Ebing, Richard Freiherr von. *Psychopathia Sexualis*. Berlin: Matthes & Seitz, 1997.
Leitner, Leo. "Volkschullehrer in Puchberg," *Haltestelle Puchberg am Schneeberg*, Gernot Schuster and Peter Zöchbauer. Vienna: Berger, 1997.
McCrary, Gregg O. *The Unknown Darkness*. New York: William Morrow, 2003. Contains a chapter on the Unterweger case.
Mrak, Bianca. *hiJACKed: Mein Leben mit einem Mörder*. Salzburg: Egoth, 2004. Bianca's account of her experiences with Jack.
Müller, Thomas. *Bestie Mensch*. Salzburg: Ecowin, 2004.
Mutzenbacher, Josefine. *Die Lebensgeschichte einer wienerischen Dirne*. Reinbek bei Hamburg, Germany: Rowohlt Taschenbuch, 1978.
Ressler, Robert K., Ann W. Burgess, and John E. Douglas. *Sexual Homicide, Patterns and Motives*. Lanham, Maryland: Lexington Books, 1988.
Schmidt, Gert, Gerlinde Wambacher, and Heinz Wernitznig. *Wenn der Achter im Zenit steht*. Vienna: ERFOLG, 1993. An invaluable source of information about the Unterweger case; when it was published before Jack's trial, a Vienna court deemed it prejudicial and prohibited its sale.
Simon, Robert I. *Bad Men Do What Good Men Dream*. Washington, D.C.: American Psychiatric Press, 1996.
Wagner, Astrid. *Und die Mörderjagd muss weitergehen!* Twimberg, Austria: Legendis,

1995. Wagner's fiercest criticism of the Austrian justice system and her most personal account of her experiences with Jack. Shortly after it appeared, Ernst Geiger sued her for libel, and a Graz court prohibited its sale.

————. *Kannibalenzeit*. Graz, Austria: Periskop, 1996. Similar to her first book, without the passages cited in Geiger's libel suit.

————. *Jack Unterweger: Ein Mörder für alle Fälle*. Leipzig: Militzke, 2001. Written in a more scholarly style, it purports to be a case study of the inequities of the justice system. Contains less of the personal narrative of her first two books.

Wallace, Edgar. *The Golden Hades*. London: Pan Books, 1966.

Wilson, Colin and Donald Seaman. *The Serial Killers: A Study in the Psychology of Violence*. London: W. H. Allen, 1990.

Wittgenstein, Ludwig. *Philosophical Investigations*. Oxford: Blackwell Publishing, 2001.

NOTES

All translations from the German in this book are my own. In the following notes, I have translated generic titles, such as the headings of police reports, into English. Documents with specific titles or headlines are cited in the original German.

CHAPTER 1: A MYSTERY

3 **a solar eclipse:** "Solar Eclipses Visible from Los Angeles, CA," http:sunearth .gsfc.nasa.gov/eclipse/SEcirc/SEcircNA/LosAngelesCA1+11.html#a+20.

3 **The men and children:** "Malibu Sheriff Station Complaint Report," July 11, 1991. The investigation of the murder of Sherri Ann Long is documented in the County of Los Angeles Sheriff's Department file 091-05820-1076-011.

4 **"Is it a decomp?":** Interview with Ronnie Lancaster. Additional details about the crime scene and autopsy provided by reports in the Sherri Ann Long file.

6 **The killer had struck first:** The investigation of the murder of Shannon Exley is documented in the LAPD's "Unsolved Murder Investigation Progress Report Fact Sheet," Victim Exley, Shannon Heather, report dated September 10, 1991.

7 **Miller had known from a young age:** Interviews with Fred Miller.

7 **In April 1989, Louis Crane:** "Man Convicted of 4 Murders," Los Angeles Times, April 27, 1989.

8 **Thirty-three-year-old Irene Rodriguez:** The investigation of the murder of Irene Rodriguez is documented in the LAPD's "Unsolved Murder Investigation Progress Report Fact Sheet," Victim: Rodriguez, Irene, report dated October 1, 1991.

10 **Dr. Lynne Herold:** Interviews with Herold and review of her notes of the case.

10 **the Los Angeles County Department of Coroner:** http:coroner.co.la.ca.us/htm/ Coroner_Home.htm.

14 **Cases have been documented of stranglers:** Depue, p. 139.

CHAPTER 2: NO APPARENT MOTIVE

18 **because he has no apparent motive:** The documentary film *Murder: No Apparent Motive* (Imre Horvath, dir., 1984) emphasizes this aspect of serial killers. In 1992, the FBI recommended the film for instructional purposes to Austrian investigators.

18 **A few serial rapists and killers:** Interview with FBI Special Agent Gregg Mc-Crary. Investigators also found videos that the serial killers Leonard Lake and Charles Ng made of themselves while committing their crimes.

18 **Centuries before the FBI agent Robert Ressler:** In the vast literature about serial killers, Ressler is most often given credit for the term.

18 In 1440, the French: Wolf, Leonard, *Bluebeard: The Life and Crimes of Gilles de Rais*. New York: Clarkson N. Potter, 1980.
19 Marquis de Sade: Wilson and Seaman, pp. 3–5. Jack Unterweger was apparently an admirer of Sade (see Kerker, p. 50).
19 In 1886, Richard Freiherr von Krafft-Ebing: *Psychopathia Sexualis.*
20 Thirty-five in the United States: Wilson and Seaman, p. 2. Conservative analysts at the FBI and at academic institutions have estimated twenty to fifty, while writers such as Ann Rule have estimated as many as three hundred. See "Number of Serial Killers in the United States as Elusive as Killers Themselves," *Financial Times*, March 5, 2005.

CHAPTER 3: THE FEAR IN THE RED-LIGHT DISTRICT

20 "Prostitute in Vienna Murdered": "Prostituierte in Wien getötet: 3 werden noch immer vermisst," *Kurier*, May 22, 1991.
21 Her killer had arranged: Details of the Moitzi crime scene from interview with Ernst Geiger, photographs, and a description in "*Sonderkommission Jack Unterweger Abschluss Bericht*" ("Special Commission on Jack Unterweger Concluding Report"), March 15, 1993.
23 The second body: Details of the Karin Eroglu crime scene from interview with Inspector Leopold Etz, photographs, and description in "Concluding Report."
24 He sent "Geigerl": Wittgenstein's stint as a schoolteacher in Puchberg am Schneeberg and his mentoring of Ernst Geiger's uncle are documented in Leitner, pp. 192–93.
25 983 murders: County of Los Angeles Department of Coroner, *Biennial Report Fiscal Years 1990–1992*. Data on homicide rates in Vienna provided by Ernst Geiger.
27 report published by the Association: *Der Kriminalbeamte*, July 1991.
27 "What if someday he returns to Turkey": "Strichweises Sterben," *profil*, June 3, 1991.
28 "She was an insanely good mother": Rudolf Prem told the story of his wife's disappearance to *profil*, June 3, 1991. Additional details from Prem's statement to the police: "Report," Vienna Police Headquarters, May 8, 1991.
29 *Viennese* magazine: "Tot, Schmutzig, Steirisch," *Wiener*, May 1991.
29 Rudolf's "dramatic appeal": "Wo ist meine Frau?" *Kurier*, May 29, 1991.

CHAPTER 5: A SPECIAL QUALIFICATION

30 The reporter introduced himself: Details of Jack's initial meeting with Chief Edelbacher from my interview with Edelbacher, Jack's diary entry for June 3, 1991, and Edelbacher's interview in *Basta*, "Wie Jack Unterweger die Polizei verhörte," April 1992.
30 "Despite a number of leads": *Journal Panorama*, ORF 1, June 5, 1991.
31 for the weekly newspaper *Falter*: *Falter*, June 20, 1991.
33 Edelbacher had been surprised: Edelbacher was repeatedly asked by reporters to recount the story of how he first learned Jack's identity. My reconstruction of the scene comes from Edelbacher's account in *Stern* magazine, vol. 36/92, and from my own interview with him.

CHAPTER 6: ONE YEAR EARLIER

35 **he was convicted**: A jury at the Salzburg Court found Jack guilty of murder on June 1, 1976. Jack appealed, and the Austrian Supreme Court upheld the verdict: "Im Namen der Republik," to the Salzburg Court, October 19, 1976.

35 **correspondence courses**: Details about Jack's education in prison from a copy of his CV and from my interview with Sonja Eisenstein, who arranged and paid for his education.

35 **the newspaper *Die Zeit***: "Ums Leben schreiben," *Die Zeit*, April 26, 1985.

CHAPTER 7: PURGATORY

36 **"My hands, sweaty with fear"**: *Purgatory*, p. 7.

36 **"Sometimes during these moments"**: *Purgatory*, pp. 8–9.

37 **one of Jack's favorite films**: *Stern* magazine, 36/92, p. 94.

37 **"Of my paternity I knew only a name"**: *Purgatory*, p. 12.

37 **Theresia Unterweger . . . committing acts of theft and fraud**: Schmidt, p. 24.

38 **She named the infant**: In the children's welfare office file on Jack Unterweger, his father is noted as Jack Bäcker (the German spelling "Bäcker" was probably a phonetic rendering of Becker or Baker). File reproduced in Schmidt, p. 27.

38 **Jack never met his stepfather**: Haller, *Nervenfachärztliches Gutachten*, p. 23.

38 **"My eyes burned from the smoky air"**: *Purgatory*, pp. 10–11.

39 **A "tramp with no time for you"**: *Purgatory*, p. 21.

CHAPTER 8: REHABILITATION

39 **premiere of his play *End Station Prison***: The January 20, 1986, event was covered by the press, and Jack noted it in his diary.

39 **"At his reading in Stein"**: Interview with Alfred Kolleritsch.

40 **"In working on this book"**: Video recording of Jack's talk at the Wels Film Festival.

40 **"Insofar as personal development"**: Letter from Dr. Arno Pilgram to President Kirchschläger, January 1, 1985, reproduced in Schmidt, p. 89.

41 **"The clarity and great literary quality"**: Letter from Elfriede Jelinek to the Krems Circuit Court, quoted in Schmidt, p. 78.

41 **"As we know," wrote senior ORF journalist**: Letter from Dr. Peter Huemer to Dr. Karl Schreiner, May 20, 1987, reproduced in Schmidt, p. 95.

41 **"Apart from general humanitarian considerations"**: "Resolution of the Austrian Authors' Council," addressed to Dr. Wolfgang Werdenich, director of the Special Facility Wien-Favoriten, quoted in Schmidt, pp. 109–11.

41 **Dr. Wolfgang Doleisch**: In a letter to Justice Minister Christian Broda dated June 7, 1982, Jack wrote: "Dr. Wolfgang Doleisch, who has helped me privately since 1977, can tell you more about my person." Jack's first patroness, Sonja Eisenstein, was privy to his relationship with Dr. Doleisch, which she described in her interview with *ERFOLG* magazine, February, 1993, and in her interview with me. In 1983, the deputy director of Stein prison told the Salzburg inspector August Schenner that Jack "was helped and supported in every way by the former section chief Herrn Dr. Doleisch." "Report," Salzburg Police Headquarters, April 5, 1983.

42 **At a closed parole hearing:** Details about the hearing, including passages from Dr. Kaiser's statement, were leaked to the press. See *Kurier*, "Gescheit genug, um alle zu täuschen?" February 16, 1992. In my interview with Dr. Kaiser, he stated simply that he had found "no manifestation of physical or mental illness in Unterweger."

42 **"Austrian justice will be measured":** Quoted in "Foregger wurde bei der Entlassung übergangen," *Kurier*, February 23, 1992.

CHAPTER 9: FREEDOM

42 **"He was polite, charming":** Recollections of Emilie Beidernickl to Schmidt, pp. 36–37.

42 **"We were alone, undisturbed":** Jack's diary entry for April 29, 1990.

43 **woman at an upscale champagne bar:** Ibid., November 18, 1991.

43 **he suggested using it as a prop:** Conversation with Martin Vukovits, photographer.

CHAPTER 10: BEST FRIEND

44 **Twenty-seven-year-old Margit Haas:** Details of Margit's experiences with Jack from my numerous conversations with Margit.

44 **In Viennese dialect, a pimp is called a *Strizzi*:** The anthropologist Roland Girtler has spent years studying *Rotwelsch*, "the language of crooks, whores, and vagabonds." *Rotwelsch* (literally "to speak falsely") is a subdialect of Viennese (*Wienerisch*)—middle-high German that has, over the centuries, been enriched by words from the various languages of the Austro-Hungarian Empire, including Czech, Hungarian, Yiddish, and Italian. The denizens of the red-light milieu use many words that are unfamiliar to the middle and upper classes, though every adult Viennese knows what a *Strizzi* is. Few, however, know its etymology (Girtler, *Rotwelsch*, p. 183).

44 **photos of him:** *free life*, July/August, 1990, p. 54.

47 **Margit's most vivid memory of *Dungeon*:** The play premiered in Vienna on the evening of November 11, 1990. Jack noted the Reiss Bar reception and his adventures with Margit in his diary entry for the morning of November 12.

49 **the sex-charged scene:** *Purgatory*, p. 139.

CHAPTER 11: PATRONESS

51 **The author and journalist Sonja Eisenstein:** Sonja told me about her experiences with Jack. She also gave a long interview to *ERFOLG* magazine, February 1993.

51 **she knew the title didn't refer to the scream:** Sonja told me that she instinctively knew the true meaning of the title *Scream of Fear*, though she never read the play.

51 **"No, I'm not aggressive":** *Scream of Fear*, p. 1.

51 **"What is the truth?":** Ibid., p. 2.

52 **he says, "Felserstrasse 28":** Ibid., p. 8.

52 **"The time of lies has passed":** Ibid., p. 6.

53 **Sonja was moved by the lyricism of the verses:** Sonja didn't realize that the poem was actually a Hermann Hesse poem titled "The Wanderer's Ode to Death." Jack changed the title to "Love Poem to Death," as well as the second line of the second stanza from Hesse's "dear brother Death" to "and are alive, Death."

   "Love Poem to Death" is my translation of "Liebesgedicht an den Tod," Jack Unterweger's plagiarism of Hermann Hesse's "Der Wanderer an den Tod," *Der Wanderer*, G. Fischer, 1920.

53 **a letter to the editor:** Letter from Sonja Eisenstein to the *Kronen Zeitung*, dated March 10, 1991.

54 **On Friday, March 29, he called Margit:** Margit remembers the call just before Easter, 1991, and Jack made a note of it in his diary entry for March 29.

54 **They met that Sunday afternoon:** Margit recalled her Easter Sunday meeting with Jack, and he also recorded it in his diary, though—in my typed version—he omitted references to the Vienna Woods.

54 **Just as they passed a sign for the Scots Court:** Margit knew from the papers that a woman was found murdered in the Scots Woods, but she didn't know the exact location, and I didn't tell her until after she showed me the spot where Jack "slowed down to a crawl"—right at the sign for the Scots Court restaurant. The body of Sabine Moitzi was found in the woods across the street from the restaurant. It appears that Jack was taking a nasty pleasure in scoping out a suitable location to commit a murder with Margit along for the ride. He used the Scots Court restaurant as a cue for when to slow down for the turn off the unlit road at night.

CHAPTER 12: A COINCIDENCE

55 **On Friday, May 31, 1991:** "Report," Vienna Police Headquarters, May 31, 1991. A group leader in the homicide section spoke with Schenner and wrote a report on the tip. The brief report (only six lines) gives the impression that it, as well as the notes of the conversation upon which it was based, was hastily written. The officer who spoke with Schenner had, three days before, made a trip to Graz to assess the possibility that the Vienna murderers were connected with murders that had recently been committed in Graz. He concluded that they were not.

55 **an old, eccentric cop from the little city of Salzburg:** Because Schenner died before I began researching this book, I had to rely on sources other than the man himself for details about his personal style. The Vienna inspector Ernst Hoffmann, who made queries about Schenner, shared his recollections with me. Schenner also made an appearance in the BBC documentary *A Stranger Murder*, 1995. See also part three of the four-part series by the German journalist Erich Follath, "Der Dichter und die Dirnenmorde," *Stern*, 38/92.

57 **was calm, thoughtful:** Edelbacher told me about Jack's mature and professional manner when he conducted the ORF interview.

57 **Edelbacher knew that true crimes aren't like the intriguing plots:** The vast majority are not, just as the majority of men and women who commit murder are not serial killers. Edelbacher told me that, at the time the Unterweger case was unfolding, he had never heard of "police groupies"—serial killers who try to establish

contact with the police. This isn't surprising, given that literature on "police groupies" had only recently been published in the United States and hadn't yet been translated into German.

CHAPTER 13: COWBOY

57 **On June 10, Jack Unterweger again appeared:** From interview with Edel-bacher and from Jack's diary entry.

57 **tell Jack about the tip from Salzburg:** One wonders if Jack sensed he might have been a suspect, and was probing Edelbacher by announcing his plan to leave the country. Up till the time of his departure, he was under surveillance. How would the surveillance unit have reacted to Jack's trip to the airport and departure if he hadn't given Edelbacher notice the day before?

57 **Jack put on a striking outfit:** Photographs that Jack had taken of himself at LAX.

58 **with his fake driver's license:** According to Bianca Mrak, the original document was a gag item he bought in a gift shop. He merely cut out the picture of a chimpanzee and replaced it with a passport photo of himself.

59 **Carolina saw the slender, fair-skinned man:** Interview with "Carolina" (a fictional name to protect the living person's privacy).

61 **Jack met a group of Austrians and Germans:** Interview with Frances Schoenberger, as well as Jack's diary entry for June 16, 1991.

61 **Jack spent the next few days:** He meticulously documented his trip to Los Angeles with photographs and his diary.

62 **Jack had a meeting with Frances's ex-husband:** Jack's diary entry. Frances Schoenberger and Michael Montfort also recalled the meeting.

62 **to shoot a portrait of Charles Bukowski:** Montfort's friendship with Bukowski is described in "The Man Who Shot Charles Bukowski," *Salon*, June 15, 2000.

62 **to track him down at the Hollywood Park:** Jack wrote in his diary that it was Montfort's suggestion to look for Bukowski at Hollywood Park.

62 **Bukowski's depiction of downtown L.A.:** Among Jack's photographs was one of what appears to be the dresser in his hotel room, on which is propped a paperback with BUKOWSKI printed across the top (the title isn't visible).

63 **Bukowski's last novel, *Pulp*:** *Pulp* was published in 1994. I wonder if Bukowski heard about Jack's attempt to track him down at Hollywood Park in 1991 and morphed it into Céline tracking down the hero of *Pulp* at the park.

63 **"We should keep":** "Subkultur der Sexualität," *Tirolerin*, Autumn 1991.

63 **Jack visited the LAPD Parker Center:** Jack wrote in his diary that he visited Parker Center from 9:00 to 12:00. At the same time, Detective Miller was on the third floor of the same building, studying the teletype about the Exley murder. It's possible that they passed each other in the lobby.

64 **"Hey, Staples":** Interview with Steve Staples. Jack also noted the ride-along in his diary.

64 **Jack read the police journal:** The Vienna police found a copy in his bedroom.

66 **saw Jack flirting:** Interview with Staples and Jack's photographs of the women.

66 **he found Zsa Zsa Gabor's house:** Jack's diary entry for June 27, 1991.

66 **He then drove out to Cher's house:** Jack did not note this in the typed version of his diary, perhaps because Cher's house is located half a mile from the en-

trance to Corral Canyon Road (a good spot to turn around if he accidentally over-shot Cher's driveway). However, Frances Schoenberger vividly recalled his failed attempt to track down Cher and his ensuing frustration. I think it is reasonable to assume that—as he did with Zsa Zsa Gabor—he found her house using his "Homes of the Stars" map.

67 **Jack told the receptionist:** Jack's diary entry for July 1, 1991.

67 **"came with dreams":** "Hollywood: Luxus, Laster, Leidenschaften," *Tirolerin*, Autumn, 1991.

67 **visit the filmmaker Robert Dornhelm:** Jack's diary entry for July 3, 1991.

67 **Robert Dornhelm was put out:** Dornhelm told me his recollections of Jack's visit. He was shocked when I told him that a woman was picked up in Hollywood and murdered a few miles from his home later that night.

69 **drove back into the city, to Carolina's duplex:** Jack's diary entry for July 3, 1991. He probably did watch her enter it with a Mexican man, and he may have, as he wrote, sat in his car, parked across the street, occasionally calling her from his cell phone. But when she didn't answer, it seems unlikely that he stayed until 6:00. He probably intended to recite the entry at his trial, as it offered a account of what he was doing on the night Sherri Long was picked up in Hollywood and murdered in Malibu.

70 **though he spoke in an intimate way:** Jack's diary entry for July 8, 1991.

71 **Austrian socialite:** Ibid., July 12, 1991, and my interview with Schoenberger.

CHAPTER 14: ZIGZAG

72 **"Jack Unterweger, murderer and writer":** All quotations in the chapter are from the ORF radio program *Zick Zack*, June 22, 1991.

73 **"In my dreams I slit open":** *Zick Zack* quotation of *Purgatory*, p. 13.

73 **"I thumbed through it to pages":** Ibid., p. 166.

74 **identified her as Silvia Zagler:** Crime scene description from "Dirnen-Killer mordet nur im Wienerwald," *Kurier*, August 6, 1991, and from *Concluding Report*, pp. 39–40.

CHAPTER 15: A TRIP TO VIENNA

74 **Carolina drifted back:** Interview with Carolina. Many of her recollections were corroborated by Margit Haas and by Jack's diary entries during her visit.

78 **The next day, Carolina asked Margit:** Both women remembered the conversation. Margit was astonished when I told her that Jack had told Carolina that he'd gone to prison for bank robbery.

CHAPTER 16: MYTHOLOGY

79 **Jack was coming to the Wimitz:** Jack's forty-first birthday celebration was covered by the press, and he noted it in his diary.

79 **Malicious lies, she'd thought:** Interview with Charlotte Auer.

79 **"the end of civilization":** Jack's schoolteacher in the 1950s, a woman named Odelia Vizthum, told me the history of Wimitz.

80 **a city dweller might be seized:** Standing in the front yard of Jack's childhood cottage at night, I was impressed by the pitch blackness of the wooded landscape. Before Jack became a suspect for the Vienna Woods murders, the investigators figured that the unknown killer must have been accustomed to being in the woods at night.

81 **He had his own bedroom:** Jack's claim that the cottage consisted of only two inhabitable rooms and that he slept in the same bed with his grandfather and various women (*Purgatory*, p. 19) is one of his most persistent myths. Though the cottage is isolated, it is not small by rural Austrian standards, and its living space is larger than most apartments in Vienna. When I visited the uninhabited cottage in 2005, I saw a hand-carved wooden airplane hanging from the ceiling of a second-floor room—probably one of the many toys that, according to Charlotte Auer, Ferdinand carved for Jack.

82 **She looked up just as a Ford Mustang:** Jack told Margit and others that he wrecked and abandoned the car in Italy at the end of March 1991. However, in my interview with Charlotte Auer, she said she was confident that he was driving a Mustang when he passed by her cottage on August 15, 1991. He may have kept it at his apartment in Tarvisio, Italy, just across the border from Carinthia, and used it for road trips in southern Austria and in Italy. Telling people at the end of March (just before the Vienna prostitutes started disappearing) that he accidentally wrecked the flashy car probably gave him an excuse for driving his inconspicuous VW Passat.

82 **She walked in to find Jack sitting:** Interview with Charlotte Auer. Jack also recorded the episode in the typed version of his diary, stating that he did not know the identity of the woman who claimed to be his Aunt Lotte. In *Purgatory* he repeatedly mentions his "aunts" and his "Uncle Fritz" (Charlotte's brother).

CHAPTER 17: A BATH

83 **Later she told Jack about him:** The chapter is from my interview with Carolina.

CHAPTER 18: DEATH BY DROWNING

86 **murdered woman found in the Salzach Lake:** The Salzburg police meticulously documented the investigation of the murder of Marica Horvath with a series of reports, starting with a crime description illustrated with several photographs. Announcement: "Unknown Offender," April 1, 1973; "Crime Scene Report": Salzburg Police Headquarters, April 1, 1973; "Report": Salzburg Police Headquarters, Zahl: II/Ref.1/1-1336/73-UT-Ro.

89 **complaint of a Salzburg girl named Daphne:** "Accusation," Salzburg, May 14, 1974.

89 **"As I tried to scream":** "Record," Salzburg Police Headquarters, May 14, 1974.

90 **"From October 1971":** "Record," Salzburg Police Headquarters, May 15, 1974.

92 **"This murder happened many years ago":** "File Record," Wels Police Headquarters, "Reference to a past murder in Salzburg," February 2, 1983.

93 **"I was a chambermaid":** "Record," Wels Police Headquarters, February 17, 1983.

93 **"We stayed in":** "Record," Salzburg Police Headquarters, March 23, 1983.

94 **Manu's story checked out:** "File Record," Salzburg Police Headquarters, February 27, 1983.

95 **an insurance claim:** "File Record," Salzburg Police Headquarters, March 24, 1983.

95 **"my stay in Kitzbühel":** "Record," Salzburg Police Headquarters, May 15, 1974.

95 **"Inspector Schenner, so good to see you!":** Schenner wrote a seven-page report on his interrogation of Jack at Stein: "Report," Salzburg Police Headquarters, April 5, 1983. Jack also made notes of the interrogation in his diary entry of April 1, 1983.

98 **To Schenner, the D.A.'s decision was a blatant injustice:** In the 1995 BBC documentary *A Stranger Murder*, Schenner reiterated his conviction that it was an injustice not to prosecute Jack for the murder.

98 **how had Manu's father come up with the story:** Schenner asked Manu if she could think of an explanation: "Record," Salzburg Police Headquarters, Wels, May 20,1983. She replied that she could think of no other possibility than that he'd heard it from one of his criminal friends.

CHAPTER 19: JUST PLAYING

99 **It didn't seem as if he was just playing:** Interview with Carolina. Jack probably was just playing a sadistic game, with no intention of murdering Carolina, but when one is being held underwater, less than a minute may seem like an eternity.

99 **"I'm thinking about renting":** Jack also mentioned in a letter that he wanted to "move into a house on the outskirts of Vienna." Letter from Jack Unterweger to Frank D. in Los Angeles, August 1, 1991.

CHAPTER 20: HOT TIP

102 **Only a well-informed:** In the typed version of Jack's diary is a photocopy of the report, the relevant passages underlined, with exclamation marks in the margins.

102 **"What is it? Tell me why":** When I interviewed Carolina in February 2005, she still didn't know why Jack had become upset on September 1, 1991, and sent her home.

CHAPTER 21: CONFRONTATION

103 **Jack popped by Chief Edelbacher's office:** Interview with Edelbacher, who documented Jack's visits in "File Record," Vienna Police Headquarters, March 18, 1992.

CHAPTER 22: CRANK CALL

105 **"At the Vienna Woods lake go left":** The Lower Austrian Police documented Rudolf's complaints about the crank calls in "Report," February 2, 1992.

106 **"on Tulbinger Hill lies Gerda":** Though the police ultimately questioned Rudolf's credibility, the date of the crank call—October 8, 1991—suggests that he told the truth about it. On a few occasions, Jack appears to have exploited the

expectations of normal people by doing exactly what they assumed a killer would never be so bold to do. Making crank calls the night after Edelbacher confronted him may have been another instance of deception by audacity, as it was likely that Rudolf would report the calls. Telling him that his wife lay on Tulbinger Hill was another way to lead the police around by the nose, as she was in fact lying on Hermann's Hill.

CHAPTER 23: ALIBIS

106 **"For the entire months of April and May":** "Record," Vienna Police Headquarters, October 22, 1991. Inspector Ernst Hoffmann was present when Jack made his statement to Edelbacher.

107 **an unusual teletype:** "Report," Vienna Police Headquarters, November 5, 1991.

CHAPTER 24: GRAZ

108 **At 12:15 a.m. a taxi driver:** "Report," Graz Police Headquarters, May 24, 1991. Hans Breitegger also depicted the Graz murders in his book (see list of sources), p. 160.

108 **her corpse lying facedown:** Description and photograph in "Special Commission Jack Unterweger Concluding Report," March 15, 1993.

109 **a prominent member of Graz society:** Interviews with Hans Breitegger and Hans Lehofer. Astrid Wagner also mentions the suspect in *Jack Unterweger: Ein Mörder für alle Fälle*, p. 105.

109 **get into a VW Golf:** Hans Breitegger, "Sechs Frauen als Mordopfer," *Kleine Zeitung*, May 4, 1991. In *Jack Unterweger*, pp. 110–11, Astrid Wagner implies that the driver of a white VW Golf with red stripes was indeed the murderer of Elfriede Schrempf. She doesn't mention the driver of the yellow VW Golf, whom the Graz police interrogated on October 22, 1991: "Record," Graz Police Headquarters. It's notable that the Graz police dismissed the VW Golf tip months before Jack Unterweger became a suspect.

109 **During further questioning of the woman:** "Statement," Gendarmerie Headquarters for Styria, October 21, 1991.

110 **"At the beginning of the eighties":** "Tod, Schmutzig, Steirisch," *Wiener*, May 1991.

110 **"I write to you about the issue of the prison inmate":** Undated letter from Prof. Dr. Ernest Borneman to Justice Minister Egmont Foregger, reproduced in Schmidt, p. 99.

111 **Elfriede Schrempf's skeleton was found in the woods:** Crime scene description and photograph in "Concluding Report," pp. 37–38.

CHAPTER 25: BIANCA

113 **Though Bianca Mrak had only:** Most of the chapter is from my interviews with Bianca, and from the dozens of press interviews she has given over the years. In 2004, Bianca published her own book (see list of sources) about her experiences with Jack.

115 **Her school didn't include the novel:** In my interview with Alfred Kolleritsch, the first publisher of *Purgatory*, he recalled giving a talk to a high school literature class that was assigned to read the book. He was dismayed when one of the students told me she considered it "the best ever written."

116 **Jack had been a master of bondage:** His dozens of girlfriends over the years included many who regularly visited him in prison. Countless observers have marveled at the strange power he exerted over them.

117 **"No theme is more poetic than the death":** Jack's handwritten reflections, found in his cell on July 16, 1975, demonstrate that he was not—as he often claimed—an illiterate and unthinking creature prior to his "rebirth" after his trial in 1976. On the contrary, his reflections, written in a pretty hand, are composed in clear German.

117 **An upscale escort service:** Bianca didn't mention this to the police in her interviews in 1992, but she gives an account of it in her book: Mrak, p. 34.

118 **He'd driven her to the red-light district:** When Carolina told me the story, I suspected that Jack was testing her. When I related it to Margit Haas (without mentioning my hypothesis), she immediately reckoned the same.

119 **his conversation with Elisabeth:** Jack's diary entry for December 17–18, 1991.

119 **an intimate hour with his other girlfriend, Elisabeth:** Ibid., December 24, 1991.

120 **the next day he told his fiancée:** Ibid., December 25, 1991.

CHAPTER 26: BREAK

120 **Nineteen-year-old Joanna:** "Record," Graz Police Headquarters, January 13, 1992, and "Record," January 17, 1992. Additional details about the landscape around the Dominion of Heaven Way from my visit at night.

123 **Hans and Bernd would pose:** Interviews with Breitegger and Melichar.

124 **"drop off the tape":** Jack did drop off the tape, which was transcribed: "Audio-tape Copy," Graz Police Headquarters, January 17, 1992. Later the police realized that Hans and Bernd had unwittingly left the speaker function of their phone engaged.

124 **"In September 1990, for my reportage":** Jack made a seven-page statement: "Record," Graz Police Headquarters, January 17, 1992.

125 **"I picked up a prostitute in Graz":** Ibid., p. 5.

126 **And so he admitted:** Ibid., p. 6.

126 **"For what purpose":** Ibid., p. 7.

127 **saw her with him at the Frankfurt:** Interview with Alfred Kolleritsch.

127 **Jack could always play:** The film director Willi Hengstler was half joking when he said that Jack would have played the role himself.

127 **But that night at the Graz Casino:** Jack's diary entry for October 17, 1990; my interview with the Graz *Kurier* reporter Ulrike Jantschner.

127 **He'd probably scoped out:** Visiting the crime scenes at night, I noticed that none of the turnoffs onto small, wooded lanes were marked or lit.

128 **He knew Hans was lying:** In Jack's diary entry for June 1, 1991, he noted reading the article about the Graz murders in the May issue of *Wiener* magazine, in which Hans was quoted. According to the owner of Café Florianihof, Jack visited the café almost every evening and read the evening editions of the following day's papers.

128 **Hans was taken aback:** The scene at the Turks' Hole is from my interviews with Hans and Bernd, and from their report in the *Kleine Zeitung*, February 16, 1992.

CHAPTER 27: KATHARINA

130 **As the schoolgirl Katharina recalled:** Katharina made two statements, the first at her parents' apartment, the second at police headquarters: "Record," Vienna Police Headquarters, January 28, 1992.

131 **"I'll see what I can find":** Hans told me about tracking Jack's movements through the culture sections of Austrian newspapers.

CHAPTER 28: A FLASH OF RECOGNITION

132 **"It's him," said Inspector Leopold Etz:** Interview with Etz.

132 **something conspicuous about the way her arms:** Ibid. What he observed is plainly visible in the crime scene photos of the Eroglu murder and the Hammerer murder.

133 **Etz imagined her:** Describing the scene to me thirteen years later, Etz expressed his anger and disgust at "the miserable dog that would do that to those women."

CHAPTER 29: A JOB IN SWITZERLAND

133 **"You could earn as much in three weeks":** Interview with Bianca Mrak.

134 **From his informants:** Wolfgang Wladkowski and Franz Brandstätter believe that Jack had *"eine undichte Stelle"*—someone who leaked information to him—in the Vienna Police. Ernst Geiger considers it possible, though he believes that a general tendency to leak (stemming from lack of discipline and professional rivalry) was to blame, and not someone intentionally trying to help Jack.

134 **he'd purchased a mobile phone:** Jack's receipt and contract for the mobile phone, dated October 28, 1991.

134 **left Vienna on February 2, 1992:** Jack's diary entry, corroborated by Bianca Mrak's statement to the police.

CHAPTER 30: SPECIAL COMMISSION

137 **So Schenner was right:** Interviews with Ernst Geiger. The intensifying investigation of Jack in February 1992 and the building of the Special Commission are also recounted in "Special Commission Jack Unterweger Concluding Report," March 15, 1993.

CHAPTER 31: ONCE A MURDERER, ALWAYS A MURDERER

138 **Jack went to the studio:** Interviews with Thomas Raab and Margit Haas.

139 **"Hello, it's me, the mass murderer":** Interview with Peter Grolig, as well as Grolig's report "Hallo! Ich bin's, der Massenmörder," *Kurier*, February 16, 1992.

140 **"where you heard that cop say":** Interview with Margit Haas. Jack was aware of the rivalries and disagreements within the Vienna police, which he tried to exploit.

140 Hans Breitegger was informed about the warrant: Interview with Breitegger.
141 Jack called and she cried into the receiver: Mrak, p. 80.
141 first meeting of the Special Commission: Interviews with Geiger and Brandstätter.
142 He knew a lot about: Jack's diary entries for February 10–11, 1992.
143 After departing Gossau: In Jack's "Miami Defense" (see chapter 42) he claimed
that a friend in Vienna happened to have called him on his mobile phone on Saturday, February 15, 1992, at 4:35. More likely the call was scheduled for 4:30,
with Jack taking or placing it near the Swiss border.
143 he called Vienna headquarters: The calls were documented by the Graz and Vienna police, and Jack mentioned them in his "Miami Defense."
144 "Get myself a pump gun": "Ich besorg' mir eine Pumpgun," *Kurier*, February 17,
1992.

CHAPTER 32: THE MISSING DIARIES
144 Jack had received generous subsidies: Documented in Schmidt, pp. 247–50.
145 Jack's diaries: See my description on pages 320–21.

CHAPTER 33: JACK ENTERS HADES
147 "The ministries are afraid": Interview with Inspector Brandstätter.
147 "Jack will probably try to enter Italy": "Mafia in Italian: Wir helfen bei Suche
nach Jack!" *Kronen Zeitung*, February 22, 1992.
147 "We all knew Regina well": Ibid.
148 he'd served as an informant: "Jack die Ratte," *Wiener*, April 1992.
148 "When the figure eight": Calls to Rudolf Prem recorded in "Report," Lower Austria Police Headquarters, February 10, 1992.
148 "To eleven": Ibid.
148 JACK ENTERS HADES: The documents found in Jack's apartment that appeared to
have a connection with the calls to Rudolf Prem are described in "Concluding
Report," pp. 94–95.
149 Greek mythology book: *Sagen des Altertums* (see list of sources). The Vienna police noted the book and its missing page in their inventory of items from Jack's
apartment, "Catalog," February 20, 1992, but they never found a complete copy
to check the missing page.
149 page 19: I obtained a copy from a seller of out-of-print books in Germany.

CHAPTER 34: COUNTEROFFENSIVE
150 "an anonymous tip": Jack apparently obtained a copy of the Vienna police report
on Schenner's tip ("Report," May 31, 1991). Because the report does not mention
the name of the caller, it gave Jack the impression that it was "an anonymous tip."
151 "The Grotesque Murder Witch Hunt": "Die groteske Mords-Hats," *profil*, February 24, 1992.
152 "The chances of catching": "Strichweises Sterben," *profil*, June 3, 1991.

CHAPTER 35: MIAMI VICE

152 **Sometimes it seemed as if:** Details about Jack and Bianca's adventures in Miami are from my interviews with her, her various press interviews, Jack's diary entries for February 14–26, her statement to the police: "Record," Vienna Police Headquarters, March 1, 1992, and her book: Mrak, pp. 83–153.

160 **"I met him":** "Report," Lower Austria Police Headquarters, February 25, 1992.

161 **his life was in grave danger:** Elisabeth told her boss, Gert Schmidt, about Jack's pressing needs: Schmidt, 206–207.

161 **"Crisis because of Elisabeth":** Jack's diary entry, February 23, 1992.

161 **he'd hit her up for $14,500:** The loans are documented in "Concluding Report," p. 12.

CHAPTER 36: BETRAYAL

163 **"I just talked to a guy":** Interviews with Geiger and Hoffmann.

CHAPTER 37: U.S. MARSHALS

165 **U.S. marshal:** Details about Jack's arrest from interviews with Conboy and Bianca.

166 **The three of them:** Jack's adventures with his two girlfriends in Switzerland and Germany in 1974 are recounted in the Salzburg D.A.'s indictment of Jack for the murder of Margret Schäfer: "Indictment," Salzburg District Attorney, February 9, 1976.

CHAPTER 38: A STAR IS BORN

169 **Kleist's *Penthesilea*:** Geiger and Hoffmann told me about the evening of Jack's arrest, and Hoffmann's trip to Miami.

170 **"It was my idea":** "Es war wie in einem US-Fernsehkrimi," *Der Standard*, March 2, 1992.

CHAPTER 39: THE TIES THAT BIND

170 **Geiger and Inspector Windisch:** Details of Bianca's initial meetings with Geiger are from my interviews with Geiger and Mrak.

171 **a tight-fitting red cotton dress:** Press photographs.

172 **Just as Geiger was hoping:** Interview with Ernst Geiger.

173 **"Hey, *Mausi*":** Bianca's telephone conversations with Jack and others were documented with wiretap transcripts. "Report," Vienna Police Headquarters, "Evaluation of Audio Recording Transcripts–Apartment of Jack Unterweger," May 23, 1992.

175 **her "incurable":** "Biancas Unheilbare Liebe," *Kronen Zeitung*, March 8, 1992.

175 **"He wants to see *Aïda*":** Interview with Ernst Geiger.

CHAPTER 40: VOLUNTARY RETURN

176 **Ninety days:** Extradition treaty between Austria and the United States, signed on September 30, 1930.

177 **"When he brought the car":** "Record," Vienna Police Headquarters, March 3, 1992.

177 **"I practice civil law":** Interview with Joseph Slama.

178 JACK UNTERWEGER WANTS TO RETURN: "Jack Unterweger will zurückkommen," *Der Standard*, March 2, 1992.

178 **"Maybe he was looking at the barber's chair":** *profil*, March 9, 1992.

178 UNTERWEGER: HOPE FOR A VOLUNTARY RETURN: "Unterweger: Hoffen auf freiwillige Rückkehr," *Der Standard*, March 3, 1992.

CHAPTER 41: A GOOD LEAD

180 **Fred Miller of the LAPD got a message:** Miller's contact with the Austrian police and his investigation of Jack's activities in Los Angeles are documented in "Chronological Sequence of Events/L.A.P.D. and Austrian Serial Murder Investigation," March 23, 1992. Miller and Harper also gave me their personal accounts.

180 **"What's going on, Fred":** Interview with Steve Staples.

181 **"I've got just one question":** Interview with Miller.

181 **"Good Lord":** Interview with Lancaster.

CHAPTER 42: JACK'S DEFENSE

182 **the defense document:** "Complaint: To the Graz Court, Re: Arrest Warrant on Friday, February 14, 1992, for Unterweger," dated Saturday, February 22, 1992, Appendix dated February 25, 1992.

183 **"Mr. Schenner reacted aggressively":** Ibid., p. 4.

183 **"On the nights of the 26th and 27th of October":** Ibid., p. 10.

184 **"That morning, at 8:30":** Ibid., pp. 12-13.

184 **"On this day I was with Martina":** Ibid., pp. 17-18.

186 **"The police know about the women":** Ibid., appendix, p. 3.

CHAPTER 43: NOT A WORD ABOUT THE CRIME

187 **He drafted his own eight-page version:** Jack's diary entry for April 5, 1983.

187 **Jack took the opportunity to tell the official:** Ibid., April 7, 1983. In 1983, Jack protested his innocence of murdering Marica Horvath, but shortly after his parole he gave his readers a tantalizing clue that he did murder her. On pages 43–46 of *Dungeon*, published in October 1990, he tells of spending a night with his girlfriend Manu in a city that he vaguely describes but does not name (unlike the dozen other cities that he visits in the story). After dinner he leaves Manu in their "second-floor" hotel room while he goes to the train station to look at the schedule. He concludes the passage ominously: "I told her nothing about my other intentions." That and other hints suggest that the passage is a veiled reference to

the night of March 31–April 1, 1973, when Jack murdered Marica Horvath in Salzburg.

188 **"Not a Word about the Crime"**: Ibid., July 14, 1983. Why exactly Jack wasn't prosecuted for the murder of Marica Horvath remains a mystery, though his diary entries strongly suggest that political influence was brought to bear on the decision. When I recounted the Horvath investigation to Dr. Peter Cardona—the Salzburg defense attorney who represented Jack at his 1976 trial for the murder of Margret Schäfer—the lawyer remarked that, even if Schenner's case was largely circumstantial, it was still odd that the authorities "didn't at least try to convict Unterweger of the murder."

CHAPTER 44: A CLEVER MEDIA LAWYER:

188 "A clever media lawyer": Quoted in "Recht im Bild," *NEWS*, June 9, 1993.

189 Zanger had been a member: Portrait of Zanger from "Der Links- und Rechtsvertreter," *WirtschaftsWoche* 6, July 1992, and "Der Linksanwalt," *Top*, August 1994.

189 Zanger told *profil*: "Miami, Collins Avenue," *profil*, March 2, 1992.

189 Dr. Zanger had "hired": "Ein US-Detektiv will sich um Jack kuemmern," *Kurier*, March 11, 1992.

190 "We'll make sure that Jack's rights are observed": Ibid.

190 Zanger was also representing Bianca: Unsigned "Agent Representation Contract" between Bianca Mrak, Dr. Georg Zanger (as legal representative), and Nestor A. Tabares.

CHAPTER 45: A CRAZY FEELING OF TRIUMPH

191 In a letter to Alfred Kolleritsch: Jack attached an autobiographical blurb for "the author's" page in *Manuskripte*, along with the request to publish "nothing about the killing." Letter dated May 14, 1983.

191 Soon Hengstler began to dread: Interview with Hengstler.

191 "Jack hasn't become a better man": Ibid.

191 Jack had learned to present his transformation: Dr. Haller told me that Jack once asked Dr. Federn: "Is it conceivable that I saw my mother standing before me when I killed the girl?" Dr. Federn replied that it was conceivable, and the story became official.

192 "I fear he didn't really interest us": "Im Spiegelkabinett," *profil*, February 24, 1992.

193 "But naturally we must ask": "Die neue Obrigkeit," *profil*, March 2, 1992.

193 "From the experiences": "Im Gespräch," ORF, January 1989. Huemer broadcast it again on the occasion of Jack's flight from the arrest warrant.

194 "what are you doing?": Jack Unterweger, *Kerker*, pp. 62–64. Compare Jack's statement, "I went to work on him without seeing him . . . I observed my movements in slow motion," with the statement of the "Texas Railroad Killer," Angel Maturino Resendiz: "Everything you see is at a distance. Everything is slow and silent." Quoted in "'Railroad Killer' Put to Death in Texas," *Washington Post*, June 28, 2006.

CHAPTER 46: OBSESSION

196 I've lost my husband to a killer: From interview with Eva Geiger.

CHAPTER 47: YOU DON'T HAVE ANY EVIDENCE

198 He consented, and at 6:00 p.m.: "Chronological Sequence of Events/L.A.P.D. and Austrian Serial Murder Investigation," case no. 127522-M/1, March 23, 1992.

198 "Have a Coke, it'll keep you cool": Details of March 13, 1992, interview with Jack from my interviews with Miller and Harper.

199 "I went to L.A.": "Statement Form," Unterweger, Jack, 3-13-92, 1800.

200 "Three black women in L.A.": Jack listed many of his conquests by both first and last names, but some are listed by first names only. Three of the entries stand out in that the women are anonymous and grouped by numbers: "3 black women in L.A.," "Seven bimbos, first names only," and "1X Romanian."

CHAPTER 48: OUR SUSPECT

202 "Our suspect": Details about the Special Commission's investigation in Los Angeles from interviews with Miller, Harper, Lancaster, Geiger, and Brandstätter.

203 "Beer, Jimmy": Interview with Miller.

204 "Who does he think he is": Interview with Eva Geiger.

CHAPTER 49: WHEN THE FIGURE EIGHT AT THE ZENITH STANDS

205 A search team found most of her bones: Details about the crime scene from interview with Ernst Hoffmann, the "Concluding Report," and crime scene photographs. Her skull was found by a hiker on Hermann's Hill in 2003, shortly after I started researching this story.

205 After sitting him down in an office: Inspector Johannes Scherz told me this story.

206 washed his car and changed its tires: Jack's diary entry for April 29, 1991. The police never saw the diary and never learned that Jack had changed his tires the morning after Regina disappeared.

206 He opened the door and saw her lying in bed: Interviews with Ernst and Eva Geiger.

206 What in hell did "When the figure eight": According to the anthropologist Roland Girtler, the Viennese criminal underworld has developed its own dialect (*Rotwelsch*) with the intention of being incomprehensible to the police. That the Vienna police were initially stumped by the meaning of "*der Achter*" is a good example, as it is one of many *Rotwelsch* words for "handcuffs." Girtler, Rotwelsch, p. 197.

CHAPTER 50: THE FEAR OF DEATH

207 "Jack, what's wrong": Interview with Miller.

208 "I feel that": Copy of letter from Fred Miller to Ernst Geiger, dated May 7, 1992.

CHAPTER 51: VLAD THE IMPALER

210 **Forty-four-year-old Wolfgang Wladkowski**: Portrait of Wladkowski from interviews with Wladkowski, Ernst Geiger, Doris Piringer, Hans Lehofer, Hans Breitegger, and Astrid Wagner. Wagner also wrote about him in her books.

211 **"Unterweger has won"**: "Jack Unterweger ist wieder da," *Kurier*, May 29, 1992.

CHAPTER 52: PRAGUE

212 **a query to the Interpol office in Prague**: Queries were also sent to Interpol offices all over Europe, but no unsolved murders that shared the same conspicuous set of characteristics were reported back.

CHAPTER 53: THE TRUTH ABOUT YOU

213 **Jack had written . . . Mrs. Müller**: *Witness Interrogation*, Graz Criminal Court, April 8, 1992.

214 **Jack told his recollections**: Interview with Wladkowski.

215 **Jack turned to Windisch**: Interview with Franz Brandstätter.

CHAPTER 54: BLANKA

216 **Blanka Bockova**: Files from the initial Czech investigation were translated into German. This information was combined with Geiger's investigation of Jack's activities in Prague on the weekend of September 14–16, 1990: "Report," Vienna Police Headquarters, "Murder Blanka Bockova," dated June 3, 1992.

217 **The landlady was a fifty-year-old woman**: Weeks before the Vienna police learned about the murder of Blanka Bockova outside the Prague city limits, a Vienna investigator traveled to Prague to interview Mrs. Bocova: "File Record," Vienna Police Headquarters, April 23, 1992. Geiger and his team followed up with a second interview: "Record," Vienna Police Headquarters, Prague, May 27, 1992.

CHAPTER 55: MANEUVER AND COUNTER-MANEUVER

218 **"The Interior Ministry is going to remove"**: Interview with Wladkowski.

219 **Jack wept and raved**: Mrak, p. 215.

220 **Even a pimp could catch a glimpse**: Ibid., p. 217. Margit Haas also told me about Jack's jealousy. He initially hoped that Margit would keep an eye on Bianca for him, but she ended up being Bianca's nocturnal companion.

220 **"I don't need your confession"**: Interview with Wladkowski.

220 **"Unterweger slashed"**: "Unterweger schnitt sich Pulsadern auf!" *Kronen Zeitung*, July 1, 1992.

CHAPTER 56: ASTRID

221 **Thank God**: Wagner, *"Und die Mörderjagd muss weitergehen!"* p. 84.

222 **Had Wladkowski decided to plant a woman**: Ibid.

222 Such a small, pitiable-looking man: Ibid.

222 "Taurus women are self-righteous": Ibid.

222 "I came two or three times per week": Ibid.

223 Here we go again: Interview with Wladkowski.

223 Wladkowski often wondered: Ibid.

223 had once read a biography: Conversation with Astrid Wagner.

224 So many briefs crossed his desk: Wladowski told me this with an ironic smile.

224 How witty of Wladkowski: Interview with Margit Haas.

224 Bianca's nineteenth birthday: The letter swap happened at the end of October 1992; Bianca's birthday was on November 7, 1992.

224 she gave an interview: "Der Mörder, der die Frauen reizt," *Wiener*, March 1992.

CHAPTER 57: FRUSTRATION

225 The American DNA test: Results of the test cited in "Gesamtgutachten in der Strafsache gegen Johann Unterweger," Institute for Forensic Medicine, Bern, p. 69.

226 Four dark hairs had been found in Jack's VW: Interview with Ernst Geiger.

CHAPTER 58: FORENSIC PATHOLOGIST

228 Andrea read in the papers: Details of Andrea's involvement in the investigation from interviews with her and Geiger.

CHAPTER 59: SPECIAL AGENT

229 "They've made an arrest": McCrary, p. 247.

230 was struck by how far and wide: Ibid., p. 249.

230 "Let's start with looking at each case": Additional details of the meeting from my interview with Gregg McCrary.

231 things the murderer didn't have to do: Ibid.

231 The technique of signature crime-scene analysis: Ibid.

CHAPTER 60: JACK, GEORG, AND THE SUPREME COURT

232 Jack became the first pretrial detainee: Before Jack's case, human rights complaints in Austria were sent to the European Court for Human Rights in Strasbourg, France, but to lessen the caseload of the European Court, the Austrian Parliament mandated in 1992 that the Austrian Supreme Court hear some human rights cases.

233 "We see the lawyer": "Der ganz grosse Jack-Plot," *Basta*, January 1993.

233 Zanger adorned his desk: From interview with Hans Lehofer.

CHAPTER 61: "ISN'T THAT UNTERWEGER'S TRAMP?"

234 "won't rent to me because they're afraid": Interview with Bianca Mrak.

234 "Hey, isn't that Unterweger's tramp?": Ibid.

234 When the Beverly Hills go-go: Mrak, p. 218.

234 **Prince Albert of Monaco hit on her:** Ibid.
235 **"I cannot fulfill your request":** Margit claims to have a clear memory of the letter, though she does not have a copy of it.
235 **"I let you stay over":** Ibid.

CHAPTER 62: REVELATION

237 **"We chatted for a minute":** Barbara Scholz's account of what happened to Margret Schäfer is my translation of her statement at the police station in Lörrach,
Germany: "Interrogation," Dillenburg Police, Special Commission, Schäfer, Lörrach (Baden), January 30, 1975.
239 **hunters found the naked corpse:** "Trace Evidence Report," Hessian State Police
Office, Wiesbaden, January 7, 1975.

CHAPTER 63: THE TRIAL OF THE CENTURY

Because I was granted limited access to the enormous court transcript, my re-creation
of the trial is based mostly on press reports and interviews. To obtain the most accurate record possible of what was said in the courtroom, I studied the reports of every
major newspaper that covered the trial: *Der Standard, Die Presse, Kurier, Kleine
Zeitung, Wiener Zeitung, Täglich Alles, Salzburger Nachrichten,* and *Kronen Zeitung.*
The magazines *profil, NEWS,* and *Der Spiegel* published weekly reports. Because of
variations from publication to publication in the way the proceedings were reported,
especially in the wording of quotations, I have relied on no one source in particular,
but have drawn my scenes and quotations from a consensus of reporting whenever I
could find it. When I couldn't find a consensus, I favored the reporting of the *Kleine
Zeitung* journalists Doris Piringer and Bernd Melichar, and the *profil* journalist Paul
Yvon, because I believe in their professional integrity.
243 **Bourcard was:** Interviews with Hans Lehofer and Astrid Wagner, who made similar characterizations of Judges Bourcard and Haas (the latter died before I began
researching this story).
244 **"Hitler was":** Recording of Doris Piringer's interview with Jack, March 14, 1994.
245 **Lehofer wanted to help Jack:** Details about Lehofer's professional and personal
relationship with Jack from interviews with Hans Lehofer.
245 **Wenzl's friendship with Zanger:** Interviews with Wladkowski and Geiger.
246 **"Alexander, a conscientious warden":** Jack's diary entry for April 20, 1994.

CHAPTER 64: OPENING STATEMENTS

248 **"He fooled a Justice Ministry section head . . . a court president":** Wenzl was
referring to Dr. Wolfgang Doleisch and Dr. Udo Jesionek, president of the Juvenile Court.

CHAPTER 65: INQUISITION

258 **"No, nor had I ever visited it by car":** In his diary entry for June 25, 1990, Jack
noted visiting a family in Lustenau and going for a walk that evening with their

dog. The Lustenauer Ried (Lustenau Marsh) has a public parking lot and is a major local attraction for walkers.

CHAPTER 67: JOKER

264 a letter that Gasser interpreted: "Wie prekär es wird," *profil*, May 2, 1994.

CHAPTER 68: MOTHER

266 "I was never a whore": "Hansi ist kein Monster," *NEWS*, April 21, 1994.

CHAPTER 70: EX-GIRLFRIEND

268 Yes, he had shown a preference: Mrak, pp. 232–33.

CHAPTER 71: DAUGHTER

269 the twenty-three-year-old girl wore a wig: Details of Claudia's appearance and testimony from interview with Hans Lehofer.

270 "This is your daughter": Claudia's story drawn from "Unterwegers Tochter Bricht Ihr Schweigen," *Wiener*, June 1992, and from Jack's diary entry for January 20, 1986.

270 "It's nothing, your honor, I promise": Interview with Hans Lehofer.

CHAPTER 75: HEIDI

276 "In my conversation with Dr. Haller": Dr. Haller told me about this episode.

CHAPTER 76: BLANKA

277 "My wife is here today": Interview with Lehofer.

CHAPTER 77: AN EXPERIMENT

279 gave Lehofer a thirty-eight-page: Unterweger, Jack, "Presentation of the Facts of the Case."

279 "Well, I'm a little guy": Hans Lehofer's student assistant Anna Schmidt told me this story. Lehofer introduced me to her because he believed she would remember more details from the case.

280 "How would you like to meet him?": Interviews with Hans Lehofer and Anna Schmidt.

281 "Really?" Lehofer asked: In reviewing the story together twelve years later, Lehofer was again surprised by how different his perceptions were from Anna's.

CHAPTER 79: THE AMERICANS

283 **Sergeant Steve Staples:** Interview with Steve Staples. Staples, Ronnie Lancaster, James Harper, Gregg McCrary, and Lynne Herold all told me about their experiences in Graz.
286 **"Despite his small stature":** McCrary, p. 256.
287 **"Have you ever heard of a man":** Ibid., p. 260.
288 **"These ligatures were":** The journalist Paul Yvon was so impressed by Herold's testimony that he wrote an entire report on it: "Der Tag der Boa," *profil*, June 14, p. 35.

CHAPTER 80: A HISTORY LESSON

290 **Zanger began his cross-examination:** Interview with Berzlanovich.
291 **"Deissen, Swoboda, Piringer":** Jack's diary entry, April 20, 1994.

CHAPTER 81: TEXTILE FIBERS

294 **"It seems to me that Lehofer's":** Jack's diary entry, June 15, 1994.
295 **no defects on her skin from fingernail scratching:** "Autopsy and Examination of Blanka Bockova," Prague, September 17, 1990 (German translation of the Czech report).

CHAPTER 82: DNA

295 **What could this little boy know:** Interview with Manfred Hochmeister.
296 **"Zanger + Dirnhofer / DNA = hot air":** Jack's diary entry, June 16, 1994.
296 **Because the police put it there:** Wagner, *Und die Mörderjagd*, pp. 205–206.
296 **Manfred conducted the final test:** Results presented in "Ergänzung zum DNA-Gutachten vom 01.07.1993 und vom 02.02.1994," May 31, 1994.

CHAPTER 85: THE LORD'S PRAYER

299 **"You could pray":** Interview with Lehofer.
299 **Astrid went up on the roof:** Wagner, *Und die Mörderjagd*, p. 303.
299 **the man in the cell had assumed the mystical significance:** Ibid., pp. 275–76. Wagner catalogs Jack's suffering and the corresponding hypocrisy of society. On page 297, she describes watching a video of him at the moment the verdict is read: "And yet his face had, at this moment, an expression of unearthly relief. Spontaneously the sentence occurred to me: 'I am not of this world.'"
300 **the rest of her life:** In her accusation that Jack's body had been desecrated, she stated that she was engaged to him: "Strafanzeige wegen Störung der Totenruhe," to Justice Minister Dr. Nikolaus Michalek, Graz, January 9, 1995.

CHAPTER 87: EXPLOSIVE

304 **"Shards bring luck," he said:** Wagner recounted her final meeting with Jack: *Und die Mörderjagd*, pp. 291–92.

304 **"Today I will hardly listen to the proceedings"**: Jack's diary entry, which appears to be addressed to Astrid Wagner, was one of several from the last thirteen days of the trial that were published in "Die letzten Notizen," *NEWS*, 27/94.

CHAPTER 89: VERDICT

309 **"Is the accused, Jack Unterweger"**: *"Im Namen der Republik,"* Graz Criminal Court, 12 Vr 426/92, June 28, 1994.

310 **the whole gang moved to a beer cellar**: Interview with Geiger.

CHAPTER 90: "IS THAT THE ANSWER?"

311 **she felt nothing, neither bitterness nor sadness**: Interview with Bianca.

312 **she would remember him as he'd been in life**: Wagner, *Und die Mörderjagd,* p. 313.

312 **"It was nothing really, I just wanted to talk"**: Interview with Dr. Leinzinger.

312 **and a sloppy suicide watch**: Dr. Lynne Herold refused to render an opinion on the ligature with which Jack hanged himself because she did not want to participate in a possible investigation of the suicide watch or lack thereof.

313 **"No one knew him"**: Interview with Margit Haas.

314 **"On behalf of Unterweger's daughter"**: "Graff muss zurücktreten," *NEWS*, 27/94. In purely legal terms, Jack did die innocent, because he announced that he would appeal but died before the court reviewed his trial. Under Austrian law, the jury's guilty verdict was not *rechtskräftig*—legally binding—prior to Jack's death.

314 **"Unterweger drives slowly through the night"**: "Unterweger fährt langsam durch die Nacht," *NEWS*, 28/94.

CHAPTER 91: PEACE

316 **"Look!" Katja said**: The final scene is re-created from conversations with Eva and Katja Geiger. Eva might not have looked at the Pacific at that precise moment, but when I ate lunch at Gladstone's, my eyes were constantly drawn to the ocean.

ACKNOWLEDGMENTS

The most rewarding thing about researching this story was getting to know the people who told me about Jack and themselves. In a world in which few of us find enough time for our closest friends and family, they made time to meet me (a random American guy they'd never heard of) and to share their invaluable experiences and knowledge.

Special thanks to Dr. Ernst Geiger, Max Edelbacher, and other police officers—Ernst Hoffmann and Leopold Etz in Vienna, Franz Brandstätter and Helmut Golds in Graz, and Fred Miller, James Harper, and Steve Staples in Los Angeles—for patiently answering my thousands of questions with care and candor. I am also indebted to Dr. Geiger's wife, Eva, and his daughter, Katja, for sharing their highly personal recollections.

Among criminal justice officials, no one had more contact with Jack than Dr. Wolfgang Wladkowski, and I am indebted to him for sharing his fascinating anecdotes, as well as his vast knowledge of criminal law. Graz D.A. Karl Gasser took time out of his busy day to tell me exactly why he prosecuted Jack with such passion and conviction.

For the defense, I will always be grateful for my many entertaining evenings in Graz with Jack's attorney Dr. Hans Lehofer, talking about Jack and the trial. Astrid Wagner helped me to understand Jack's charisma—his immense vital energy, which enveloped her the instant she met him. She also pointed out with great clarity the faults of Jack's opponents (though she never persuaded me that they outweighed Jack's own).

I am indebted to Bianca Mrak and Carolina for telling me about their lives with Jack. Both women have had to come to terms with the fact that they were intimate with a serial killer, and they were generous to talk to me about it.

Thanks to Margit Haas for our many fun nights in Vienna, talking about Jack and everything else.

The reporters who covered the case at the time—Peter Grolig and Paul Yvon in Vienna, Hans Breitegger, Bernd Melichar, and Doris Piringer in Graz—made time for me even when they themselves were under deadline pressure. The late Günther Nenning generously shared his candid and contrite reflections on his participation in the campaign for Jack's release.

Thanks to the Austrian director Willi Hengstler for his fascinating account of writing a screenplay with Jack and for granting me full access to his voluminous correspondence. Alfred Kolleritsch also gave me copies of his correspondence with Jack when he was a fledging author. Thanks also to the American director Robert Dornhelm, who called me during a break in his hectic schedule to tell me his bizarre account of hearing Jack's pitch for yet another film. In Hollywood, Frances Schoenberger met with me to discuss my project, just as she'd met with Jack to discuss his projects fourteen years earlier.

On countless afternoons, Dr. Andrea Berzlanovich regaled me with coffee and cakes at the Vienna Institute of Forensic Medicine, carefully answering my questions. Dr. Manfred Hochmeister gave me a crash course on DNA, and Professor Peter Leinzinger told me about the findings of his autopsy on Jack. In Los Angeles, Dr. Lynne Herold told me dozens of fascinating stories about her work at the crime lab. Dr. Reinhard Haller was an invaluable source of information about Jack's psyche from a clinical perspective.

Maybe it's just my own insecurity, but I have sensed that few people have much faith in an author's first book. From the moment John Marciano first suggested that I write a book about Jack, he has been a tireless supporter and counselor. I don't think I would have written it without him. Amy Fine Collins and Jay Fielden also gave me support and helpful advice from the beginning. Jack Radisch, a dear friend and former California prosecutor, carefully reviewed the entire typescript.

In the same spirit, I wish to express my profound gratitude to my agent David Halpern, who has always kept the faith in this project, offered invaluable editorial advice, assuaged my anxieties, and demystified the publishing business. Last but not least, I wish to thank my brilliant editors Sarah Crichton and George Miller. They placed their bets on an unproven author and showed me how to shape this wild story into a book.